# The New Retirement

# The New Retirement

*The Ultimate Guide to The Rest of Your Life*

**Third Edition**

**Jan Cullinane**

# WILEY

Published by John Wiley & Sons, Inc., Hoboken, New Jersey.
Published simultaneously in Canada.

For general information on our other products and services or for technical support, please contact our Customer Care Department within the United States at (800) 762-2974, outside the United States at (317) 572-3993 or fax (317) 572-4002.

Wiley also publishes its books in a variety of electronic formats. Some content that appears in print may not be available in electronic formats. For more information about Wiley products, visit our web site at www.wiley.com.

*Library of Congress Cataloging-in-Publication Data*

Names: Cullinane, Jan, author.
Title: The new retirement : the ultimate guide to the rest of your life / Jan Cullinane.
Description: Third edition. | Hoboken, New Jersey : Wiley, [2022] | Includes index.
Identifiers: LCCN 2022010301 (print) | LCCN 2022010302 (ebook) | ISBN 9781119838159 (paperback) | ISBN 9781119838173 (adobe pdf) | ISBN 9781119838166 (epub)
Subjects: LCSH: Retirement—United States—Planning.
Classification: LCC HQ1063.2.U6 C85 2022 (print) | LCC HQ1063.2.U6 (ebook) | DDC 646.7/9—dc23/eng/20220314
LC record available at https://lccn.loc.gov/2022010301
LC ebook record available at https://lccn.loc.gov/2022010302

Cover Design: Wiley
Cover Image: © Westend61/Getty Images

SKY10033975_032522

*To Roger, my sounding board, cheerleader, and supporter extraordinaire.*

# Contents

Foreword                                                                ix

Acknowledgments                                                         xiii

Introduction                                                            xv

**Chapter 1**    What Makes Retirement Successful?                        1

**Chapter 2**    168 Hours a Week                                        31

**Chapter 3**    Working in Retirement: It's Not an Oxymoron             55

**Chapter 4**    What and Where Is Home?                                 73

**Chapter 5**    Locations, Locations, Locations                        109

**Chapter 6**    Forever Young                                          161

**Chapter 7**    Dollars and Sense                                      207

**Chapter 8**    The Taxman Cometh                                      259

**Chapter 9**    Money Saving Tricks and Tips                           281

**Chapter 10**   The Final Chapter                                      299

# Contents

References     317

About the Author     325

Index     327

# Foreword

## by Kerry Hannon

*– Best-selling author of* Great Pajama Jobs, Never Too Old to Get Rich, *and* Great Jobs for Everyone 50+, *career/retirement strategist*

**D**emographic transformation and population aging are occurring at a blistering pace around the world. Increasingly, our lifespans are topping 100 years, and this will become increasingly commonplace in the years to come.

That's the backdrop for my curmudgeonly views on retirement. I am not a fan. At least not in the way it has been approached in the past.

I guess you'd have to say I'm the anti-retirement expert. I routinely remark: Let's retire the word *retire*.

I say this for myriad compelling reasons. In large measure, it's spurred by deep-seated financial concerns. A striking number of Americans have little saved for retirement and do not have access to an employer retirement plan to help them sock away funds for their future financial security.

The ability to *choose* to retire is tangled in thorny financial choices and more than a little crystal ball gazing.

How much longer will you be able to work from a health perspective and in an ageist workplace culture that resists retaining older workers? How will you pay for healthcare after you leave your employer's plan? Importantly, how will you create a life in this chapter that balances your budget and allows you to embrace new challenges and meaningful experiences?

For many people, the decades that lie ahead, should they step out of the workforce in their 60s or are not financially prepared, are a daunting prospect.

For nearly two decades, I have been concerned, speaking, and writing about the looming elder poverty crisis in this country. That crunch is evolving as Baby Boomers retire and are faced with longevity without the savings to support the years ahead, including surging medical costs, particularly at the end of life. My mother died recently on the cusp of turning 92, and I can assure you, her annual living and healthcare costs in her last few years were staggering.

Experts at Fidelity have estimated that about 15% of the average retiree's annual expenses will be used for healthcare-related expenses, including Medicare premiums and out-of-pocket expenses.

According to the Fidelity Retiree Health Care Cost Estimate, an average retired couple age 65 may need approximately $300,000 saved (after tax) to cover healthcare expenses in retirement.

Clearly, that figure comes with provisions that depend on when you step out of the workforce and your health, luck, and so on.

But a successful retirement involves far more than whether you will outlive your money or whether you have saved adequately. To me, work in some fashion engages the mind and provides a social connection and network that is vital to healthy aging.

This doesn't necessarily mean full-blown work scenarios. Part-time, seasonal, contract or consulting positions, a side entrepreneurial gig, can all serve as a financial safety net.

That income is the fourth leg of the retirement stool along with retirement savings, personal savings, and Social Security. Meantime, work can also provide future retirees the ability to delay tapping Social Security retirement benefits.

Social Security's rules essentially give you an 8% bigger benefit for each year you postpone claiming benefits after your full retirement age (currently 66 to 67), until age 70. Put another way, if you're now 66 and wait until 70 to start claiming, you'll see 32% larger benefits than if you filed at your full retirement age.

Jan Cullinane's enlightening new book highlights the significance of a holistic approach to retirement. I'm pleased she includes vital advice on the role working longer can play.

"For some, a long and (hopefully) rewarding job/career, followed by non-working years is the retirement goal," Cullinane writes. "For others, retirement is more of a process, perhaps involving several forays into and out of alternative projects, pastimes, and careers/jobs.

Many people hope to do a 'phased transition' to retirement and combine more leisure time with work, and some insist they will *never* retire. Some want to retire by age 55. Others want to be part of the FIRE movement – financial independence, retire early – where the goal is to live on your own terms by the time you're in your 30s or 40s".

*The New Retirement: The Ultimate Guide to the Rest of Your Life* is a persuasive reminder that retirement is vastly different today than in previous generations and will continue to mutate. But it can be a time of great adventure and purpose if you carefully prepare the foundation for a period of life that may outlast your primary working career.

Different flavors of ice cream is a metaphor for how we all seek different things in the next chapter of our lives.

Cullinane shows us that it *is* possible to step away from a career and create our own bespoke retirement chapter. She provides solid resources and actionable steps for those nearing retirement as well as those decades away to begin to plan intentionally and embrace the rich possibilities ahead.

For me, the new story of retirement for those who have saved adequately is that it will be in fact a sequence of shifts over time as one calibrates and re-jiggers the puzzle of our next phase from a practical and a deeply personal perspective that centers on that cosmic question we all grapple with: What ultimately matters in a life well led?

As my friend Ken Dychtwald, psychologist, gerontologist, and founder and chief executive of Age Wave, a consulting and research company, told me: "During this transitional period, some people feel unsettled, anxious, or bored, but eventually they realize that 'I can be fresh. I can be new.'"

A 2021 study by Age Wave, Edward Jones, and the Harris Poll found that most retirees say that all four pillars – health, family, purpose, and finances – are crucial to optimal well-being in retirement, which is common-sense to me. And retirees, when compared with younger Americans, are far more likely to say that "having a sense of purpose" in life is essential to achieve peak well-being.

One of the big takeaways from the report: being *useful* makes retirees feel *youthful*. I like that notion. (And it's far cheaper than Botox.)

It plays into my concept that, if you're financially secure, this should be a time of life of engaging in the world, moving to something new, certainly not fading away, or, ahem, *retiring*, in the time-worn sense of the word.

The new retirement movement needs books like Jan's because, as a respected retirement specialist, her advice is realistic and honest. It resonates. She understands the demographic reality of longevity and shows us the positive pathways to create financial security and a future of opportunity and joy.

# Acknowledgments

". . . some things just take time. You can't produce a baby in one month by getting nine women pregnant." I came across this Warren Buffett quote while writing this book, and it resonated with me. Although a book will often have just one name on the cover, it's truly the work of many talented, dedicated, smart, and generous people. And, I'd like to thank them.

I appreciate the anecdotes and comments contributed by friends, acquaintances, and people who have retired or are planning to retire who willingly shared their experiences, thoughts, stories, challenges, and wisdom. And thanks to the CPAs, CFPs, and other experts who shared their technical knowledge.

The people at Wiley are phenomenal. A huge thank-you to Senior Acquisitions Editor Kevin Harreld, Senior Managing Editor Susan Cerra, Assistant Editor Samantha Enders, Editorial Assistant Samantha Wu, and Wiley Creative Services. They are dedicated, enthusiastic, and provide prompt and excellent advice. Much appreciation to Kerry Hannon, who wrote the Foreword to the book, and who is a great source of wisdom.

Finally, endless thanks to my agent, Linda Konner. I was told she's the best, and is she ever!

# Introduction

If you're reading this, congratulations and welcome! Congrats for recognizing the importance of thinking about and planning for retirement in a holistic way, and welcome to the book that's going to help you in your journey.

You may be considering this book for a number of reasons:

- You may be one of the 10,000 people who will reach the age of 65 *every day* until 2030, when all Boomers will be at least 65.
- You may be among the approximately 12 million households in which the primary wage earner says he/she "aspires to retire" by the age of 55.
- You may be among those who left a primary career (by choice or not) and are technically "retired" but looking for more information about health, wealth, relocation, and second careers.
- You may have a YOLO (you only live once) approach and want to live life to its fullest.
- You may be a digital nomad, wanting to work on your terms, and looking to combine a remote job with an ideal place to live.
- You may want to not run out of money before you run out of life.
- You may want a book that contains both solid and specific lifestyle and financial advice.
- You may want to find out how to make a difference, have a purpose, and leave a legacy.

- Your life may have been transformed by Covid-19, and you're ready to make some changes.
- You may define yourself as married, always single, widowed, divorced, a person of color, and/or LGBTQ+. This book is for everyone.
- You may want to create more than just a financial plan – you're looking to create a life plan.
- You may subscribe to this advice from a wise academic friend of the author: "If you read a book or go to a conference and pick up one or two good ideas you can integrate into your life, career, or relationships, it's a success."

This book is different because it combines all the following aspects into one readable, actionable book:

1. It explores health issues, lifelong learning opportunities, opportunities for working after leaving a primary career, and what to do with 168 hours a week.
2. It describes specific retirement locations, as well as how to age in place successfully (including reasons why you should *not* age in place).
3. It lays out a blueprint for sound financial planning.
4. It provides concrete suggestions for meeting others, deepening existing relationships, having purpose, and leaving a legacy.
5. It is unbiased – the goal is a *Consumer Reports* approach to retirement.
6. It is easy to read, practical, and interactive. It can be read cover to cover, or individual chapters can be accessed for specific topics. The use of subheadings, bulleted lists, quotes, and humor make it extremely reader-friendly.
7. It includes worksheets, references, and helpful forms.
8. The author continues to support the readers and provide relevant information through the book's Facebook page, Twitter, LinkedIn, and the author's web page.

9. "Big-box" retailers like Target, Walmart, Costco, and Amazon thrive because so many people want one-stop shopping. This book provides the same type of service to you, the reader.
10. At the end of each chapter, you'll find a list of additional helpful resources, including checklists, websites, and books.
11. This book will be invaluable to those who are looking to make the rest of their life the best of their life.

Like the old L'Oréal commercial, you should read this book "because you're worth it." Ready to get started? Let's go!

# What Makes Retirement Successful?

■ ■ ■

**D**id you take the SAT or ACT? If so, did you try a few practice tests or take a prep course to familiarize yourself with these assessments prior to the actual test? If you had children, did you help prepare them for kindergarten by teaching them numbers and shapes and colors and letters? If you had a job interview, did you research the company, prepare questions to ask the interviewer(s), dress appropriately, and show up on time? For most of us, the answers would be yes. Preparation is an important ingredient for achieving our goals.

Yet, you have probably heard that many people spend more time planning a two-week vacation than they do planning for retirement. It's understandable – you're caught up in day-to-day living, you have a lot on your plate, you have competing demands for your time, and retirement may seem far away. Thinking about retirement can cause "analysis paralysis." So many choices – whether to stay or relocate, how to structure your time, aging parents and/or boomerang kids, whether to continue working in some fashion, and so forth. And, of course, if you're part of a couple, aligning retirement goals may be a challenge (such as the couple at a talk I was giving told me they had never discussed it, but the wife assumed they were moving to the East Coast when they retired and husband assumed they would relocate to the West Coast!).

To demonstrate how significant retirement is, consider the Holmes and Rahe Stress Scale. Two psychiatrists, Thomas Holmes and Richard Rahe, developed a list of 43 common life events of varying severity, and ranked them based on more than 7,500 participants' responses. For example, the top stressful event on the scale is the loss of a spouse or child. The forty-third event on the list is a minor violation of the law (such as a parking ticket). Retirement ranked number 10, right above "a major change in the health or behavior of a family member." Pretty telling.

When you consider how much time you may have after leaving a primary career, recognize that women in the United States have an average lifespan of 81 years and retire on average at age 63 (according to the Census Bureau), so retirement averages about 18 years for women, and a little less for men, with their few years' shorter lifespans. So, let's see: 18 (years) × 365 (days/year) = 6,570 days of retirement; some people will spend 20 or 30 or more years in retirement. It's obvious that it's vital for peace of mind to spend time planning, both from a financial and nonfinancial standpoint.

Think of this book as a prep class for retirement. A prep class that will help you become confident as you approach this transition, and formulate what specific actions to take (with your significant other, if there is one) to make these years the best years. And, this class is "taught" by an award-winning expert (with contributions from other experts) with more than 40 years of experience in both the financial and nonfinancial areas of retirement.

## A Brief Retirement History

Before going forward, let's go back. The concept of retirement is fairly recent. At the beginning of the nineteenth century, few people retired, because they simply could not afford to do so. In the United States, the average lifespan for white men was 47; for men of color, it was 43. For white women, the average lifespan was 49 years and only 34 years for women of color. No time/not enough money = no retirement for the vast majority of people in the 1800s.

As white-collar jobs replaced a predominantly agricultural economy, however, incomes rose, and people had more money, along with longer lifespans. Improved sanitation, housing, education, the development of vaccines and antibiotics, and the subsequent decline in death rates among all ages increased average life expectancy. FDR signed the Social Security Act into law on August 14, 1935. Besides replacing some of the income that was lost due to retirement and creating somewhat of a safety net, Social Security was also an incentive to create job opportunities for younger workers. In January 1940, Ida May Fuller of Ludlow, Vermont, became the first recipient of Social Security benefits. And did she benefit! Ida lived 35 more years, and collected almost $23,000 in benefits before passing away at the age of 100. That's the equivalent of about $430,000 today.

Our current labor force, compared to Ida May's time, is larger, more diverse, older, and more female. In 2020, women held the majority of jobs for the first time (if you exclude farm workers and the self-employed), according to the Bureau of Labor Statistics. Declining births, coupled with longer lifespans, reduces the number of workers supporting each retiree. In 1975, there were about 3.2–3.4 workers per retiree. In 2013, there were about 2.8; in 2034, it's estimated that only 2–2.3 workers will be supporting each retiree, according to the Social Security Administration. There is a deeper exploration of Social Security in Chapters 7 and 8.

Many reading this book are in the Boomer cohort, defined as those born between 1946 and 1964. This group, about 75 million strong, has been described by demographers as a "pig in a python" due to the huge number of births fueled by the end of World War II coupled with a booming economy. And now Boomers are retiring or semiretiring. As mentioned in the book intro, 10,000 people will reach the age of 65 *every day* until 2030, when all Boomers will be at least 65. But you may be part of the 12 million households who "aspire to retire" by age 55.

## The "New" Retirement

Is the word *retirement* outdated? Most say yes, because the word conjures up images of withdrawing, being sedentary, old (in attitude if not age), and non-contributing members of society. Terms like Zoomers, Arrivement, Life 2.0, Next Act, Encore, Third Act, and so forth have been suggested as alternatives (my favorite is the Spanish word to describe retirement, jubilación). But, for the sake of name recognition, I'll continue to use the word *retirement*.

For some, a long and (hopefully) rewarding job/career followed by nonworking years is the retirement goal. For others, retirement is more of a process, perhaps involving several forays into and out of alternative projects, pastimes, and careers/jobs. Many people hope to do a "phased transition" to retirement and combine more leisure time with work, and some insist they will *never* retire. Some want to retire by age 55. Others want to be part of the FIRE movement – financial independence, retire early – in which the goal is to live on your own terms by the time you're in your 30s or 40s. With FIRE, you can work full-time, work part-time, or not work – it's your choice. Needless to say, unless you hit it rich when you're young or get a big inheritance, FIRE involves very aggressive saving and investing, and perhaps living a radically different kind of lifestyle. So there are lots of choices. But whichever flavor of retirement you think you might want to pursue, this book will help guide you.

## Expectations versus Reality

"Work 'til you drop" – that is the professed retirement plan for a number of people, whether it's because they love what they do, they need the money, it's something with which they are familiar, it's easier to avoid change, or some combination of these. But retirement can happen whether you're ready or not. Some professions have mandatory retirement ages, including airline pilots, firefighters, FBI agents, and certain judgeships. In other cases, people are unexpectedly downsized, "right-sized," need to retire to care for an aging parent, they or their spouse or child have an illness, the business changes, or a calamity (such as Covid-19) hits.

There is a disconnect between what many people think will happen and what does happen regarding retirement timing. I refer to it as expectations versus reality. Each year, the Employee Benefit Research Institute (EBRI) publishes a "Retirement Confidence Survey." The 2020 version, which surveyed more than 2,000 workers and retirees in January 2020 (prepandemic), offers important insights. For example, looking at recent retirees' experiences:

- They expected to retire at a median age of 65; they actually retired at a median age of 62.
- 31% expected to retire at 70; only 6% actually worked until the age of 70.
- Only 11% planned to retire before age 60; 33% retired before age 60.
- 18% planned to retire between 60 and 64; 37% actually did retire during that age range.
- 48% left the workforce earlier than planned.

The results have been consistent over the years – many of us think we will work longer than we actually do (the EBRI has been doing this annual survey for 30 years). We may get another job or start another career, but it's important to know the reality versus the expectation. Speaking of which . . . the EBRI looked at this statistic, too, and found that 74% of retirees *planned* to work for pay in retirement; but only 24% *did* work for pay in retirement. As Antoine de Saint-Exupéry said, "A goal without a plan is just a wish."

What did the 2021 EBRI survey of more than 3,000 Americans *during* the pandemic show? The median expected age for retirement was still 65, and the actual age was still 62; 23% of retirees said the pandemic made them "somewhat or significantly less confident they will have enough to live comfortably throughout retirement."

## Working and Sense of Self

Set aside financial considerations for the moment (they'll be addressed in detail in Chapters 7, 8, and 9). What is your relationship between work and your identity? There are two competing theories. The first, called continuity theory, is the perspective that our levels of self-esteem and life satisfaction stay the same, independent of work. Under this theory, it wouldn't matter if a person worked or not; he or she would maintain the same feelings of well-being. The second perspective, role theory, has two sides. Although role theory considers working to be vital to a person's identity, retirement can improve feelings of well-being if the career/job being left was considered very difficult or stressful; or retirement can cause distress if people feel they have lost a valuable role by not being employed. The effect of leaving your career/job (again, disregarding money) is more a function of how you perceive your employment – does working play a crucial role in your life, is it something to give up with relief, or is it immaterial to how you think about yourself?

Now, think about your "elevator speech" – the blurb you'd give to someone you meet for the first time (called an elevator speech because it takes about the same time as a short elevator ride – 30 to 60 seconds). How would you describe yourself if you had left your job and just met some new neighbors in a new community – would your elevator speech be about your previous career? If so, working may be integral to your self-worth. And that's okay. It may have defined you for many decades. But you will need to find a substitute for it if you do not find/create another job or career. More about that in Chapter 2.

My tip/confession: I've moved seven times, and my husband and I have lived in our present home for more than 14 years. The majority of people in our community are retired and some have started new businesses. Most do not talk about their previous careers, and many had quite illustrious ones. They are present and future-oriented, not reliving their past glory days. I do feel work is integral to me as a person, which is why I still like working, although now it's on my terms and my office is in my house. My husband, on the other hand, had a long career as a tax partner in a major accounting firm, and, although he enjoyed and excelled at his job, he claims he doesn't miss a day of working, and wonders where the day goes.

## *Why* People Decide to Retire

A friend of mine named Jim said you should ask yourself these three questions to decide if you are ready to retire: Do I have enough? Have I had enough? Do I have enough to do? This is simple, clever, and to a large part it reflects what studies have shown as the major reasons why men and women decide to retire:

- To do other things
- Financial incentives/have enough money to retire
- Spouse retired
- Poor health
- Didn't like working
- Didn't get along with boss
- Family health issues
- Not appreciated
- Job terminated

There's no one correct answer to the question "When should I retire?" A 2018 Fidelity survey found that half of Boomer couples disagree about when they should retire, and for Millennials, more than half disagreed what time was/will be the right time. If you are reading this book because you're considering retiring, take the fun and informative "Are You Ready to Launch Your Retirement" quiz at the end of this chapter. And, if you have a spouse or significant other, she/he should also take the quiz . . . and be sure to have an in-depth discussion about your results.

As you can see from the preceding list , some people retired not because they wanted to, but because they had to. It's important to recognize that it's not always a choice. As the popular idiom succinctly states, "Forewarned is forearmed."

## Retirement Timing for Couples: Same Time or Staggered Times?

If you're part of a couple, should you retire together? Around 50% of married couples in the United States retire within two years of one another. According to a study involving more than 500 working couples in their 50s, 60s, and 70s, they reported greater marital satisfaction if they retired at or around the same time. This is especially true if accumulating additional money is a nonissue, and the couple has shared interests, such as relocating to a new place, travel, getting in shape, or seeing/helping out their children/grandchildren. Interestingly, but perhaps not surprisingly, men who were retired but had working spouses reported the most marital discord. You may have heard the saying "Twice the husband but half the money." According to Ronald J. Manheimer, founding director of the North Carolina Center for Creative Retirement at the University of North Carolina, women's fears in retirement include losing one's identity, being responsible for their spouses'/significant others' social lives and entertainment, and experiencing a disruption of their established patterns.

However, there are sound reasons for couples to stagger their retirement:

- Several years of additional income from the working spouse could make a huge difference in total retirement savings.
- The extra income may allow later claiming of Social Security benefits, resulting in an increase in benefits.
- Additional years of working by one spouse may shorten the years money needs to be withdrawn from retirement savings.
- If there is family medical coverage provided by an employer, this can be a great money-saving move, especially if the other person is under 65 and not eligible for Medicare.

- Although "too much togetherness" can be an issue for some couples, having one spouse retire first may help ease the transition to a new lifestyle. Consider creating two separate offices that provide a bit more breathing room if a little space is a desirable thing. Distance can be beneficial sometimes, but Arthur Aron, a relationship researcher at the State University of New York at Stony Brook, has a great suggestion for couples to revitalize their relationship. It's to do something novel that neither of you has done before – and do it *together*. Examples? Go whitewater rafting, try an Escape Room, take a trip to an exotic place, eat at an ethnic restaurant, help out at a Habitat for Humanity build, take up ballroom dancing. It's found that fresh kinds of activities activate the same systems of the brain that are involved in the rush of romantic love – and cocaine highs! – the dopamine reward system. Aron's research found new experiences among couples boost marital happiness.

## Single and/or a Solo Ager?

You may be single by choice or single due to divorce or death of a spouse. As a single, you are among a large and growing cohort of adults. According to 2020 Pew Research figures, 28% of U.S. adults aged 50–64 are single, and 36% over the age of 65 are single. In the over-65 group, 21% of males over 65 are single, and 49% of women are single, partly reflecting, of course, men's shorter life expectancy, along with "gray divorce." That is why there is a common saying, "Men die married; women die single." And what about "solo agers" – those without children, without a spouse, and without close relatives? Solo agers comprise about 20% of Boomers.

Being single or a solo ager can have a big effect on retirement planning: It can simplify planning – you only have yourself to look after and you are responsible for your own choices; or it can complicate them – you don't have a partner and/or children or relatives to help navigate retirement (although friends can and often do fill in that gap).

## Where to Retire

The 1981 punk rock band The Clash released the catchy "Should I Stay or Should I Go?" They obviously weren't singing about picking up stakes and moving after leaving your primary career or at some point in your retirement, but it's an important question to consider and discuss. Are some places better than others? The short answer is yes.

As mentioned in the Introduction, the pandemic has had an effect on migration patterns within the United States. People realized working remotely is not only an option, but in many cases it's a new normal. Good weather and open spaces that allow you to walk, bike, eat, and play outdoors year-round have become much more desirable. I live in Florida, and I have seen a huge influx of people of all ages relocating and purchasing homes and condos. For example, Marie L.'s oceanfront condo in Florida sold in two days to a New York buyer who purchased it without checking it out in person.

A clever way of determining overall migration patterns is seeing where moving companies are packing up people – and unpacking them. The 2020 U.S. Moving Migration Patterns Report from North American Moving Services lists these states with the most *outbound* moves: Illinois, New York, California, New Jersey and Maryland. Inbound moves? Idaho, Arizona, South Carolina, Tennessee, North Carolina, Florida, Texas, and Utah.

If we drill down and look at Boomer migration patterns, Realtor .com analyzed who looked up home sales on their site throughout the United States from ZIP codes where at least 4 out of 10 people were Boomers. (As an aside, it's a little disconcerting to see how we are tracked.)

The top 10 locations that these Boomers looked for online were cities in . . . Florida! If we examine their data a little more broadly, areas in North Carolina, South Carolina, and Georgia were represented. I guess it really is "better at the beach."

When those who recently retired are asked about relocating after leaving a primary career, the fairly standard answer is that they want to "age in place." I get that – you may have lifelong friends, children, grandchildren, many ties to the community, and love where you live. For example, David K. is a homegrown Florida guy. He grew up, went to college, founded his financial services company, and continues to happily live in Florida. I grew up and went to high school and earned my bachelor's and master's degrees in Maryland, but also lived and worked in New Jersey (and was working toward my doctorate there), relocated to Ohio due to my husband's corporate transfer, and moved to Florida in 2006. I can work virtually.

You may be born, grow up, retire, and die in the same area. That plan works for many. But, Chapter 5 suggests possibilities for relocation (including "niche" communities such as living on a ship or in a new "green" city), things you should consider when buying or renting a home or if you're considering more than one retirement location, what you must do if you decide to age in place, and what to do when you can no longer care for yourself or your loved ones.

## Retirement and Lifespan

There's a lot of research regarding timing of retirement and lifespan. Some studies show early retirement prolongs longevity; other studies show it decreases longevity. A recent study published in the *Journal of Epidemiology and Community Health* recognized that people sometimes must retire early because of health issues, so this study only enrolled subjects who were similar in health, socioeconomic, and lifestyle factors. The results? Among healthy retirees, a one-year-older age at retirement was associated with an 11% lower risk of all-causes mortality. The researchers' conclusion? "Early retirement may be a risk factor for mortality and prolonged working life may provide survival benefits among U.S. adults." Food for thought.

# Six Secrets for a Successful Retirement

So far, there has been a little retirement history, some statistics, a few important questions to consider, a quiz you should take ("Are You Ready to Launch Your Retirement?"), and a smattering of research about this transition. Now we'll condense what is known about optimizing the chances for a joyful and satisfying retirement, into "The Six Secrets for a Successful Retirement." Let's briefly address each "secret," and then do a deeper dive in subsequent chapters.

## Secret 1: Have Something to Wake Up For

In addition to a paycheck and perhaps health coverage, work can provide status, intellectual engagement, social interaction and support, purpose, pride, joy, accomplishment, and structure. After leaving your primary career, you'll still want to experience these benefits in your everyday life. Chapters 2 and 3 explore a host of specific suggestions for a rich, full life, including possibilities for a paycheck after leaving your primary career. (The "Pertinent Quotes" below are from attendees at my retirement talks.)

**Pertinent Quote**: "Retirement brought a quick collapse to the daily environment I had known for a long time. This gave rise to a lot of issues I had never faced before and working through those issues took time and a lot of work." – Michael K.

## Secret 2: Renegotiate Roles/Cultivate Resilience

There are two chief ways of looking at the world, according to research, that increase the chances for smooth sailing through the transition to retirement: having both an internal locus of control (the belief that outcomes are under one's control), and retirement self-efficacy (the belief or self-confidence that one can cope with the changes retirement brings). Adopt these mind-sets to help ensure a satisfying retirement.

Retiring can be similar to your adolescent years, exciting, but at the same time, often turbulent. Leaving your primary career/job results in shifts in thinking – about time, wants and needs, relation-ships, perhaps where you live, and thoughts about this "third age" of your life. It's time to concentrate on the present and future – your past doesn't need you anymore! Prior to retiring, if part of a couple, you may have worked out patterns or divisions of labor that worked for you – from making meals to taking out the garbage to washing the dishes to food shopping to doing the laundry to supervising work done around the house to yard work to taking care of children and/or assisting your parents . . . you get the idea. Now is the time to reconsider and to renegotiate these roles. If old patterns still work, great. If not, it's time to discuss which ones need to be changed or renegotiated.

Author C.S. Lewis said, "You can't go back and change the beginning, but you can start where you are and change the ending." Lewis is talking about resilience, which is the ability to bounce back after adversity. It's an important ingredient in the recipe for a suc-cessful retirement, whether single or coupled. You can cultivate this desirable quality by accepting that change is part of life; by concen-trating on changing adverse circumstances that can be altered; by acting decisively rather than wishing problems would just disap-pear; by maintaining perspective; and by taking big problems and breaking them into smaller, manageable challenges.

It can be beneficial to talk to friends and relatives about their own shifts to retirement. For example, although my friend Carol loves to cook, she hated doing the dishes, but felt it was her "duty" to do them since she did not work outside the home. Now, Julian is doing the dishes, and they do the food shopping together, which they both enjoy. A small but important change. Ramona and Car-los were having a difficult time adjusting to "too much together-ness." They pulled out their 1992 copy of *The Five Love Languages* by Dr. Gary Chapman, and reviewed and discussed which of the ways they liked to "receive" love: acts of service, gift-giving, physical touch, quality time, and words of affirmation. Carlos was doing lots of repairs around the house he never had time to do while working, and although Ramona was pleased with his "acts of service," she really craved words of affirmation. Ramona liked surprising Carlos with little gifts, but he was really hoping for her to initiate sex . . . discussing what they wanted and needed went a long way toward smoothing the adjustment to an almost 24/7 togetherness.

You could also consider consulting with a counselor or couples' therapist or life coach, and/or attending retirement seminars, particularly if they address more than just financial issues. Think of redefining/renegotiating roles as a process, and gradually build that muscle called resilience. The process of adapting to retirement can be more like slowly turning a dimmer on a light rather than flipping a switch.

**Pertinent Quote:** "I was used to having a large team to whom I could delegate many of the things I didn't like to do; my husband would say that after I retired, I sometimes treated him as if he were one of them." – Linda R.

### Secret 3: Have Strong Social Support

This "secret" is a biggie. Bette Midler is famous for it and Donkey sang it in the movie *Shrek*: "But ya got to have friends." There is an abundance of research linking social connections to longer life-spans. And, strong connections result in more than just additional years – they are healthier and happier years as well, which is why I prefer the term "healthspan" to "lifespan." An ad for a 1946 book about aging got it right: "The important thing to you is not how many years in your life, but how much life in your years!"

A few specifics:

- Harvard Health Publishing/Harvard Medical School (2019) summarized research showing that positive family, friends, and religious and community connections are as beneficial to your health as sufficient shut-eye, a healthy diet, and being a nonsmoker. Their newsletter also cited a study involving more than 300,000 people that found that a "lack of strong relationships increased the risk of premature death from all causes by 50% – an effect on mortality risk roughly comparable to smoking up to 15 cigarettes a day, and greater than obesity and physical inactivity."

- Lynn Giles, PhD, and three other researchers followed 1,500 people for 10 years and found that those with extensive social networks outlived those lacking social support by 22%. Interestingly, their research showed friends had a more powerful effect on longevity than family.

- A 13-year study showed that men and women 65 years and older who were more socially active lived an average of 2.5 years longer. This study was notable because the activities included things such as playing cards, eating out, or going to movies with others. It demonstrated that social engagement alone can increase lifespan.

- An interesting 2019 study, titled "Friendships That Money Can Buy," reported by the National Center for Biotechnology Information, looked at the connection between money and social support. The authors of the study found that "greater financial security predicted greater social connectedness, which in turn supported better health." Their conclusion? Financial security "increases opportunities for social connection." Makes sense. If you have the financial wherewithal to join a gym or tennis center, travel, eat out socially, spend time volunteering, go to the theater, and so forth, you increase your opportunities for social interactions and creating friendships. (More on achieving financial security in Chapters 7, 8, and 9.)

We've heard the expression "friends with benefits." Well, friends *are* the benefit! We all want – and need – to have someone to "play with" in retirement. It's worth noting that many of us worry about making new friends. We tend to have a lower opinion of ourselves and think we are more boring than others think we are. It's called the "liking gap," and a study in 2018, pairing strangers together for conversations, found that people were better liked and made better impressions than they thought they did. It's very helpful to know we're more likable than we think we are!

### Secret 4: Have a Healthy Body and Mind

"Heartache." "Gut-wrenching." Money worries that cause head-aches. When we think of "mind," we need to go beyond just the analytical structure of the brain; our mind includes beliefs, atti-tudes, and emotions. There has been tremendous research demon-strating the powerful effect of the mind-body connection:

- One study investigated the link between positive thinking and the risk of frailty. The researchers followed 1,558 older adults for seven years and compared frailty (determined by speed of walking, strength of grip, weight loss and fatigue), with positive thinking by asking participants how many par-ticular positive thoughts they had over the course of the study (such as "I feel hopeful about the future"). As a group, frailty increased among the aging adults, but those with posi-tive emotions and thinking were less likely to become frail.
- Another study followed 545 men for 15 years and found that the most optimistic men in the group were half as likely to die from cardiovascular disease as the men who were least optimistic.

Why does optimism work? It's thought that positive emotions may directly influence body chemicals in a way that affects health. And, positive people tend to have increased social interactions (back to Secret 3), which may result in more access to resources.

University of Pennsylvania psychologist Martin Seligman, PhD, has studied happiness and optimism for decades. Seligman sug-gests we go beyond seeking pleasure and instead look for gratifica-tion. What's the difference? Pleasure is not necessarily meaningful and does not always result in a greater good. For example, eating a piece of cheesecake may be pleasurable and feed your stomach, but it doesn't feed your soul. Gratification involves cultivating and nurturing your strengths and putting them to positive use. As an example, Darlene V. and Jonathan tragically lost their first child just prior to childbirth. Although devastated by the loss, they set up a foundation at a local hospital to provide indigent women with the financial resources to bury children who died under similar circumstances. Darlene and Jonathan took their strengths of compassion, generosity, and financial savvy and parlayed them into a gratifying experience in the midst of their sorrow. Likewise, we can cultivate happiness by incorporating strengths such as kindness, humor, optimism and courage into everyday life. Happiness is more of a by-product than a goal.

Martin Seligman coined the term "learned helplessness," the concept that we internalize that nothing we do matters – that we cannot control our environment, even if we're placed in a new situation. Seligman's findings originally applied to dogs who received unavoidable mild shocks in a lab setting; when the dogs were placed in a new situation, they had "learned" they could not avoid/change their situation, and did not try to do so. Seligman says we can escape this belief that we have no control with "learned optimism." He suggests ". . . not to ruminate about bad events that happen to you . . . I recommend fun distractions, because studies show that if you think about problems in a negative frame of mind, you come up with fewer solutions." We can train ourselves to think more optimistically and put a stop to distorted ways of thinking. When you think negatively about something, note it, evaluate it, and replace the thought with something more realistic. It takes practice, but it's an effective tool for increasing happiness.

Having a sound body and mind is so important for a successful retirement that Chapter 6 is devoted to this "secret." I've mentioned the word "healthspan" before, and it's worth repeating that this is the goal: "live long and prosper" – not only financially, but also physically and mentally.

### Secret 5: Have a Strong Financial Plan

Ah, yes . . . money! For many retirement books, finance is the dominant or only topic. It's tremendously important, which is why three chapters are devoted to this "Secret." A few stories and studies about money and retirement that are worth mentioning:

- Most of us want to project a confident, got-it-together façade. So, it's very concerning that two-thirds of those in a 2021 Retirement Risk Readiness Study by Allianz Life reported they were concerned about healthcare costs, the rising cost of living, and not having enough money to do what they want in retirement, *but* they were not bringing up these issues with their financial professionals. Yet, the survey takers also said they would like to discuss them with their advisor. Ironic that the people who could help them may not know what is really bothering their clients. Kind of like when we go to a doctor's appointment and we are not really forthcoming on what's troubling us or symptoms we may have. So, speak up! And financial professionals . . . be proactive in your questions.
- Does money bring happiness? Recall the ancient fable "The Golden Touch." A king named Midas performed a good deed and was granted a wish by a god. Midas wanted everything he touched to turn into gold. The god warned him this was not a good wish, but Midas persisted, and his wish was reluctantly granted. At first Midas was thrilled with his new power, but then when he became hungry and his food turned into gold and he could not eat it, he realized he had made a BIG mistake. His beloved daughter, trying to comfort him, also turned into gold. Not scientific, but a good message that money isn't everything. (But, let's face it – it *is* important.)
- A 2020 study in *Social Psychology and Personality Science* involved almost 1,300 adults who reported their income as well as how *frequently*, on average, they felt happy and how

*intensely* happy they felt. The results found a higher income was related to feeling happy slightly more often, but there was no relationship to the intensity. So, money itself did not bring a giant boost in happiness, but may allow people to experience happiness more often.

- "Keeping up with the Joneses." Sarah Newcomb, PhD, a behavioral economist at Morningstar, cites three studies that found that "where a person believes they stand relative to others has a much larger effect on happiness than absolute income." The power of social comparisons is huge; even those participants in the study making large salaries felt bad about themselves when they made upward comparisons to others. Advice: Compare yourself to those who make the same or less. Or think about how far you've advanced financially compared to your younger self – use your younger self as a reference rather than others. You'll be a *lot* happier than obsessing about the rich guy or gal down the block.

Best view of money? It's valuable because it can buy time, freedom, and choices (although too many choices can be a negative). And, as my CPA friend says, "Retirement planning doesn't have to be hard, complicated, or stressful." You'll agree when you read the financial chapters.

## Secret 6: Have a Purpose

Recall that Secret 1 is "Have Something to Wake Up For" – what gets our juices flowing and keeps us engaged with life. But Secret 6, "Have a Purpose," is more about the legacy we want to leave when we *won't* be waking up anymore! It's about making a positive, lasting change. More than 90% of preretirees in an Age Wave/Edward Jones study agree purpose is key to a rewarding retirement. Ways to do this financially and nonfinancially for our children, for our grandchildren, for causes we are passionate about, and/or for charities that represent our values are discussed in Chapter 10. It may involve money, time, or both. And, purpose and legacy are also addressed in the final chapter. As George Eliot (the Victorian novelist who was actually a woman) said, "It's never too late to be what you might have been." Having a purpose helps us do just that.

## Retirees' Regrets

We can learn a lot from people who have done or are doing something we're contemplating doing – whether it's picking a friend's brain about traveling to a particular place he/she has been to several times, asking for recommendations for dentists or doctors, conversing with people who are living in a community we are considering for relocation, and so forth. So what about those who have already retired – what financial and nonfinancial pitfalls can they warn us about? According to financial planners who work with retirees and retirees themselves, these are some of retirees' top regrets:

1. Not starting to save early enough/not saving enough (biggest regret for most).
2. Holding too much debt (car loans, mortgages, credit card, educational loans).
3. Not figuring out how much they'll need in retirement.
4. Not knowing where their money was going prior to retirement to form a basis for a budget when they retired.
5. Not knowing how to effectively invest their money.
6. Not considering major life events, such as unexpected illness or death of a spouse.
7. Claiming Social Security too early.
8. Not making catch-up contributions to retirement plans.
9. Retiring too early (not enough money) or not retiring earlier (to enjoy the gift of being in control of your own time).
10. Not considering how they will use their time in retirement (what are they retiring to – not from).
11. Not traveling more when they had the opportunity to do so.

12. Not discussing, if part of a couple, their expectations for retirement ahead of time.
13. Not enough diversity in their retirement portfolio.
14. Buying/staying in a bigger house than they really need or one that is not aging-friendly.

## Lessons from the Pandemic

It would be an omission to discuss retirement without exploring the effects of the pandemic on retirees' beliefs and attitudes. A 2021 study by Age Wave, Edward Jones, and the Harris Poll provides some important insights:

- 61% of retirees reported that "the pandemic has given them more appreciation for what makes life meaningful."
- 92% of retirees agree that "purpose is a key to a successful retirement."
- 67% of retirees said "spending time with loved ones provides them with the greatest source of meaning."
- 93% of retirees believe it's "important to feel useful in retirement," and 87% said being useful "makes them feel youthful."
- 89% of retirees feel that "there should be more ways for retirees to put their talents and knowledge to use for the benefit of their communities and society."
- Regarding finances of those not yet retired, a third are "contributing more to their retirement savings because of the pandemic" and a third plan to "delay retirement because of the pandemic."
- Finally, 77% "wish there were more resources available to help them plan for an ideal retirement beyond just their finances." (And that, of course, is a major purpose of this book.)

It will be interesting to see how – or if – these beliefs and attitudes will change as we return to a postpandemic "normal" or a "new normal."

*Freedom, purpose, enjoyment, stress-free.* These were the most common words when more than 5,000 workers were asked in a Transamerica Center for Retirement Study what the word "retirement" meant to them. Let's turn those words into reality by exploring what to do with your "168 hours a week" in the next two chapters. And, remember, much of learning is trial and error – retirement is a brand-new experience. Keep these wise words of Nelson Mandela in mind: "I never lose. I either win or I learn."

## Just for Fun

Since you're thinking about retirement, it's helpful to know some of the vocabulary. Here are a dozen words/acronyms you "need" to know:

- **KIPPERS** (kids in parents' pockets eroding retirement savings): Hint – save for your own retirement *first*. Kids have more time than we do to save for the future.
- **SKIER** (spending the kids' inheritance): SKIERs plan to spend all their money before they die . . . travel, have multiple homes, eat out, own luxury vehicles, and so forth.
- **Kidults:** Offspring between the ages of 18 and 25, often financially and psychologically dependent on their parents. They are caught in the transition between childhood and adulthood, also known as "adultolescence."
- **Splitters:** Those who split their time between two (or more) homes. About 15% of adults over 50 own a second home, according to the Research Institute for Housing America.
- **FANBY** (find a new backyard): People who relocate multiple times, perhaps moving to a resort style area, then closer to children/grandchildren, then to an active adult community, and then a CCRC (continuing care retirement community).
- **Freemales:** Women who choose to be single (remove "spinster," "old maid," and "crazy cat-lady" from your vocabulary *now*).

- **Wusband:** Self-explanatory.
- **Gray Divorce:** Divorce among those 50 and older. The divorce rate in this age group has doubled over the past decade, and now makes up 25% of all uncouplings, according to Susan Brown, professor of sociology at Bowling Green State University. You may recall that Bill and Melinda Gates put out this statement after 27 years of marriage: "We no longer believe we can grow together as a couple in this next phase of our lives." Two-thirds of gray divorces are initiated by women. Most common reasons for divorce from a survey of almost 2,400 recently divorced couples: falling out of love by one or both spouses (the most common reason); issues communicating (a close second); lack of caring, trust, or respect; a desire to move in a different direction because they had grown apart. For many, "'til death do us part" is no longer valid when life is long . . . and life is short.
- **Returnment:** Going back to work after leaving a primary career.
- **Jhobby:** Turning a hobby into a paycheck.
- **LATs** (living apart together): Couples in committed relationships who maintain separate residences. Kevin R., for example, had a number of corporate transfers that required him to live in several different states throughout his career, but his wife, Caroline, a nurse, remained in their home in Michigan until Kevin retired.
- **LTAs** (living together apart): No longer a couple, but remaining in the same household because of finances, children, or the perception of social stigma.

## Quiz: Are You Ready to Launch Your Retirement?

*For each question, please choose the statement which best fits your thinking and frame of mind at the present time. More than one answer may seem appropriate but you must pick only one.*

# The New Retirement

1. **How do you feel about giving up your job and career?**

   A   My career is history. I'm ready to open a new chapter.
   B   I would enjoy meeting other retirees from my profession.
   C   I would like to stay up to date with trends and developments in my profession just to keep my hand in it.
   D   Once retired I'll be happy to mentor younger people in my profession.

2. **How open are you to new adventures in your retirement?**

   A   I'll probably do things I've done in my past, but now I'll have more time for them.
   B   I'm itching to try some things I never had time for during my career.
   C   I don't plan on changing my leisure activities that much.
   D   I earned my retirement so I'm going to have fun doing nothing.

3. **What part will exercise play in your retirement?**

   A   My outdoor activities will keep me in good shape.
   B   I'll keep my weight in check by walking.
   C   I plan to have a regular daily exercise program.
   D   I probably won't have a planned exercise program.

4. **Do you plan to include weight training?**

   A   Weight training may do me more harm than good.
   B   Weight and resistance training will be part of my exercise program.
   C   I'll get enough exercise through aerobic activities.
   D   Body building for seniors doesn't make sense to me.

5. **How "home-based" will your retirement be?**

   A   I'll spend a lot of time at home doing at least one of these activities – watching TV, talking on phone, doing household chores, working on computer, reading.
   B   Chilling out at home is my idea of retirement.
   C   If I am home too much I have to get out.
   D   I expect to spend a good deal of time carrying on activities outside the home.

6. **How does your spouse's retirement coincide with your own?**

   A   My spouse has already retired.
   B   My spouse does not plan to retire any time soon.
   C   My spouse and I plan to retire together (within an 18-month period).
   D   I don't have a spouse.

## 7. What is the status of your children?

A   I still have children living at home.
B   I have no children living at home.
C   I have "boomerang kids" who may want to return home for a while.
D   I have no children.

## 8. Are you at risk for depression?

A   I have suffered bouts of depression in the past.
B   My spouse has had some problems with depression.
C   I have no history of depression.
D   I get anxious now and down at times but not what you'd call clinical depression.

## 9. Are you a "hobby person"?

A   I have no major hobbies but I may find one during retirement.
B   I have some hobbies to keep me busy.
C   I don't really need any hobbies to enjoy retirement.
D   There is at least one current hobby that I can devote more time to during retirement.

## 10. How active are you in community organizations?

A   I'm not a joiner.
B   I plan to become active in some organizations once I retire.
C   I'm already active in several church/social/civic organizations.
D   I belong to some organizations, but I'm not very active.

## 11. Do you like volunteer work?

A   I already do volunteer work when I find time.
B   I have other activities that keep me busy and don't need volunteer work.
C   I prefer to work for pay.
D   I plan to volunteer some of my time during retirement.

## 12. What friends do you spend the most time with?

A   I have close friends from work and outside of work.
B   I make friends easily and my time with them varies widely.
C   I spend as much as half of my social time with friends I know from work.
D   I spend only a small part of my time socializing with work friends.

### 13. Do you have a good support network?

A    I have at least five close friends that I see often.

B    My social circle includes more than a dozen good friends.

C    I enjoy my own company and am not really a social person.

D    I have one or two friends I see regularly.

### 14. How will travel play a role in retirement?

A    I enjoy travel more than my spouse.

B    I enjoy being close to home.

C    I enjoy travel and look forward to many trips during retirement.

D    My spouse enjoys travel more than myself.

### 15. How important is family time in retirement?

A    I look forward to family visits during retirement.

B    I plan to spend more time with family during retirement.

C    Visits to family members won't play much of a role in retirement.

D    Visits to my spouse's family are too frequent or too long.

### 16. Do you and your spouse (or significant other) enjoy doing things together?

A    We don't have the same interests.

B    We have some interests in common.

C    We like doing things together and separately.

D    I don't have a spouse or significant other.

### 17. Will learning and study play a role in retirement?

A    It may play a role if I find something I like.

B    I finished school a long time ago. Why go back to the classroom?

C    My spouse or friends have encouraged me to take some courses.

D    Taking courses on various subjects will make retirement more interesting.

### 18. How's your work/play ethic?

A    I earned my rest so I don't plan to work at anything too hard.

B    I'll throw myself into my retirement just as I did my work.

C    The less the work the less the stress in my retirement.

D    I won't mind work as long as it's not too taxing.

### 19. Will you be acting your age during retirement?

A    Now that I'm older I will be restricting some of my activities.

B    I expect health problems will have some effect on my retirement.

C    For the immediate future I expect only a few physical limitations.
D    I don't feel my age. Mentally I am decidedly younger.

**20. Does the TV keep you company?**
A    On a typical day I have regular TV shows I watch.
B    I watch TV but I prefer to be doing other things.
C    On a typical day TV is my main source of entertainment.
D    I watch TV fewer than three hours a day.

**21. How easily will success come in retirement?**
A    I succeeded in my career and I'll be just as successful in retirement.
B    I will have to change gears and think differently in retirement than I did during my career.
C    Succeeding at retirement may take a little work.
D    I'm not sure.

**22. Will you have enough money for retirement?**
A    Good financial planning will pave the way for my retirement success.
B    I plan to work part-time to make sure ends meet.
C    I'm not sure how financially prepared I am.
D    It will be touch-and-go on the money but I'll get by.

**23. Will your native skills help you in retirement?**
A    I'm still at the top of my game.
B    I'm not as mentally sharp as I was 20 years ago.
C    Retirement means I won't have to push myself, so I'm not concerned about skills.
D    Employers don't want an over-the-hill person like me for good-paying jobs.

**24. How's your health?**
A    Good. No chronic diseases and the same for my spouse (if you have one).
B    I'm okay but my spouse has a serious health problem.
C    I have some health issues but my goal is to not let them slow me down.
D    My health is a problem and may seriously affect my retirement activities.

**25. Are you prepared for retirement?**

A   I've been looking forward to it for a long time, so I'll be okay.
B   Of course. I don't have to prepare for goofing off.
C   I've planned a few things that should be fun.
D   I've done a lot of planning and research on what I will do with my time.

## "Are You Ready to Launch Your Retirement?" Scoring

 1. (A)4; (B)2; (C)1; (D)2
 2. (A)3; (B)4; (C)1; (D)0
 3. (A)3; (B)3; (C)4; (D)0
 4. (A)0; (B)4; (C)3; (D)0
 5. (A)1; (B)0; (C)3; (D)4
 6. (A)4; (B)0; (C)4; (D)2
 7. (A)0; (B)4; (C)2; (D)4
 8. (A)0; (B)0; (C)4; (D)3
 9. (A)2; (B)3; (C)1; (D)2
10. (A)0; (B)3; (C)4; (D)1
11. (A)4; (B)2; (C)2; (D)4
12. (A)3; (B)4; (C)1; (D)2
13. (A)3; (B)4; (C)0; (D)1
14. (A)1; (B)0; (C)4; (D)1
15. (A)4; (B)4; (C)0; (D)1
16. (A)2; (B)0; (C)2; (D)4
17. (A)2; (B)0; (C)2; (D)4
18. (A)0; (B)4; (C)0; (D)1
19. (A)2; (B)1; (C)3; (D)4
20. (A)1; (B)3; (C)0; (D)4
21. (A)2; (B)4; (C)2; (D)2
22. (A)4; (B)3; (C)3; (D)2
23. (A)4; (B)3; (C)0; (D)0
24. (A)4; (B)0; (C)0; (D)1
25. (A)2; (B)0; (C)3; (D)4

## Total Points: Scoring

**Below 50** – Abort your retirement mission immediately. Key systems are not functioning properly.

**50–59** – A launch hold is in effect. More preparation is recommended.

**60–69** – A launch is possible but prepare for a bumpy ride.

**70–85** – You're cleared for takeoff. A few system checks and repairs may be necessary during the flight.

**Above 85** – A-OK. All systems are a go.

Source: RetirementRocket.com

# More Resources

## Books

Dychtwald, Ken, and Robert Morison. *What Retirees Want.* Wiley, 2020.

Gilbert, Fritz. *Keys to a Successful Retirement: Staying Happy, Active, and Productive in Your Retired Years.* Rockridge Press, 2020.

Leider, Richard. *Who Do You Want to Be when You Grow Old?: The Path of Purposeful Aging.* Berrett-Koehler Publishers, 2021.

Moss, Wes. *What the Happiest Retirees Know: 10 Habits for a Healthy, Secure, and Joyful Life.* McGraw-Hill Education, 2021.

Petrow, Steven. *Stupid Things I Won't Do When I Get Old: A Highly Judgmental, Unapologetically Honest Accounting of All the Things Our Elders Are Doing Wrong.* Citadel, 2021.

Singletary, Michelle. *What to Do with Your Money When Crisis Hits: A Survival Guide.* Mariner Books, 2021.

## Websites (General)

AARP (www.aarp.com)

Next Avenue (www.nextavenue.org). This site also has a great section for solo agers.

TopRetirements (www.topretirements.com)

## *Websites (Targeted to Women)*

National Association of Baby Boomer Women (NABBW)
    (www.nabbw.com)
Sixty and Me (www.sixtyandme.com)

## *Podcasts*

**Retire Sooner Podcast with Wes Moss** (over 60 podcasts):
    https://podcasts.apple.com/us/podcast/retire-sooner-with-wes-
    moss/id902749218

# 2

# 168 Hours a Week

■ ■ ■

Does the idea of planning 168 hours a week for two or three decades (or more) sound thrilling or intimidating? If you deduct eight hours in a 24-hour period for sleeping (and I'm guessing not too many of us get a full eight hours of sleep every night), that still leaves 112 hours a week to "fill" mindfully or mindlessly. It was noted in Chapter 1 that it's important to replace the benefits, in addition to a paycheck, that working provides. That is what this chapter is about. Retirement doesn't mean sitting on the sidelines of life. It's the freedom to choose and forge new paths, pursuits, relationships, and opportunities. You can decide who you are and who you want to be. You can re-invent yourself. Kind of like our GPS, when we need to "recalculate."

Assuming you have the financial means, you can play golf, pickleball, tennis, watch television, and eat all your meals out, but what other options exist? What types of volunteer and lifelong learning opportunities are there? Hobbies? Travel? Play a new sport? Volunteer? Learn a new language? Use the time to deepen relationships with family/friends? Decide to finally lose those 20 or 30 extra pounds you've been carrying around for several decades? Create or do something that will make a lasting impact, long after your death (see Chapter 10)? Start a second (or third or fourth) career (see Chapter 3)?

But, is there a "sweet spot" for how much *unscheduled* time per day is best? You may have spent or you are spending much of your preretirement life with so many demands on your time, you feel you can barely make a trip to the bathroom. Retirement can change that time crush, but many retired people continue to over-schedule and still feel under constant time pressure. A 2021 study addressed this exact question about time – it turns out people are generally happiest with about two to five hours of unstructured time per day. Fewer than two hours created stress, while more than five hours each day of free time negatively affected feelings of well-being and feeling purposeful. So, just as in the story of Goldilocks (as in many facets of life), there is a balance that is often "just right." And, what's the best thing to do with that "free time"? The researchers found exercising (I know, for some it's more of a job/obsession), learning new things, or spending time with others increased happiness – in other words, doing things by choice, not obligation. And, the free time doesn't have to be done in large chunks of time to have a beneficial effect. Reading a short chapter of a book or taking a mile hike or just watching the clouds passing overhead for 15 minutes can all be good uses of discretionary time. A reminder – what's considered "free time" for some (walking the dog) could be considered obligatory by others.

Now is a good time to complete the "Time on Your Hands" worksheet at the end of this chapter to get a preliminary sense of how you think you will/do spend your time. The results may be eye-opening. If part of a couple, compare and discuss your results.

### *Personality and Goal-Setting*

Are you a planner? Martha H. is. She took care of her grandchildren for about 10 years after leaving her primary career of teaching Environmental Science and running the Science/Math department at a community college. Martha commuted from New Jersey to Boston for several years, staying Monday–Thursday to babysit, and then for several more years she commuted from New Jersey to New York City to take care of her grandchildren from her other daughter. When the kids were older and the weekly babysitting stint was over, travel (deferred for a year because of Covid-19), reading, snowshoeing (at her second home in Colorado), genealogy, and walking are high on Martha's list of things to do – and she makes sure it happens. Family is at the forefront of many retirees' lists of what is important.

On the other hand, my single friend Jean M. lives very much in the moment. She will go on a trip without hotel reservations, embraces each day as it comes, and is willing to drop whatever she's doing and help out family members if they need assistance, including caring for her mother for several years as her mom slowly succumbed to Alzheimer's.

Gordon C. loosely structures his time. He plays occasional golf, some tennis, maintains the house, and is catching up on all the books he wanted to read as a busy professional but never had the time to do so. He also serves on the Board of his community association, and volunteers at a food bank. He and his wife care for their grandchildren at least once a week to give their adult children a break and to enjoy some quality time with the kids. As Gordon likes to say, "I feel youthful when I am useful."

Teresa G. divorced after a long marriage and a fulfilling career as a counselor, and is now a realtor. She lives in Florida, loves working with and helping people find their ideal place, and immensely enjoys her second career. She finds her counseling background provides many skills she can use in her new role.

These examples of different people with different personalities share this in common: They all have goals they want to accomplish.

For most people goal setting is important. The research shows that people who aren't engaged in purposeful activities are generally not as happy as those who are. Whether you're talking about starting a new business, taking up birding, becoming a mentor, or trying out for a community theater production, it's best to be flexible, try out new things, have a natural curiosity about life, and have at least a general plan for your future.

Make lists! Take the time to think about what you want to accomplish, and write down your goals. If you are part of a couple, set down both individual and joint ideas relating to family, working, travel, health, lifelong learning, volunteering, friends, making a difference, learning a new sport or language, or any other area. Recognize that each person in the relationship has valid needs and wants. Decide which interests you share, and recognize that having time apart for separate interests is also important. Brainstorm all possibilities, then evaluate and prune the unworkable ones.

## Be SMART

I love mnemonics and acronyms. They make things much easier to remember. As a kid, you may remember "ROY G BIV," a clever way of remembering the order of the hues of the rainbow: Red, Orange, Yellow, Green, Blue, Indigo, Violet. I took many, many science classes as an undergrad and grad student, and remember the taxonomic hierarchy of organisms by making up this crazy sentence (can recall it decades later) . . . **K**eep **P**utting **C**heese **O**n **F**resh **G**ravy **S**oup . . . which represents **K**ingdom, **P**hylum, **C**lass, **O**rder **F**amily, **G**enus, **S**pecies.

**SMART** is an easy-to-remember acronym describing the characteristics of goal-setting: **S**pecific, **M**easurable, **A**ttainable, **R**ealistic, and **T**ime-Sensitive. So, when coming up with your goals, be SMART. Rather than saying "I want to continue to learn new things," say "I will sign up for a European history class at my local community college for the upcoming spring semester." Rather than "I want to exercise more," say, "I will walk from 9 a.m. to 10 a.m. every Monday, Wednesday, and Friday." Writing out your goals and posting them where they are visible will help reinforce them. Creating self-imposed deadlines can be very motivating.

You may already have a list of goals, or you may be open to suggestions. Let's take a look at some possibilities in the areas of education, sports, hobbies, volunteering, the world of work, and travel. The next chapter will address working or starting a business after leaving your primary career. The last chapter in the book will address leaving a legacy, financial or otherwise, so that will be addressed later.

## Lifelong Learning

"Live as if you were to die tomorrow. Learn as if you were to live forever." Brilliant guy, that Mahatma Gandhi. Until relatively recently it was believed that once nerve cells (also called neurons) were formed, that was it – our brains were pretty much "fixed." But, scientists have discovered that not only can neurons regenerate to an extent, but as importantly, the connections (called synapses) that allow nerve cells to communicate with one another can also sprout and create new pathways. This is called "neuroplasticity." More about this concept in Chapter 6, Forever Young, but it's important to know what is needed to "grow" our neurons: novelty, active learning, upending routines, solving problems, social interactions, and mental and physical engagement.

To quote Steppenwolf, let's explore ways to "get your motor runnin'" and mesh some of your SMART goals with these suggestions to wisely use those 168 hours a week.

### In-Person Learning

There are suggestions for *living* in a college town in Chapter 5, but let's take a look at how you can enjoy learning for free/low cost in person at educational institutions such as universities, colleges, and community colleges. Most offer tuition-free classes on a space-available basis if you meet certain criteria. You may not be awarded any credits, and you'll need to pay for any books and perhaps some associated fees, but what a gift.

As an example, I will use my alma mater for my undergrad and master's degree, the University of Maryland (Go Terps!). Their "Golden ID Program" permits you to enroll in up to three classes/

semester on a space-available basis – tuition-free. You must be 60 years of age or older, a legal resident of Maryland, and retired, which is defined as "not engaged in gainful employment for more than 20 hours a week." There is a fee for the Golden ID (about $260 per semester), which allows the use of the libraries, shuttle buses, and some additional services. With a three-credit in-person class normally around $1,000, if you're enrolling in three classes, it's a good deal. Community colleges can be a lot cheaper. I was an Assistant Professor at Sussex County Community College in New Jersey for a number of years. Their deal is a bargain. You need to be 65 or older, a resident of the county, meet any prerequisites for the class (some, like lab classes or trade classes are excluded), and register in person the final two business days before the start of the semester. No fees, no tuition. Taking in-person classes provides the additional benefit of social connections along with the sheer joy of learning – without the tests and papers. Sweet!

If you're thinking about getting a formal degree, many colleges exempt "mature" students from the SAT or ACT. CLEP, the College Level Examination Program (https://clep.collegeboard.org ), allows you to earn college credits by passing exams in a variety of subjects. Cost per exam is about $90 (often free for military personnel).

OLLI (Osher Lifelong Learning Institute, www.osherfoundation.org), offered in more than 120 U.S. institutions of higher learning, is a philanthropic organization that supports lifelong learning for adults 50 and older. OLLI offers member-driven classes (no credit/no assignments/no grades) facilitated by peers and college faculty. Using Arizona State University as an example, there is a small membership charge (about $20/semester) and then a reasonable charge for a class (Example: $14 for a 1.5 hour class); you may need to pay for parking/transportation on campus. Classes can literally range from A to Z. For example, "Ancient Etruscan and Roman Art" to "Zhivago: The Novel and the Movie."

Be sure to investigate what your local library, community center, school system and/or county offers. You'll be surprised how many quality and free (love that word!) classes/lectures/workshops are out there. (I am on the Board of Trustees of my local library and the number of no-cost courses that are offered, both in person and virtually, is impressive.)

### Online (Free)

**Podcasts** (audio files) have exploded in popularity. Americans aged 55 and better are among the fastest growing listeners, comprising 40% of the podcast audience in 2019, according to Marketing Charts. Download and learn from your laptop/phone/computer/ mobile device while you're comfy and sitting at home or at Starbucks, on the beach or taking a walk, or in your car. A few suggestions from various genres (all of these sites offer free podcasts):

- History: Dan Carlin Hardcore History (www.dancarlin.com); Fall of Civilizations (www.fallofcivilizationspodcast.com); The Explorers (www.explorerspodcast.com/urdaneta/); Malcolm Gladwell's Revisionist History (www.revisionisthistory.com).
- Health/Science/Culture/etc.: How Stuff Works (https:// www.howstuffworks.com/about-hsw.htm), is "an award-winning source of unbiased, reliable, easy-to-understand answers and explanations of how the world actually works."
- Psychology: Hidden Brain (https://www.npr.org/series/4233 02056/hidden-brain); Freakonomics (https://freakonomics. com/). This last is a personal favorite of mine.

### MOOCS (Free)

- Massive Open Online Courses are known as MOOCS (www .MOOC.org). There are approximately 3,000 free courses in all disciplines from stellar universities such as MIT, Yale, and Princeton. You can spend your 168 hours/week on this site alone.
- Coursera (www.coursera.org) is another MOOC with free offerings from more than 200 top-tier universities such as Duke, Stanford, and the Imperial College of London. Sign me up!

## Masterclass ($180/year)

If you want to learn from titans in their respective fields, check out Masterclass (www.masterclass.com). Writing for TV? Shonda Rhimes is your instructor. Songwriting? Alicia Keys. Photography? Annie Leibovitz. Cooking? Gordon Ramsay. Chess? Gary Kasparov. You get the idea. More than 100 classes covering nine categories, and a PDF workbook for each class, which averages approximately 20 ten-minute lessons. New classes are added monthly.

All this accumulated knowledge at your fingertips, *and* the time to indulge your interests. Sweet!

# Volunteering

Besides the obvious perk of making a difference for others, volunteering bestows benefits on the volunteer: new friends, meet others with similar interests, learn new skills, gain confidence, tackle challenges, have fun, find purpose, combat depression, lower stress levels, become healthier physically, and perhaps delay or reverse declining brain function, according to a study at Johns Hopkins University. As Gandhi noted (yes, I am quoting him again!), "The best way to find yourself is to lose yourself in the service of others."

AmeriCorp reports that more than 30% of American adults volunteer (women volunteer more than men), and the economic value of their time contributions equals $167 billion. More than half of all Americans donate money to charity as well.

If you plan to give money to an organization, it's important to know the percentage of donations that go directly to the cause. For example, the American Red Cross spends more than 90% of its income on programs that directly benefit communities. Choose a charity that dedicates fewer than 30% of its total costs to fundraising and administrative expenses. Two websites to check out a charity you're considering are Charity Navigator (www.charitynavigator.org) and CharityWatch (www.charitywatch.org). Be sure your donation gets the biggest bang for the buck.

Here's a list of in-person and/or virtual volunteering opportunities from (literally) A–Z. Of course, there are many, many worthy organizations and most gladly accept monetary donations as well, but check them out on CharityWatch and/or Charity Navigator first.

- **Adult Literacy** (www.proliteracy.org). Provides basic literary, math or computer skills to the more than 20% of adults in the United States who struggle with literacy issues.
- **Big Brothers/Big Sisters** (www.bbbs.org). "Ignite the power and promise of youth." Connects volunteers to children in mentoring relationships.
- **Create the Good** (www.createthegood.org) is an AARP site (you don't have to be an AARP member.). Find volunteer opportunities, virtual or in person, based on your ZIP code. When I put in my ZIP code, hospice helper, teaching a one-hour virtual class to older adults (with the volunteer's choice of topic), and being a garden volunteer at a local state park popped up.
- **Disaster Response.** Provide food, drinks, snacks, and donated goods following a disaster through The Salvation Army (www.salvationarmyusa.org).
- **E-volunteering.** As an example of volunteering from your home, check out https://www.dosomething.org/us/articles/9-places-to-volunteer-online-and-make-a-real-impact. This site lists a number of ways to volunteer online; how about volunteering at a crisis text line?
- **Food for the Homebound.** As Meals on Wheels (www.mealsonwheelsamerica.org) notes, "Nine million seniors in America face the threat of hunger" and "millions more live in isolation." The first meal was delivered in 1954, and 221 million meals are served to 2.4 million older adults by two million volunteers *each year*.
- **Guardian ad litem** (www.guardianadlitem.org). Represent the best interests of a child in judicial proceedings that include child abuse, custody issues, child support, and so on.

- **Hospice Foundation of America** (www.hospicefoundation. org). My dad had incredibly compassionate volunteer hospice workers at my parents' home when my father was in the final stages of lung cancer. (Background checks, orientations, and training are required as a prerequisite to volunteering.)
- **Income tax preparation** (https://www.irs.gov/individuals/irs-tax-volunteers). Volunteers learn how to prepare tax returns and help those who need assistance through VITA (Volunteer Income Tax Assistance) or TCE (Tax Counseling for the Elderly). Nothing better than perhaps learning a new skill and making a difference in others' lives.
- **Job assistance.** The stated mission of Dress for Success (www. dressforsuccess.org) is to "empower women to achieve economic independence by providing a network of support, professional attire, and the development tools to help women thrive in work and in life." Ladies, a great opportunity to declutter your closet and assist disadvantaged women.
- **K** (as in Martin Luther King) **Day of Service** (https://ameri-corps.gov/newsroom/events/mlk-day). This is a national day of service on the third Monday in January in honor of MLK. Suggestions include "tutoring and mentoring children, painting schools and senior centers, delivering meals, building homes, and reflecting on Dr. King's life and teachings."
- **Library.** Book lover? Contact your local branch and share the love by volunteering to shelve books, assist in clerical work, prepare children's programs, and so forth. I've been on my local library's board of trustees for more than a decade, and am astounded by all the things libraries do beyond lending books and DVDs. And check out all those classics you swore you'd read one day. Donate those books you have laying around that you'll never read/won't read again.
- **Mentor** (www.mentoring.org). Love their quote: "Potential is equally distributed; opportunity is not." Fill out a simple form and find mentoring opportunities near you. Or, ask

about opportunities at your local church, school, or civic organizations.

- **Nurture.** Being a "baby cuddler" in a NICU is a very popular volunteer activity. Contact your local hospital/children's hospital for specifics on volunteer opportunities and how to apply.
- **Offer assistance to the elderly and homebound.** AmeriCorps Seniors Senior Companion Program (https://americorps. gov/serve/fit-finder/americorps-seniors-senior-companion-program). "Serve as a friend and companion to older neighbors making sure they can live in their own homes for as long as possible." Must be 55 or better to volunteer.
- **Poverty reduction through affordable housing.** "Housing is the key to reducing intergenerational poverty and increasing economic mobility" according to the National Low Income Housing Coalition. Check out Habitat for Humanity (www. habitat.org). I volunteered on two builds, and learned to lay tile in a kitchen and help erect the outside walls of the house (our group was very closely supervised by someone who knew what they were doing, of course).
- **Queen for a Day Foundation** (www.foradayfoundation. org). Now renamed "For a Day Foundation," this charity is "committed to creating emotionally therapeutic experiences for seriously ill children and providing them and their families with a joyful and much needed diversion from the strain of chronic treatment" in the hospital using play-oriented programs like "Queen for a Day" or "Hero for a Day."
- **Reading.** Volunteer to be a reader to children. Reach out to your public elementary schools and/or public library. Or, contact your local United Way (www.unitedway.org – look for "Find Your United Way" tab) for other possibilities. Reading is vital for brain and language development, comprehension, and expanding children's imaginations. Be a role model.
- **Special Olympics** (https://www.specialolympics.org/get-involved/volunteer). Volunteers are needed as "coaches,

trainers, officials, event organizers, fundraisers, and managers." Volunteers can also play "alongside athletes with intellectual disabilities—or fans cheering in the stands."

- **Tutoring (Learn to be).** Learn to be (https://www.learntobe. org/apply). "Help K–12 underserved youths in math, science, reading and writing from wherever is most convenient and whenever is most convenient." Or, contact your local school system for additional options.
- **Usher.** Assist audience members and see performances for free? Contact your community theatre, high school, college theatre department, or performing-arts centers. A win-win.
- **Voter Registration.** Contact your local election office and volunteer to be an election worker. There may be requirements, such as age, residency, and proof that you are a registered voter.
- **Walk a Shelter Dog.** Contact your local shelter. Besides walking a dog, you may want to help in the office, collect donations, or best of all, adopt a furry friend.
- **Xenophon Therapeutic Riding Center** (http://xenophontrc. org). "To enrich the lives of individuals with disabilities through a high-quality program of equine-assisted therapies." For additional therapeutic equine programs, see https:// www.ridinghome.com/page-us.
- **Your imagination.** What can you do to make a difference or give back? Perhaps think locally: Which of your friends, neighbors, or relatives could use a hand with household or yard chores, grocery shopping, or babysitting? Volunteer to organize a meal train for someone who is ill or whose loved one has passed away; walk dogs for a friend who has had recent surgery.
- **Zoo.** Perhaps for you, "It's all happening at the zoo," like Simon and Garfunkel sang. Be an exhibit host, assist with day-to-day care of the animals, or perform administrative duties.

This list is a snapshot of volunteer possibilities; training, background checks, and certain time commitments are often required. If you're still looking, go to www.volunteermatch.com, put in your ZIP code and see the opportunities, both in person and virtual, that await.

Research shows it really does feel better to give than to receive. Volunteering is a great use of some of those 168 hours.

## Learn New Things/Hone Old Skills

"Broadly speaking, human beings can be divided into three classes: Those who are toiled to death, those who are worried to death, and those who are bored to death" (Winston Churchill). If life-long learning opportunities through classes or volunteering aren't enough, let's explore some other activities that enrich your life by broadening your knowledge, sharpening your skills, improving your health, or that are just plain fun:

**Move.** I took up tennis in my late 40s, and quickly became a huge devotee. It checks off a lot of what I like – exercise, social support, friendly competition, structure, and enjoying nature (I live in Florida, so it's outside play year-round). Tennis has led to many warm and lasting friendships (and lunches!). If you're looking for something a bit easier on the joints, consider pickleball, which is the fastest-growing sport in America, according to *The Economist.*

If racquet sports aren't your thing, perhaps join a gym (consider a few sessions with a personal trainer to get you on the right track), golf, bowling (a group from our community bowls weekly, with dinner afterward), belly dancing/ballroom/square/swing/line dancing (some studios provide a partner for you if you need one), and swimming and biking (easy on the joints). Snowboarding is so popular among older adults they are called "grays on trays." Plant a garden. Climb a mountain. Try a SUP (stand-up paddle-board). Of course, there is always walking, which is easy, free, and can be social or solitary. And, if you have a dog, he/she will love it.

**Think.** Join or start a book club – with your neighbors, through your local library, or online (check out www.goodreads.com for lots of suggestions). Linda and her husband Pete started a couples' book club in their new neighborhood by mailing an invitation to their neighbors (they didn't know all their names, so just a "Hello Neighbor" and an invite to come to their home on a specific date/time with the book selection included). It was the beginning of a decades-long book club, and decades-long friendships. Or, organize a monthly game night – Euchre, Train Dominoes, Bunco, Pictionary, Mahjong, and so forth. Strengthen your brain by learning a new language or instrument. Do crossword puzzles (I love the free online daily mini-crossword from the *New York Times*), Sudoku, acrostics, "Words with Friends," and jigsaw puzzles. Try an "escape room" – work as a team to escape a locked room within an hour by solving clues and puzzles. Addictive and mind stretching.

**"Be Curious, Not Judgmental."** Although this phrase is attributed to the poet Walt Whitman, according to Snopes (a fact-checking site), this is not Whitman's quote. However, if you watch/watched the miniseries *Ted Lasso*, "Be curious, not judgmental" is how the main character approaches life. Ted asks questions; he doesn't jump to conclusions; he's open; he doesn't assume; he explores all possibilities; he doesn't make snap decisions. This fictional character and this phrase are great models for making the most of retirement.

The benefits of being curious are backed by science. A 2013 study in *Psychological Science* found that improved memory was found only in those who engaged in activities that were "unfamiliar and mentally challenging, and that provide broad stimulation mentally and socially." Examples included quilting and digital photography. The lead researcher in this study, Denise Parks, said this about keeping our minds sharp: "When you are inside your comfort zone you may be outside of the enhancement zone." Push yourself to do things outside of your wheelhouse.

**Create.** Indulge your inner chef, if you're so inclined, or take up painting or sculpting or photography. Perhaps consider community or local theater. Helene G. performed in the musicals *The King and I* and *South Pacific* at Leisure World, an active adult community in Silver Spring Maryland, as well as in a performance of *Our Town*. (If you have stage fright, you can always work behind the scenes.) Or, sing at your place of worship; St. Augustine said, "To sing is to pray twice."

**Family.** A study by Age Wave/Merrill Lynch found that retirees ranked staying healthy, improving health, and relaxing at the top of their "Everyday Leisure Priorities" list, followed by family connections. Certainly "family connections" can fill lots of hours. But what does that phrase mean to you? Living a short distance from children/sibs/aging parents? Staying in touch via technology? Frequent in-person visits? Following your adult kids if they move? Having a second home near adult children/parents? Acting as a full-time sitter for your grandchildren while their parents work? Moving closer to your kids when you're elderly and need help? This is an important area to consider and discuss, particularly if you're part of a couple – are you both on the same page? To find out, take the survey, "Retire Close to Family . . . Or Not Too Close!" from TopRetirements.com at the end of Chapter 4, What and Where Is Home?

**Travel.** Travel is usually close to the top of the list of "wants" in retirement. No surprise – there's a big and exciting world out there to explore, and retirement provides the time (and hopefully the money – more on that in Chapters 8, 9, and 10). One of Rosemary and Ed G.'s retirement goals (Rosemary was a high school counselor and Ed is a retired CPA) was to visit every continent. It took 12 years to accomplish, but they did.

45

Of course, there are many types of travel. Recall the Greyhound bus commercial, with the tag line "Leave the driving to us." Do all the planning, do some of it, or be like the Greyhound ad, and purchase a complete travel itinerary with most, or all decisions preplanned. All you need to do is show up with your luggage and travel documents and the tour company will take it from there. What kind of traveler are you? Do you want a knowledgeable guide to lead you, or are you more likely to strike out on your own, meet the local people, and create your own itinerary? Or perhaps you're a hybrid of the two approaches, or you want to experience travel in a variety of ways. You could be like Carol and Phil White, who bought a small RV and lived in it for a year as they traversed the United States.

Here are Carol's thoughts and suggestions:

---

Of all the many ways to travel, RVing may be the most flexible. You can stay in a cozy RV park in the city, in a friend's driveway in the suburbs, in a beautiful national park, a full-amenity recreation complex – or something as unglamorous as a parking lot anywhere along your way.

Phil and I did all of those things in our year-long trip around the United States. We also "cheated" and stayed in a beautiful National Park Lodge or even a cabin by a lake when we were tired of doing the camping life. The beauty of it is that the choice is yours and you are always ready for whatever may come your way. We traveled in a small Class B RV, so we had total flexibility to park downtown or under a tree and call that home for the night.

We recommend having some goals for your trip – see all the state capitols, all the National Parks, something quirky in each state, hiking a famous trail in each area – whatever strikes your interest. Those goals will help shape the planning for your trip.

My sister called it traveling with "our shell on our back," which is an apt expression because you have everything you need with you. That was a major appeal to us versus taking a car on our long trip. On more than one occasion, being able to pull over at a rest stop or a park and heat up last night's left-overs for lunch proved to be one of the unexpected things we enjoyed – we were always prepared for an impromptu meal. Another plus was that you were always prepared for a "pit stop" – no more looking for the rest area or dying until you got somewhere. This was especially handy when we were stopped in summer construction – sometimes for an hour or more.

Choosing the type of RV that you want to travel in is one of the most challenging aspects of your planning. You have to think carefully about your own driving abilities and desires, about your mechanical adaptability, and what kind of a trip you are planning. If you are planning a mostly urban experience, a 45-foot Class A "bus" would probably not be your first best choice in New York City or Chicago. On the other hand, if one of you is adept at driving a big rig, knows the ins and outs of mechanics and you are planning a week at a time in a beautiful RV park or National Park, then a big rig may be perfect for you. The smaller sized RVs are great for maneuverability, fitting in tight spaces (city parking), and stopping at an auto repair place when something doesn't sound right (most are built on some type of truck chassis). The other option is, of course, a towable – either a trailer or a fifth-wheel that attaches in the bed of a truck. The advantage of this arrangement is you can disconnect and take your vehicle with you and not your entire "house." Depending on your trip plans, that can be very handy. Towing a car behind a larger RV is also an option that might serve your needs.

If you are planning a long trip, we recommend that you don't overplan it. If you've made reservations ahead and something happens, which it will, then you have all those plans to undo. Have an itinerary of roughly where you want to be when, just to keep you on track, but please don't try to plan it all ahead – most of the fun is the whimsy of each day. Some days we traveled 5 miles, some days a hundred, but our longest day was 380 miles to meet up with some traveling friends. Just let your trip unfold in front of you. Because you have an RV of some type, you can always sleep in a parking

47

lot and if you have a small rig, many "full" RV parks can tuck you in someplace. We had some of the best RV spots that way. They once put us on a tennis court near Zion National Park on a busy holiday weekend with an extension cord for electricity. Fun!

RVing is a great way to meet people, see our country (or another!) and have the time of your life. We were never at a loss for something to talk about from every state (we are part of only 2% of our population who has been to every state) and travel enriches and informs your life forever. Don't wait. Do it now while you have your health. If you need more direction to begin planning your dream trip, grab a copy of our award-winning book, *Live Your Road Trip Dream.*

---

Some other options:

**Cruises.** Someone else cooks, serves, cleans, makes your bed each day, provides entertainment and enrichment programs, and transports you from destination to destination. What's not to like? Obviously, the pandemic affected the 2020–2021 travel season, but in 2019, there were 30 million cruise passengers with more than half coming from North America. Ships range from the mega (almost 7,000 passengers) to the intimate. Having cruised quite a bit, I've noticed over the years that some people never disembark at the ports because they have been on so many cruises (and they tend to win all the Trivia games since they've heard all the questions before!). Recent welcome additions to many cruise ships include dedicated solo staterooms, so a single doesn't have to pay the dreaded "single supplement."

**Escorted Tours.** Ann and John B. love escorted tours through OAT (Overseas Adventure Travel). My spouse and I took an OAT tour to Israel/Palestine and absolutely loved it. It included visiting residents' homes, and having an open political dialogue with both Israelis and Palestinians.

Hotels, transportation, transfers to the airport/hotel, most meals and some sightseeing are usually included in escorted tours. (OAT also offers exclusive women's tours.) Brian P., who is single, loves Smart Tours, which are all-inclusive and pride themselves on being affordable. Brian is a worldwide traveler and we value his advice, and indeed my spouse and I took a Smart Tour to India and loved it. Steve and Debbie L. did a bike tour in Europe through Backroads Rhine River Cruise Bike Tour, riding bikes through four countries in eight days while also enjoying the food and luxury of a small AMA Waterways ship along the Rhine. Those on the trip decided how many miles they wanted to ride during the day, and were transported back to the ship when ready.

**Singles' Travel.** The travel industry is finally recognizing that not everyone is coupled. Check out the all-women Oh Solo Mio (www.ohsolomio.travel) or male/female Singles Travel International (www.singlestravelintl.com). Many companies will help match you with a suitable roommate if you want one, using a questionnaire to match up like-minded travelers.

**African American Travel** (www.Africanamericantravelers.com). This company was founded in 2013 by Lawrence McLean to "broaden the reaches, horizons and perspectives of our community by bringing them to the world."

**LGBTQ+** (Lesbian/Gay/Bisexual/Transgender/Queer or Questioning, and the + represents inclusion of all people). If you've cruised, you may have seen "Friends of Bill W" or "Friends of Dorothy" listed in the daily cruise activity program. Although many might know that "Friends of Bill W" is an invitation for Alcoholics Anonymous members to meet, "Friends of Dorothy" is an opportunity to gather with LGBTQ+ persons. The large cruise companies offer these get-togethers, and more cruise ships are tailoring itineraries and sailings to various groups.

**Educational Travel.** It's almost an oxymoron – all travel is educational, in my opinion (even if it's learning how to make a trendy alcoholic drink on a cruise ship). However, there are some companies, such as Roads Scholar (https://www.roadscholar.org/) (formerly known as Elderhostel – the company wanted to eliminate the word "elder"), National Geographic Expeditions (https://www.nationalgeographic.com/expeditions/) and Smithsonian Journeys (https://www.smithsonianjourneys.org/) that really shine with their emphasis on learning. Greg T. went on a tour to the Amazon with National Geographic, which employs professional photographers, regional specialists, and naturalists. He learned so much about the flora and fauna of the area he felt he should have earned four college credits for a lab course in Biology.

**Voluntourism.** Travel with a noble purpose? That's what a volunteer vacation should be. There are a large number of organizations that sponsor travel nationally and internationally, but there are a few cautions about this type of travel. Some experts say it would be better to pay for those who live in a village to perform work (such as digging wells) than have unskilled people who fly in from another country for a week to do the labor. And, it's been documented that sometimes orphanages, a popular voluntourism destination in some countries, aren't always what they seem; some places have "created" orphanages to receive money from the volunteers. Vet all organizations carefully. For voluntourism close to home, a good site is AARP's CreatetheGood (www.createthegood.org). Put in your ZIP code, and see what good things you can do in your own backyard.

**Multigenerational travel.** What about several generations vacationing or traveling together? With three adult children, their spouses, and five grandchildren, my husband

and I solved this by living on the ocean in Florida, with a pool in the backyard. That's an instant magnet for all generations, as well as siblings and their spouses and children. But for multigenerational travel that doesn't involve buying a house, consider cruises. The megaships have something for everyone, including free childcare and acres of swimming pools. The Disney ships cater to children. Our grandchildren loved the ship, including the three years and older youth clubs the ships offer and the ship's live theater performance of *Beauty and the Beast* that was Broadway caliber. Other suggestions include dude ranches, all-inclusive resorts, skiing, a safari, camping, and national parks. Paula K. takes each grandchild to a destination of his/her choosing (within reason) when he/she turns ten. Want someone else to do the planning? Search for "Tauck Bridges tours" or "Sierra Club family." And heed this wise travel advice: "When preparing to travel, lay out all your clothes and all your money. Then take half the clothes and twice the money" (Susan Heller).

Travel not your thing or you don't have enough money for this luxury? Think like Queen Latifah: "I don't have to take a trip around the world or be on a yacht in the Mediterranean to have happiness. I can find it in the little things, like looking out into my backyard and seeing deer in the fields."

**Working/having a second (or third or fourth) career.** Are you interested in pursuing work-related opportunities after leaving your primary career or considering starting your own business? That's up next in Chapter 3.

"The best time to plant a tree was 20 years ago. The second best time is now." This period of your life we call retirement allows us to grow, change, and experience new things. Let's heed this Chinese proverb and make the most of it.

## Time On Your Hands

Will your retirement days be time-filled or time-empty?

To get an idea how well you'll handle time once you're retired, or how well you're presently doing in retirement, take this simple quiz. For a typical one-week period, estimate in half-hour increments (0.5, 1.0, 1.5, etc.) how much time you think you'll spend, or are spending, on the following activities:

| | |
|---|---:|
| Meal preparation | ___ |
| Housework, yard work and maintenance | ___ |
| Gardening | ___ |
| Exercise (walking, jogging, swimming, aerobics, weight training, etc.) | ___ |
| Sports (bicycling, golf, tennis, hiking, canoeing, pickleball, etc.) | ___ |
| Organizational activities (committees, civic meetings, social, religious services) | ___ |
| Volunteer work (church, civic, school or special causes) | ___ |
| Classes of any kind | ___ |
| Studying or prep for classes | ___ |
| Computer time (email, web surfing, IM, etc.) | ___ |
| Social events (lunch with friends, parties, get-togethers, plays, movies, concerts, entertaining at home, etc.) | ___ |
| Hobbies (not sport-related) | ___ |
| Plan/prep for a trip | ___ |
| Pet care ___ (walks, grooming, vet visits, playing with pet, etc.) | ___ |
| Family visits | ___ |
| Reading | ___ |
| Shopping | ___ |
| Miscellaneous errands (nonshopping) | ___ |
| Part-time job/new career | ___ |
| TOTAL | ___ |
| If male, add 77 hours (for sleep, eating, and personal hygiene) per week | ___ |
| If female, add 80.5 hours (for personal hygiene) per week | ___ |
| NET TOTAL | ___ |

Subtract the net total from 168 (the number of hours in a week)

Total "additional" time per week ____

For an average day, divide by 7 ____

Source: retirementrocket.com.

## More Resources

### *Books*

Fodor's Travel. *Best Road Trips in the USA.* Fodor's Travel, 2021.

Maxwell, John. *Change Your World: How Anyone, Anywhere Can Make a Difference.* HarperCollins Leadership, 2021.

Shultz, Patricia. *1,000 Places to See Before You Die.* Workforce Publishing Company, 2015.

Smith, Hyrum. *Purposeful Retirement: How to Bring Happiness and Meaning to Your Retirement.* Mango, 2019.

Yogerst, Joe. 100 Drives, 5000 Ideas. *National Geographic*, 2020.

### *Websites*

Volunteer or donate to a charity near you: https://greatnonprofits.org/nonprofits/Q/1

# CHAPTER

# 3

# Working in Retirement: It's Not an Oxymoron

■ ■ ■

Want to *learn, earn, and return* (go to school/college, have your job/career, and then go back to work after retiring from your primary employment)? As mentioned in Chapter 1, *nearly half* of recent retirees in the latest Employee Benefit Research Institute (EBRI) survey left the workforce earlier than planned, so the idea of working in retirement, especially doing something that aligns with your passions and interests, can be a terrific idea, assuming that if there is a spouse/significant other, you're both on the same page. And, 74% of recent retirees in that same survey planned to work in retirement, but only 24% did so. It reminds me of something a wise friend said long ago that resonates: "The vital part of every plan is to plan on your plan not going according to plan." You may want or need a side hustle/side gig. Close to 60 million Americans are participating in the "gig economy."

Desiring or needing extra income, wanting to unload some things you no longer need, feeling bored, wanting a sense of purpose, and/or choosing a new path that feeds a passion can be an exciting adventure and a very meaningful part of your 168 hours a week. You may have enough saved for retirement so that you don't *have* to work (but want to), perhaps you love the structure (and paycheck) of a job, perhaps you want a bridge until Social Security / Medicare kicks in, or you may really need the money . . . but whatever the reason, here are some suggestions, many of which have very reasonable entry requirements. Interestingly, for the first time in history, there are now five generations participating (potentially vying for jobs) in the workforce: The Silent Generation, Boomers, Generation X, Millennials, and Generation Z.

## Where the Jobs Are/Will Be

It's helpful to know the jobs that are in demand, and if you can pair that info with your interests, you're on your way. The *Occupational Outlook Handbook*, published by the U.S. Bureau of Labor Statistics, predicts areas of highest job growth through 2029 (www.bls. gov/ooh/ and click on "Most New Jobs (Projected)"). Median pay, entry-level education requirements, growth, work environment and other valuable information is included on the site. Jobs in high demand with low or no educational barriers include: home health aides and personal care aides (2.5 million employees are needed by 2030 in long-term care, according to McKnight's Senior Living), fast-food workers, waiters/waitresses, passenger vehicle drivers (think Lyft, Uber or school bus drivers), hand laborers, and material movers (Amazon, UPS, etc.). A short descriptive video accompanies each job description. It's a treasure trove of information.

If you enjoy your job, but would like additional free time, perhaps you can have a "phased" retirement at your current place of employment, by either job-sharing or becoming a part-time employee in a different capacity. It doesn't hurt to ask.

## AARP Recommendations for Part-Time Jobs for Retirees

AARP's top 25:

1. Full-charge bookkeeper (a full-charge bookkeeper manages all the accounting needs of the business)
2. Bookkeeper

3. Dental hygienist
4. School bus driver
5. Office manager
6. Registered nurse
7. Administrative assistant
8. Secretary
9. Licensed practical nurse
10. Paralegal
11. Nanny
12. Home health aide
13. Orderly
14. Dental assistant
15. Receptionist
16. Office clerk
17. Nurse assistant
18. Security guard
19. Merchandise displayer
20. Customer service representative
21. Pharmacy technician
22. Housekeeper
23. Retail sales worker
24. Sales associate
25. Cashier

## Companies That Welcome Mature Workers

**CAFÉ.** "The Age-Friendly Institute's Certified Age Friendly Employer (CAFÉ) program is the nation's only certification program that identifies organizations committed to being the best places to work for employees aged 50+." CAFÉ has a list of 100 employers from Adecco to Verizon. Check CAFÉ out here: https://institute.agefriendly.org/initiatives/certified-age-friendly-employer-program/.

**AARP Employer Pledge Program.** More than 1,500 companies have pledged to be age-diverse. You can search by your ZIP code and/or keywords: https://jobs.aarp.org/.

## Start Your Own Business – Know the Five Ps

Always dreamed of being your own boss? The Center for Retirement Research at Boston College published a paper by Joelle Abramowitz in 2020 that stated that 17.1% of workers aged 55–65 and 33.8% of workers aged 65 and older are self-employed. And, research from the Kellogg School of Management at Northwestern University found that it was middle-aged entrepreneurs who were most successful. A 60-year-old is almost four times as likely to start a successful start-up compared to a person who is 25. Age does have its benefits, including wisdom.

If this is something you're considering, think about what I call the "Five Ps" to increase your chances of success: *Passion* (you have an interest and competency in the area); *People* (there are many people who want/need your services/products); *Persistence* (you can/will persevere in spite of setbacks); *Platform* (you have or can create ways to promote your business); *Patience* (you're like a new parent, willing to invest the time and resources to watch your "baby" grow).

You may have heard these stories about famous authors: Stephen King's *Carrie* was rejected 30 times before being picked up by a publisher; J.K. Rowling of *Harry Potter* fame was rejected by the first 12 publishers; Louisa May Alcott of *Little Women* fame was told by one publisher "Stick to your teaching, Miss Alcott. You can't write." Talk about people having passion, persistence, and patience!

Joan M. was widowed in her mid-50s, and needed/wanted additional income to supplement what she and her husband had amassed prior to his death. Although she could get by, Joan loved both dogs and exercise. So she started a dog walking/dog-sitting business ("It's Potty Time!") that grew by word of mouth among neighbors and through repeat clients to the point Joan now has to turn away business. Joan's business keeps her busy, keeps her moving, facilitates meeting people, and pays for her tennis club membership . . . and of course, her furry clients love it (if you don't want to start your own dog-walking business, you can check out www.rover.com and sign up as a dog-walker).

Others have taken their skills/passions/hobbies and parlayed them into their own businesses, such as Kate K., who loves photography and takes pictures of newborns in adorable poses (the warmed-up bean bags really relax those babies), and captures family and wedding photographs that will be treasured for years to come. Brian F. is a whiz with his drone, and takes aerial videos of houses and the neighboring area for local real estate companies. John R., a former Midwest builder who retired and relocated to the Southwest, has a great gig working with homeowners who are building houses, many for the first time, providing advice about building materials and design, as well as keeping an eye on the building process, particularly for those who are building homes but live in another state. Kevin L. was a high school art teacher, and now creates unique pieces of jewelry that he sells at craft fairs, through small boutique jewelry stores, and to the clientele he has built up over the years. Brianna L. loves to bake and sells her "Divine Delicacies" at farmers' markets (check with your local Department of Health that this is okay – there is something called "Cottage Food Laws" which vary by state). Tanya B., a solo ager, is an in-demand sitter at a high-end resort hotel, charging $25/hour. After being vetted by the hotel, Tanya's name was put on the hotel's list of recommended sitters. Thomas K. is a huge Disney fan. He knows the California theme park so well he is privately hired as a "paid guide" to take small groups through the park, so they can maximize their time. Claudia E. became a fitness instructor and personal trainer. She lives in a 55+ community, as do her clients, many of whom love seeing someone similarly aged who is fit and a great role model (40% of the National Federation of Professional Trainers are in the age range of 42–60, according to their site). Rich T. is a jack-of-all-trades and after working for home builders for 20 years he is now a handyman, doing all those pesky jobs no one wants to do – or knows how to do. For help starting a business, check out the U.S. Small Business Administration (www.sba.gov), which provides free advice on planning, launching, managing, and growing your business. "Never let your memories be bigger than your dreams." Go for it.

## Additional Suggestions

**Work for a Charitable Nonprofit.** If you want to work . . . and at the same time work to make the world a better place, consider employment with a charitable nonprofit. These are examples of well-known charitable nonprofits: Salvation Army, American Red Cross, United Way, Habitat for Humanity, Goodwill Industries International, National Wildlife Federation, UNICEF (United Nations International Children's Emergency Fund), National Audubon Society, and Human Rights Watch.

**Food Delivery.** The Coronavirus pandemic spawned a huge increase in food delivery and shopping services, and people realized they liked the convenience of food/goods being brought to their doorstep. Look into companies such as Doordash, Grubhub, Postmates, UberEats, and Instacart (at Instacart, you both shop and deliver).

**Casinos.** Most states have some sort of gambling, whether it's traditional land casinos, riverboat casinos, or Native American casinos. Casinos employ hundreds of thousands of people, not only as dealers, cashiers, and security personnel, and if you've visited some of the larger ones, you know there may be spas, entertainment, restaurants, lodging, retail, and so forth. As a multi-billion dollar industry that often operates 24/7, there are jobs in many categories, both full and part-time.

### Online Sites to Sell Your Stuff/List Your Skills

Do you have items you want to sell or do you have the skill to design a website, create a book cover, make a personalized product, and so forth? Each site lists its procedure, including any fees for listing, shipping, marketing, promoting, and the like.

A few suggested sites:

- Amazon (www.amazon.com). An NPR/Marist poll found that 44% of online shoppers start their search on Amazon. It's the monster of online selling.

- Etsy (www.etsy.com/). I recently used this site to order an adorable fleece "lovey" personalized blanket for a niece's baby's baptism. The emphasis is on selling handmade and vintage goods.
- eBay (www.ebay.com). Kevin D.'s mom, Valerie, is a manicurist, and has affluent clients who often give away perfectly good items. Valerie's son Kevin picks them up for free, then re-sells them on eBay. According to Valerie, it's his full-time job and he makes a lot of money doing this.
- Fiverr (www.fiverr.com). Have a skill such as designing websites, presentations, or logos? Resume writing or proofreading? Fiverr is a site where freelancers offer their services. (It's named Fiverr because all services were originally $5 at the company's inception in 2010.) There are more than 10,000 sellers for more than 120 different services.
- Freelancer (www.freelancer.com). Find a wide variety of jobs by skills or language. For example, there were bids to design a WordPress website from $4 to $25 an hour. Competition can be stiff.
- Nextdoor (www.nextdoor.com). This is a local neighborhood social platform site, and connects neighbors based on geographical location. There's a newsfeed; you can buy and sell products and services on it, as well as post free items. Very interactive and very easy to use. Nextdoor is a great way to learn more about your community.
- Poshmark (www.poshmark.com). Ready to purge your closet? Poshmark allows you to sell clothes, shoes, and accessories, perhaps including business attire you never want to wear again. Poshmark takes a 20% cut of each sale. It's an easy, fun, intuitive site. (Of course you could also head to your nearest consignment shop or donate to Goodwill, Habitat for Humanity, or another good cause.)
- DeCluttr (www.decluttr.com). Want to get rid of old phones, CDs, books, games, tablets, DVDs and wearable tech? Or even Lego bricks in good condition? Using their site or using

the DeCluttr app on your phone, you can get an instant price from DeCluttr, mail your stuff to them for free, and get paid by direct deposit, PayPal or check. One hitch . . . if your items don't pass DeCluttr's quality control, the company will not return your items to you (although tech items will be returned free of charge).

- Taskrabbit (www.taskrabbit.com). This site allows sole proprietors to register and provide paid assistance in a variety of areas. Examples (for Jacksonville, FL) include pet sitting ($15/hour), carpentry ($34/hour), furniture assembly ($31/hour), and event staffing ($18/hour). Here's a site that you could use at both ends – as both a provider and a consumer.

## Real Estate

A popular "encore" career is real estate. The pandemic generated a huge increase in the number of sales and purchases of residences and lots, and real estate boomed. Peoples' homes became their offices, retreats, gyms, and in some cases, their classrooms. Becoming a realtor is relatively easy (for most states, a minimum age of 18, a high school diploma, a prelicensing education requirement, passing the licensing exam, working for a real estate broker or brokerage, and continuing education requirements). However, the number of active agents goes up and down with the housing market, so a hot market means more realtors vying for more listings and more sales.

People may also rent rooms in their homes for additional money, or become whole-house investors and rent entire dwellings on a short-term basis. Companies such as Airbnb or VRBO thrive on this model. Before you go down this route, check to be sure it's allowed where you want to rent short-term. Many communities – and many Homeowners' Associations – have very specific rules regulating short-term rentals in residential neighborhoods.

## Education

Have a master's or law degree or you're a CPA? Most community colleges (and a few colleges/universities) will allow you to teach if you have a credential in an area of need. For example, my brother retired from his career at a telecommunications firm, and taught accounting at a private university near his home. His CPA credential and his years of industry experience were great assets, and he was able to provide many real-life examples to his business students. Many high school/elementary teachers earn a master's degree while teaching, and can parlay this into an adjunct (part-time) or perhaps full-time position at the community college level. And, depending on your background, you could tutor for an ACT/SAT prep company, or go to students' homes for tutoring gigs.

Consider becoming a substitute teacher. Certain requirements such as education, background screening, drug testing, and training courses may be required. Depending on the location and type of sub, substitute pay ranges from around $75 to $120 per day, with $200 and up per day for long-term subs with a degree in the needed subject area.

Positions such as daycare/child care/camp counselor are considerations as well.

## Direct Sales

Most of us are familiar with Tupperware, one of the first direct sale products. A bit of history: Earl Tupper, a chemist, created these tight-sealing pliable plastic containers in 1946, but they didn't sell well in the stores, which prompted in-home demonstrations. Direct sales have been sullied in the past by pyramid schemes and scams, but many are legit. These companies tend to be associated more often with women, but there are some that are popular with men. People who work in direct sales are independent representatives (not employees), and for a fairly nominal fee (from free to about $300), the company provides you with a starter kit containing what is needed to launch your own business. The average monthly income ranges from about $300–$500/month doing this on a part-time basis.

Direct-sales companies include Mary Kay (cosmetics), Pampered Chef (kitchen supplies), Traveling Vineyard (wine), Discovery toys (toys/books/ games), Touchstone Crystal (Swarovski jewelry), CAbi (clothing), Herbalife (nutrition and weight management), and Kaeser & Blair (promotional products for businesses). These last two have a number of men involved. If you like people and want to be in control of your own schedule and make a little money, this could be an option.

---

*True Life: Robin R., a Mary Kay consultant*

Dipping my toes into the direct-sales market began 16 years ago when my daughter was a sophomore in high school. I had been a practicing dental hygienist, raising a family, and helping my husband while he grew his advertising agency. Our daughter was on the high school swim team, attending two practices a day. Five hours in the pool and her skin begged for moisture. No matter what I brought home for her to help quench her moisture-deprived skin, it didn't work. An acquaintance sold Mary Kay skin care. She gave me a bottle of classic moisturizer for my daughter to try. Voilà! Our daughter's skin was clear, moist and beautiful again!

This consultant moved away and stopped selling the product. I found another consultant and purchased the product from her. She had me try on the skincare and I fell in love with the product, as had my daughter. I had always shopped at the cosmetic counter but never purchased products through direct sales. I now wanted to tell all my family and friends about this unbelievable find. That is how my journey in direct sales started. It really has never been about the money for me. It has been more about making women feel good about their skin. I became their personalized skin-care consultant. It made me feel great and brought an additional level of fulfillment to my life. For me, it's about building relationships. Whether I sit across my kitchen table and hold a one-on-one beauty session, or host an open house of 20 women, I am thrilled to see how this product can renew damaged or dry skin. This will never get old for me.

There are no quotas or territories that I have to worry about in my Mary Kay business. I started my Mary Kay business in Cleveland, Ohio, and for the past 10 years I have lived in Palm Coast, Florida. I continue to send product to my customers in Cleveland and build my business here in Florida. Meeting new people, sharing my knowledge of product, and building relationships is something I plan to do for a very long time.

My business is woven into my everyday life. Handing out samples, delivering product, and chatting about new products is often done informally in exercise class, club functions and at our club's coffee bar! Yes, there is money to be made in direct selling such as Mary Kay. This all depends on how much time one is willing to put into it. I look at my source of income as a way to treat myself, treat my family, and now spoil my grand-kids. Lastly, one of the things about my business that I really love is that I have total flexibility to spend as much or as little time as I want; I run my business exactly how I want to so it fits within the framework of *my* overall life. This alone is a wonderful feeling and benefit.

---

## Seasonal/Temporary Work

If you watched the movie *Nomadland*, you got a (rather depressing, in my opinion) view of people who move from place to place for seasonal work. However, for many people, this is an adventure, not a forced way of life. Check out www.coolworks.com. It's a great site that shows seasonal job openings at ski resorts, national parks, summer camps, dude ranches, and so forth. Many seasonal employers provide housing and food for the workers, and Cool Works offers a dedicated site for the "Older and Bolder." About a fifth of their employees are retirees. They've been around since 1995. As their site notes, "Great places lead to great experiences."

---

*True Life: Don Kostyal and CoolWorks*

After 28 years in the military, I retired from the United States Air Force, and then worked in a management position an additional five years for a major U.S. airline. I relocated to Marco Island, assuming I would retire, but I like and need to stay busy, so I worked during the Florida winters and took summers off to visit grandchildren and friends up north. I returned to school and became a registered nurse, but after about six months in a fast-paced cardiac step-down unit, I realized it wasn't really for me.

My CoolWorks discovery was sheer luck. I visited a friend in Montana, and realized how much I hadn't seen of the United States. As I drove through Yellowstone National Park and the Big Horn National Forest, I asked people who were working there how they got their jobs, and they told me it was through CoolWorks. That winter I applied to places through CoolWorks, and was offered a job managing the gift stores at Signal Mountain Lodge in Grand Teton National Park. Since then, I have returned on and off to Signal Mountain Lodge for five seasons, including during the crazy COVID season.

CoolWorks is a great clearing house for all kinds of jobs, including Dude ranches and resorts, from various employers in every state and even foreign destinations. The employees at CoolWorks are former seasonal workers, so they know the industry. The CoolWork's website has a forum for job seekers to share stories, questions, pictures, and so forth. I consider those who I've met through CoolWorks true friends.

---

I worked for Kelly Services (www.kellyservices.com) years ago during my college spring breaks. Kelly Services has been around – with a few different names – since 1946. With more than 440,000 workers, Kelly Services can help you find both temporary and full-time positions. Placements range from administrative to tech to finance to education. There is no fee to join, and a lot of potential perks.

For some retirees, working around the holidays or other busy times fits the bill. Think retailers (cashier, shelf stocking, customer service, etc.), package delivery services such as Amazon, FedEx, or UPS, the post office, and Tax Prep companies such as the IRS, H&R Block, or Jackson Hewitt. In addition to doing tax returns, consider all the support services that go with it, such as data entry and customer service. Or, consider Vicki F., who took a job at Macy's at Christmastime to stay busy after her spouse passed away; several years later she is still there, but as a full-time HR employee.

Mark K. became a bus driver for his local school system after leaving his career in local government. The job provides paid training and a benefits package, an annual salary of $33,800, and Mark likes that he has free chunks of time each day and can pick up additional income doing field trips. He loves kids and knows his morning cheery "hello" is a nice start to the kids' mornings and afternoons, and that the children can go to him for fatherly advice if needed.

## Peace Corps Volunteer

Did you know about 6% of Peace Corp volunteers are 50 or better and that there's no upper age limit to volunteer? If you're looking to make a difference for others while gaining a new perspective for yourself, this could be a smart choice. There are opportunities for couples as well as singles. How about volunteering as an English education teacher in Nepal (no other language is required). The Peace Corp provides housing, a living stipend, multiple training opportunities, transportation to and from the country of service, medical and dental care, two paid vacation days/month, and after two years of service, $10,000 (pretax) to use as you'd like.

Go to www.peacecorps.gov and click on "Volunteers."

## Work from Home Customer Service/Virtual Assistant Jobs

We have all contacted those friendly voices on the phone when we've called a store or company because we ordered something in error, have a question about the organization, need to straighten out a billing issue, require help with our computer, didn't receive our newspaper, need technical info from a company, received an incomplete order, and so forth. These can be full or part-time jobs, and many companies/organizations have their own customer service agents. Although these can also be in-person positions, here are a few sites to find a virtual position: www.indeed.com, www.glassdoor.com, www.flexjobs.com, www.virtualvocations.com, and www.zirtual.com. This last site, for virtual assistant positions, states: "All of our virtual assistants live in the United States and have a college education. They have administrative experience and know how to serve their clients online."

## Work Part Time with Health Benefits and/or Other Perks

I mentioned at the beginning of this chapter that some people may want/need to work for paid health benefits. A number of companies have discontinued health and/or retirement plans and other perks for part-time employees, but the following companies still offer them (there are often days of consecutive service or minimum hours/week required to qualify): Costco, Lowe's, Starbucks, UPS, REI, Staples, U-Haul, and Chipotle.

These are just some examples to get you thinking about options if you need/want to work after leaving your primary job. And, of course, with perhaps 30 or more years in your second act, you could return to college and get a degree in an entirely different area and still have time for a new career. "Dear Abby" famously responded to a reader when a reader asked Abby about going back to school to become a physician as a mature adult. The reader said it would take seven years to finish medical school. "And how old would you be in seven years if you don't go back to college?" asked Dear Abby. Wise woman, that Dear Abby.

## Networking and Resumes and Interviews

Don't forget to network. Who are the people with possible connections doing what you'd like to do, and who can direct you to those people? This can be vital. Most people like to be helpful, and you'll be surprised how many will take the time to talk/communicate with you a little bit about how they "got there" or who they know. Be sure you have a presence on LinkedIn, a polished resume at the ready, see who is doing what you want to do, and reach out to them. Ask your family and friends about possible connections they have to your area of interest. Volunteer in an area where you'd like to work. For example, Dimitri K. volunteered to walk dogs for his local animal shelter. When a position opened up, guess who the shelter hired? And, Donna P. volunteered at her church as a Eucharistic minister for a number of years, and decided to return to teaching a year after her spouse passed away. The parish had an elementary school associated with it. Guess who the school hired when they had an opening? Follow people on Twitter who are doing what you'd like to do, and sincerely comment on their posts. Join organizations that have people in the field that you're interested in pursuing. For additional tips on networking, resumes, and acing interviews, see the "More Resources" section at the end of this chapter.

So, will it be "everyone back in the (labor) pool?" Some will be forced in, some will tentatively test the water, some will jump in wholeheartedly, and some will avoid the (labor) pool like hydrophobes.

## Core Pursuits

Chapter 2 provided food for thought regarding what to do with your 168 hours a week, and this chapter provided some specific suggestions for earning money in retirement. It's good to ask yourself what are the things (such as tennis, running your own business, volunteering, interacting with grandchildren, working in a field you love, reading, travel, taking classes) that get you up and rarin' to go in the morning. These are your core pursuits.

Wes Moss, an investment strategist, author, and managing partner of Capital Investment Advisors in Atlanta, surveyed more than 1,350 retirees to correlate how happy they were in retirement with their number of passions. Moss found that the happiest retirees had an average of 3.6 core pursuits; those who identified themselves at the low end of retirement happiness had an average of 1.9 core pursuits.

We often hear or read about the financial gurus discussing our "number" – namely, how much money we need to comfortably retire. And, although money is vital, and will be addressed in later chapters, it's as important to concentrate on your "core pursuits" for a fulfilling retirement. A "core pursuit" of Phil T. is to visit all 63 "elite" National Parks in the United States. He's halfway there (the pandemic delayed his progress for a year), and it's keeping him busy, happy, and in awe of the beauty of our country.

Need some inspiration to help develop your "core pursuits" list? Check out the link under "Websites" at the end of this chapter for a great list to get those brain gears turning.

Instead of retirement being about what you're *not* doing (working full-time at a job you did/didn't like, rushing from one commitment to another, raising children), make it about what you *are* doing: reinventing yourself, learning and trying new things, connecting/re-connecting with others, giving back, getting paid for what you love, and "smelling the roses."

In Chapters 4 and 5, we'll talk about places to live . . . where you can smell those roses!

## More Resources

### *Books*

Bolles, Richard. *What Color Is Your Parachute? 2021.* Ten Speed Press, 2020.
Collamer, Nancy. *Second-Act Careers: 50+ Ways to Profit from Your Passions During Semi- Retirement.* Ten Speed Press, 2013.
DeCarlo, Laura. *Resumes for Dummies* (8th ed.). For Dummies, 2019.

Feiler, Bruce. *Life Is in the Transitions: Mastering Change at Any Age.* Penguin Press, 2020.

Hannon, Kerry. *In Control at 50+: How to Succeed in the New World of Work.* McGraw-Hill Education, 2022.

## Websites

https://www.newretirement.com/retirement/what-to-do-in-retirement/ ("120 Big Ideas for What to Do in Retirement" by Kathleen Coxwell)

https://www.mylifestylecareer.com/ (second-act careers and reinvention)

www.Workforce50.com (search for opportunities by state)

https://www.monster.com/career-advice/article/best-companies-lgbt-0617 (best companies for LGBTQ workers)

https://www.presentslide.in/2019/07/best-interview-preparation-websites.html (interview prep sites)

https://www.abstraktmg.com/st-louis-business-journal/15-simple-ways-to-expand-your-network-remotely-in-2021/ (easy ways to network)

https://www.kiplinger.com/retirement/602951/great-jobs-for-retirees (more job ideas)

CHAPTER

4

# What and Where Is Home?

■ ■ ■

"Home is where the _____ is." For many, that adage is true; it is where the "heart" is. But others may want to fill in the blank with a different word(s) – ocean, good weather, hiking, culture, golf, social support, job opportunities, friends, adventure, family, and so forth. "Should I/we relocate in retirement?" is an important question, and one in which the answer may change as physical health, mental health, financial health, marital status, and family and personal dynamics evolve. After all, home is *how* you live, as well as *where* you live. The majority of retirees and preretirees, when asked about relocation, say they want to stay where they are, and "age in place." But, that could simply mean they don't want to transition to an assisted-living facility. They may, however, want to pick up stakes and move someplace else because they *choose* to do so, rather than because they *are forced* by circumstances to do so.

We are a mobile society, and the question "Where is home?" can become difficult to answer. For example, I grew up in Maryland, but also lived in New Jersey, Ohio, and now live in Florida. When I'm asked where home is, I say "Florida." But my sister-in-law, who moved to the United States when she was 17, is now in her mid-70s, and has lived in Washington, DC, for about 60 years, invariably refers to Ireland as home.

"Where is home?" has no one answer – it can be where you were born, where you grew up, where you are now, where most of your family is located, or the place that holds special meaning for you, even though it's not where you are presently living. Let's face it – many of us are living in a particular location because of job considerations, but now you can focus more on lifestyle than livelihood. If your job is no longer the major driver of where you presently live, and you add in remote working, scattered adult children/grandchildren, a change in health or other factors, the number of relocation options can become overwhelming. There's a name for it – "analysis paralysis" – choices become so numerous that it's easier to just stay put.

## Reasons to Stay Put . . . or Not

The moving process itself can be difficult. Caroline V. had several corporate transfers, and her company paid all costs for each relocation, so she took everything, figuring that she'd deal with it later. However, when she finally retired and moved to a smaller (and warmer) place – and one without a basement – and had to pay for it all herself – she found going through years of accumulated stuff (trophies from seventh-grade basketball, college English books, etc.) very difficult. With a smaller new house footprint and limited storage, she *really* had to downsize. In a way it was cathartic, and she felt good about donating so many usable things, but it wasn't easy.

Then, of course, there are family, friends, and your existing social group. These are often the biggest drivers of staying put or "aging in place." Surprisingly, a questionnaire by Shari and Clyde Steiner, the authors of a book about moving, surveyed more than 400 people who paid for their own moves, and found the third most commonly cited reason for a move was to move *away* from relatives and friends!

We know that as our grandchildren get older and develop their own social groups, they are often less inclined to want to hang out with their grandparents on a regular basis; and some retirees do not want to become regular sitters for young grandchildren. Eileen and Kevin A. have five adult children in the area, and a total of 12 grandchildren of various ages. Most of their adult kids/ spouses have demanding professions, and there is usually some kind of emergency every week that necessitates them helping out their adult children. For some retirees, this provides purpose; for others, it becomes a duty and a disruption to their daily routine. Harsh words? Perhaps. Solution? Eileen and Kevin did relocate, but they are happy to visit often and stay with the grandchildren so their parents can take a hard-earned vacation, go to an out-of-town wedding, or just to offer them a weekend respite. Their children and grandchildren also love visiting them in their new location. This may not work for everyone, but it works for them. What to do? At the end of this chapter, complete (and discuss with your significant other if there is one): "Retire Close to Family. . .Or Not Too Close!" from TopRetirements.

Friends, of course, are a major source of happiness, and/or you may be heavily involved in church activities or clubs that you are loath to leave. All are good reasons to stay. There are no right or wrong answers – it's what is right for you. Just don't let "status quo bias" – it's easier to do nothing than something – prevent you from making a move that you think would be beneficial.

As important as it is to think about why you're considering aging in place, it's just as important to think about why you're considering moving. Do you want to escape from something unpleasant in your current situation (shoveling snow, meddling in-laws, high cost of living, a house that won't suit your needs as you age, your adult children/friends have moved away)? Do you have the desire to use this time to create and experience a new chapter of your life – perhaps even in another country? Divorce? Death of a spouse? A second (or third) marriage? These could all be reasons to pick up stakes and move. AARP found that about a fourth of people age 50 and older plan to relocate to a new area altogether.

What are retirees looking for regarding house size? A recent survey by Del Webb found that 65% of those between 50 and 60 years old don't want to downsize their home at all: 43% desire a home around the same size, and 22% plan on larger digs. Why is bigger better for some? Reasons for more square footage include more room for visiting family/friends; space for family members to move in if necessary; a more desirable house or location; dedicated home office space(s); entertainment options; room to hold all their "stuff"; a place for hobbies/crafts; and a desire for privacy. The pandemic made many people realize that living spaces, both indoors and outdoors, were fine when working outside the home, but were not adequate as a 24/7 living and working space. Let's take a look at what Americans in general are doing about picking up stakes.

## What We Can Learn from the 2020 U.S. Census

If you're wrestling with where or if to relocate, knowing where other Americans are moving within the United States could be informative. Dr. William Frey, a noted demographer and sociologist, analyzed the 2020 census data, including statistics for "migration" patterns in the United States over the past decades. Frey found that there's been a big shift in our country's population from the Midwest and Northeast to the South and West. In 1920, the Northeast and Midwest accounted for 60% of the U.S. population; by 2020, that had shrunk to 38%. The South and West did the reverse; in 1920, the South and West accounted for 40% of the population; by 2020 that percentage had ballooned to 62%. If we look at the fastest-growing states over the past 20 years, they include what are considered desirable areas for relocation in retirement: Arizona, Nevada, Utah, Idaho, Texas, North Carolina, Georgia, Florida, Colorado, and the state of Washington.

In Chapter 1, a clever study was cited involving moving companies in order to get a sense of where people are relocating. Smart Asset, a financial technology company, used the 2020 Census data to see where people aged 60 and over were moving. However, because people move *out* of a state as well as *into* a state, looking at net migration is informative. These are the top 10 states with the highest net migration (those 60 and older moving in minus those 60 and over moving out): Florida, Arizona, North Carolina, South Carolina, Texas, Tennessee, Idaho, Oregon, Nevada, and Alabama.

Not to beat these statistics to death, but Smart Asset reported that people aged 65 and over, although comprising only 17% of the population in the United States, were responsible for 29% of all United Van Lines' moves in 2020. And, 20% of *all* those who moved said it was a retirement relocation. In brief, that's a lot of moving vans heading to new retirement digs!

Yes, the majority of people, when asked, say they want to "age in place" (perhaps some of the respondents had already relocated), but like the 2010 song by the Jamblasters, we've got a lot of movin' and shakin' going on.

## What Makes a Place Ideal?

"Ideal" is a personal word. Someone who loves the vibrancy and culture of New York City might cringe at the idea of relocating to a laid-back, sleepy beach town. Those who want a walkable town would be turned off by a location that requires them to hop into their car or take public transportation every time they want to go someplace. Some want the most bang for their retirement bucks; others might want to relocate where there are other like-minded people, or to be close to children, grandchildren, and/or in-laws, regardless of where they live, whereas many others will stay put. Some with medical issues want to be in close proximity to their healthcare providers, others want to move to a less expensive place, or buy a condo or rent an apartment and not worry about doing maintenance chores. Some are "serial locators" who want to sample a number of lifestyles in their retirement years; others are looking for entirely new/newer ways of living – what we call "niche" com-munities; these could include living on a ship, cohousing, home-sharing, LGBTQ+ communities, and so forth. (More about these kinds of communities in the next chapter.)

*True Life: Jane A. fits the definition of a "serial relocator." Here is her journey:*

Growing up, my family rarely traveled. Yet, when we did, I loved it. My father instilled in me my sense of curiosity about different locales. I grew up in the country, basically on a farm, and I couldn't wait to move away. Things were too slow and boring for me. Luckily, my dream came true. At the age of 21, I moved to Johnstown, Pennsylvania, for a job with the International Ladies Garment Workers Union. While living there, I met my first husband. Shortly after we married, we moved to Killeen, Texas – for a whopping six months. Then, my husband took a different job in a northern suburb of Chicago. Moving there was heavenly for me. I found everyone so hospitable. And, there were oodles of wonderful restaurants, fantastic shopping, and lots to do. At the end of six years, my husband dragged me away when he accepted a new position in Midland, Michigan.

For the first six months of the 18 years I lived in Midland, I cried quite a bit. The move to a small town in the middle of Michigan from the Chicago area wasn't the easiest transition; but, I became determined to make the most of it. I joined an intramural soccer team, something I loved; and shortly after that, I started to play tennis. This paved the way to meeting lots of nice people and I started making inroads. Additionally, I found employment with an orthopedist, and put to use my degree from a medical arts school. After working in the medical field for eight years, I left the job . . . and my husband. My husband had become content with the routine of everyday life, whereas I continued to yearn for something new. I went back to school at night and accepted a full-time position with a major international accounting firm. The work was challenging, and the work environment exposed me to an ever-changing mix of people from all over the United States and around the world. Through these people, I learned about other parts of the United States and the world, all of which continued to whet my curiosity.

At the end of 18 years, I moved from Midland, with my second husband, to Cincinnati, Ohio, a wonderful small "big" city. After joining the Newcomers' Club and a local country club, I had a full calendar of things to entertain me when not working—the gym, book club, cooking club, golf, tennis, skiing, bridge, museums, and theaters. While living in Cincinnati, my husband and I started thinking about where we'd like to retire. Any place we traveled, we'd look at our destination through the eyes of possible transplants. At the top of my list was Vancouver, Canada, but my husband said absolutely not— something about not wanting to move out of the United States. I also liked the Santa Fe, New Mexico, area but wasn't keen on all the shops closing at 5 p.m. After 10 years of life in Cincinnati, and my husband and I not agreeing on a place to retire, I overheard another tennis team member saying she'd be moving to Boquete, Panama, in about a year. Intrigued, I started asking her about Panama. Liking what I'd heard, I mentioned it to my husband, who said he'd like to visit Panama, but wasn't interested in moving outside the United States. But, next thing we knew, we were off to tour Panama. While there, we fell in love with the mystique of Boquete and bought a piece of property. In the two years we had before we'd retire, we had a home built and prepared mentally for the move. Of course, during this time we visited Boquete several times; with each visit, we continued to feel we'd made the right decision.

Once in Panama, we had the time of our lives—some of it good, and some of it bad. Yet, for every tale we could tell, pleasant or not, another expat could tell you another unbelievable story. Thus, even when going through something not to our liking, we were able to laugh about our and our fellow expats' (silly) expectations. An example of a tough time for us was when a car mechanic kept our SUV for an inordinate amount of time, while he waited for a part to arrive from the U.S. Obviously, he hadn't ordered it on a priority basis, and he didn't care that we needed to pay for a rental car in the meantime. Most of the expats in Boquete were from various parts of the United States and Canada. Additionally, there were people from Switzerland, Holland, Germany, and elsewhere. For the most part, mingling with all of these people was wonderful. A number of the expats were into causes; it seemed I was always helping with one benefit or another, be it for an animal clinic or to raise money for a local charity. Additionally, I volunteered at the local library, did some painting, and played bridge, golf, tennis, and euchre.

After six and a half years of fun, we opted to move back to the United States for two reasons: to help with my mother-in-law, who was elderly, and to be closer to family (in particular, my husband's sons and their families). Initially, I was sad to leave Panama; yet, once in the Delray Beach area of Florida for a week or two, I was ready for my new life. Unfortunately, my mother-in-law became quite ill shortly after we arrived. As upsetting as that was, we were thankful to be there and pretty much made being with her our vocation. When my mother-in-law passed away, my husband and I discussed where we'd prefer to live in Florida. While doing this, my younger stepson and his wife asked if we'd consider moving to Memphis, to be near them and their soon-to-be-born son. Because we had no real ties to Florida, we agreed to move to Memphis. Thus, after 14 months in Florida, we moved to Memphis, hoping we'd spot Elvis.

We never did spot Elvis, but we did enjoy a lot of what Memphis offers. Memphis hosts quite a few fabulous festivals (beer, BBQ, hamburgers, music, etc.), especially during Memphis in May. Additionally, there is always something going on, year round, on Beale Street; and, seasonally, one can take in a Memphis Grizzles basketball game or enjoy outdoor music at Levitt Shell. It seemed that we'd no sooner finished decorating our house and making some changes to it than my stepson let us know he'd accepted another job – one in Vancouver, Canada – the city I had initially picked for retirement. What's more, my stepson and his wife asked if we'd move to British Columbia. Once we got over the shock of the news and had time to think about moving – again – we opted to travel to the northern part of Washington state, to see if we liked the area. We fell in love with Bellingham, Washington, and moved from Memphis almost one year to the day from when we'd moved there. We actually moved before my stepson and his family moved. We have now been here for four years. We love the town and what it has to offer and are happy that it's not too far from Vancouver, B.C.

For now, we're content to remain in this area. Yet, as we age, we can foresee being inclined to move to an active adult community – one where we can get around in a golf cart, if need be. Wherever we next move, we'll adapt and adjust and enjoy what it offers. For anyone reluctant to step out of his/her element, I would recommend giving change a try.

## Second Homes

If finances permit, others may choose to have two or more locations. Karen and Steve C. have a house in South Carolina, but also have a home in Vermont on a lake to escape the hot and humid southern summers. Pete and Jane K. have their primary home in suburban Washington, DC, but can drive to their beach townhome in Bethany Beach, Delaware, in a few hours. Susan L. lives in Chicago where her daughter and granddaughter live. She's a therapist, and works virtually. Her second home is a condo in Breckenridge, Colorado, where she can work, hike, ski, and enjoy the beauty of the mountains, and can rent out her condo short-term when she isn't there. Brad R. and Thomas G. live in Cincinnati, and although they own one home, they will rent a condo for several months in warm-weather states to "try out" and explore different places in case, one day, they decide to relocate. Although the pandemic caused an acceleration of second home purchases, normally about 20% of home sales are second homes, with a median distance of about 350 miles from the main residence, according to the National Association of Realtors.

## International Relocation

A June 2020 survey by the Aegon Center for Longevity and Retirement found that 13% of those still working or already retired in the United States would like to live abroad. And in 2019, almost 432,000 retired U.S. workers living abroad received Social Security benefits.

Here's an interesting story:

---

*Janet S.'s fearless "semiretirement" experiences: Living, working, growing, learning, and thriving . . . in China, Thailand, and Portugal . . . starting at the age of 61.*

I was born in Indiana, but spent most of my adult life in the Washington, DC, metro area. I sold computers, became a LAN administrator, and then became an interior designer. In 2008, my husband passed away, the housing market collapsed, and my income dried up, so I rented out my basement and my two upper-level bedrooms. Survivor mode is something I know how to do. It was impossible for me to make enough money to continue my life in Virginia, so I knew there had to be another way. I've always wanted to live overseas and teach English, but it took me five years to develop and execute my plan. When I make a decision, I never look back. I was ready for a big change. There was no fear, no question – I was ready for the unknown! I became certified to teach ESL (English as a second language) in early 2013, sold my house in June, had an estate sale, and moved into a rental for several months.

The ESL course was for four weekends and cost $1,000. When I passed my certification, I was told I could only be placed in China, because of my age. I was 61. You are placed in countries where companies can easily obtain a work permit. Korea, Japan, and China pay the best, and they provide work permits for Americans up until ages 62–65. I researched the best places to live in China. Xiamen was my first choice, and I was offered a position within a few weeks. On December 23, 2013, I arrived in China and was picked up by the Headmaster, a 29-year-old Chinese woman. For the next year I shared a large apartment with her. We could walk the two blocks to the language school. My students were between three and nine years old, the classes were after school from 4:00 p.m. to 9:00 p.m. Tuesday through Friday, and Saturday and Sunday from 10:00 a.m. to 7:00 p.m. Teaching little kids is no easy task. I signed a one-year contract, learned a lot, and worked hard.

Few people spoke English in the suburb where I lived, but I managed to get along fine with the help of my three fellow teachers. I could take the bus downtown and explore the beautiful city of Xiamen by myself. Chinese food in China is not anything like it is in the states. Eating out was a challenge. I mostly cooked for myself and learned how to find familiar food at a wet market where no one spoke English. Starbucks was a treat and the only place to get a decent cup of coffee. It was quite an experience watching the rats, not squirrels, run from trash can to trash can. I loved the adventure but did not love teaching very young children. I decided to look for a position teaching older kids. One of my ESL classmates told me there was an opening at her school in a nearby city. On the train ride to the interview, I met a professor from Ningbo University, and he recruited me to work there. A few months later I started teaching Oral English to Freshman English majors at Ningbo University. I loved it! The university, located in Ningbo, housed all the foreign teachers in a building on campus. I had my own one-bedroom apartment, and walked to my classes twice a day. I could take a 20-minute subway ride to get downtown. I would have stayed longer than two years but the air pollution was causing me problems.

So, off I went with my three suitcases to Chiang Mai, Thailand. Once again, I researched the job opportunities in Chiang Mai. Everything I had read said just look for a job when you arrive. I gathered all my professional information, and talked to all the ESL schools. Two days later I had two job offers. I accepted a full-time position at a school that taught preschool through high school. For one very hard year I taught reading to seventh through twelfth graders. I was picked up at 7 a.m. and returned home at 6 p.m. As soon as I completed my contract, I quit. Teaching English online had to be easier. Within a few weeks I was teaching English 16 hours per week online for the same amount of money I had been making working 40+ hours a week. You can live amazingly well in Thailand for around $1,000 per month. Thailand is really HOT and humid. It's like living in a steam bath every day. I could not adjust to the weather so . . . .

Off to Portugal I went. I have always dreamed of living in Europe. Portugal is the least expensive place to live in the EU. It's much closer to the United States and you can fly anywhere in the EU for less than 100 euros round-trip. Porto is at the mouth of the Douro River and the Atlantic Ocean. It is beautiful, and for me the weather is perfect. It's usually around 78 degrees in summer, and winters are short and mild. There are lots of things to do and you can drive to Spain in three hours or take a day trip to several smaller cities in Portugal. The Portuguese people are welcoming and friendly. Most young people in Porto and Lisbon speak some English. The Portuguese language is quite difficult for those of us who do not know another foreign language. I am impressed with the excellent quality of the healthcare in Portugal. Private insurance is around 135 euros per month. I am still teaching ESL online.

The expat communities in all the places I have lived have made the experience of living abroad amazing! It is easy to make friends and people who choose to live abroad are adventurous, fun-loving, professional, interesting people. We can afford to eat out and travel because the cost of living is so much less than in the United States. We enjoy a simple life, we live with less, and we have time to walk, talk, drink, and explore. I have made Porto my forever home. Five years of living in a suitcase is enough for this 68-year-old single woman. It's difficult to even think about a trip back to the United States. I have spent a lifetime visiting friends – they can come and visit me! I promise they will be surprised and charmed by the calm beauty and variety that this small, often forgotten country can offer. And, Portugal is one of the easiest countries in the EU to immigrate to. They welcome retirees, single women, and people in the LGBTQ+ community.

---

(Specific recommended places for retirement abroad are listed in Chapter 5.)

## What Do People Want in a Retirement Location?

*Where to Retire* magazine asked its 200,000 subscribers which features were most important to them when thinking about a place to live in retirement. The majority of responses (in order of importance) fell into these 18 categories:

- Low crime rate
- Good hospitals nearby
- Active, clean, safe downtown
- Low overall tax rate
- Mild climate
- Scenic beauty nearby
- Friendly, like-minded neighbors
- Low cost of living
- Active social/cultural environment
- Good recreational facilities
- Walkability
- No state income tax
- Low housing costs
- Airport with commercial service nearby
- Major city nearby
- Friends, relatives in area
- College or university town
- Full- or part-time employment opportunities

*ideal-LIVING* **Insights.** First, full disclosure. I have been the "Healthy Living" columnist for *ideal-LIVING* magazine since 2015.

This company provides in-person events in addition to digital and print media to help people find their "ideal" retirement location at no cost to those looking for information (*ideal-LIVING* partners with generally large, master-planned communities predominantly located in the southeastern United States). In just the past two years, more than 50,000 buyers have relocated using their services.

*ideal-LIVING* did a survey of those who purchased a home and were asked "What is the most important feature that prompted you to choose your "ideal" community?" Responses (one caveat – these communities are located primarily in the southeast, so a warm climate was already a given):

- Sense of community/broad range of activities: 42%
- Proximity to natural amenities (ocean, lake, mountain): 22%
- Home styles and design: 15%
- Closer to friends and family: 12%
- Pricing: 9%

To get to that final decision to purchase, 42% visited five to nine potential locations; 40% visited 10 or more; and 18% visited one to four communities. More than half of those who purchased a home visited the community two or three times before deciding to buy; about 25% visited three or more times, and about 20% purchased after one visit. Of course, we realize that some people prefer to rent, and not own, but these guidelines of what most people find desirable still apply.

## Narrowing (or Expanding) the Possibilities

It's a big world out there if you're looking to relocate, and if you can keep your list to five or so "nonnegotiables," it makes the process easier. For my husband and me (remember, we had moved several times, so it wasn't a wrenching decision to pick up stakes), it was warm weather (as one friend said, "At least you don't have to shovel heat"); by the ocean; a reasonable distance to an airport and good healthcare; and a new all-ages community on the east coast designed to make it easy to meet new people; be active (must offer tennis and biking/walking paths); and act as a lure for our adult children, their spouses, and their five children to frequently visit, along with sibs and extended family members. So, our successful corporate relocations made it easy for my husband and me to move; deep-rooted family, professional, and personal ties can make the decision for others to relocate more difficult.

The average time for finding a place to relocate, according to *ideal-LIVING's* survey, was more than a year. As with any big transition, take your time (similar to the advice about not making any major life decisions for at least a year after a divorce or loss of a spouse). And, of course, you may realize the best place for you to retire is right where you are.

Need some suggestions for places to move based on *your* preferences? Look at the More Resources section at the end of this chapter for a few fun and informative quizzes that will suggest places customized by your answers to a number of questions. Some of these take a bit of time to complete. If you don't want to spend the time doing the quizzes, at least read through the lists – something may jump out at you that you realize you MUST have in your ideal location.

And, of course, a quick search on the Internet of "best places to retire" will provide you with a multitude of lists – although *their* list uses criteria that aren't necessarily on *your* list. However, you may find helpful insights or become tempted by a location that wasn't on your radar.

## Food for Thought

Based on visiting hundreds of possible places for retirement over the past two decades, looking at the research, and talking to many people who have either relocated (or not), these additional observations and suggestions may be helpful if you're considering pulling up roots:

- **Travel and vacations.** Just because you go back to a place to *vacation* year after year, or you've been to some incredible travel destinations, it doesn't necessarily make them great places to *live*. Loved visiting stunning Antarctica, but . . .
- **Are the basic amenities in place?** Check out developers' and builders' solvency with the Better Business Bureau and the local builders' association.
- **Trial run.** Many large communities offer a "try before you buy" or "sneak a peek" or "stay and play" opportunity – an invitation to stay a few days at a very reasonable rate to experience the community, talk to people who live there, and sample the amenities. And, consider renting in a potential location for a year before you purchase.
- **Amenities.** Do you really need/want all the amenities a community offers? For example, Doreen and Nolan A. bought in a community that allows you to purchase a social membership (tennis, pools, exercise classes), or a full membership that also includes golf. They were not interested in becoming golfers, so for them, the social membership was perfect. No need paying for more than you need. Or, perhaps the larger community where you decide to relocate offers public tennis courts, pickleball, pools, and so forth and you can pick and choose what you want to join and save money. That can be a good financial trade-off, but you could miss out on meeting more neighbors within your neighborhood if you take that route. Food for thought.
- **How old is the community?** In successful communities, people tend to "age in place." For example, the median age of residents in The Villages in Florida, which started in the early 1980s, is 71; in Sun City Arizona, which opened January 1, 1960, it's 74. Newer communities have younger median ages. So, if you're investigating, be aware that a well-established community will generally have older residents.
- **Sample all seasons.** A crisp fall day in New England may seem a faraway dream when you're shoveling a foot of snow in

February; a balmy 75 degrees at the beach in the Southwest in October may feel different when it's 98 degrees in July.

- **Politics.** The real estate brokerage company Redfin recently reported that 42% of 3,000 U.S. residents surveyed would be reluctant to relocate to an area with differing political views. Polarizing politics could be a deal-breaker if you have strong feelings about politics and you find you're surrounded by the "other side." Top 2021 Democratic states: Hawaii, Vermont, California, and Maryland. Top Republican states: Wyoming, Utah, Oklahoma, and West Virginia. See this link for a general U.S. "Blue State/Red State" map: https://www.gkgigs .com/list-of-blue-states-and-red-states/, although there may be areas within the state that may be "purple" or completely the other color.

- **Crime/Livability/Real Estate/Cost of Living.** We all want to live in a great community. Check out AreaVibes (www.area-vibes.com) to see how a potential community is rated. For example, Claudia O. is considering Fort Collins, Colorado. Using AreaVibes, she found that Fort Collins has a livability index of 75 (considered excellent), the crime rate is 20% lower than the Colorado average, cost of living is equal to the Colorado average, and real estate prices are 8% higher than the Colorado average. A helpful and informative comparison-shopping site.

- **Relocate and live longer (or not)?** A creative study involved researchers examining 1999–2014 Medicare records of more than six million Americans between the ages of 65 and 99. The study collected health information from people who lived in a particular location and who had similar health profiles, then followed them when they moved to a variety of new locations and tracked how they long they lived. The results showed that the "before the relocation" health of people accounted for approximately 70% of their lifespan, and that the new location added to or reduced their expected lifespan by about 15%. Why did people live longer or shorter in some locations than others? Factors such as quality of health care, weather, and pollution were cited as possibilities, but additional research needs to be done on this interesting approach to see how relocation impacts longevity.

- **Schools.** Even though you won't have children attending K–12 (unless you retire *really* early or are raising grandchildren), strong schools indicate a vibrant, involved community, they're a future source of employees, and they often offer continuing education or activities that can be enjoyed by all. A good ranking site is www.greatschools.org (only public schools are rated). And, note where the closest community college or university is located for lifelong-learning opportunities.

- **Leverage "Nextdoor."** If you're not familiar with this popular site, it's a virtual meet-up of local neighbors/neighborhoods in your area. In order to join, you need to own or rent a home, own property, or own a rental unit in one of the several communities your particular Nextdoor encompasses. The site provides lots of feedback on restaurants, businesses, things to do, and so forth. It is monitored, so inflammatory postings are promptly removed. Local businesses can post basic info about their companies. If you know someone in a community you're considering moving to, ask to see Nextdoor conversations. Nextdoor is also an easy way to give away (or sell) things – Rosemary T. has given away her 40-year-old console piano, a number of lamps, a large rug, and some furniture by listing it on Nextdoor – available for free to anyone who wants to pick it up. She's found her giveaways are usually gone within a day.

- **Size can matter.** People have told me they regretted moving to very small, established towns. Although it was scenic, and checked many boxes, they felt like outsiders and were unhappy with their choice. Just an FYI. May not apply to you. (And see "Tiny Homes" in Chapter 5 if you want to significantly downsize your house!)

- **New residence/resale/or rental?** The right answer is what's right for you. A new house will allow you to customize, but you'll have more upfront costs; resales will tend to have more mature landscaping and lower upfront costs than a new house; renting a place allows more flexibility, and less of a commitment, but many considering owning a home a better financial choice, since you're paying your own mortgage instead of someone else's, and won't be forced to move if the owner decides to sell or just stop renting. You can do a simple calculation called a price-to-rent ratio: Take the average price of a property you're considering in your new location and divide it by the average yearly rent for a similar property. For example, if Jonathan can purchase a condo for $400,000, but rent it for $36,000/year, his price-to-rent ratio is 11.1. What does that number mean? When the price-to-rent ratio is 15 or below, it's usually better to buy a house; if it's 16–20, it's usually better to rent, and if it's 21 or higher, it's almost certainly better to rent than to buy. But don't forget equity, the tax benefits of Jonathan living in his investment, and his pride of ownership.

- **Selling your home.** You know you need strong curb appeal (it provides the biggest return on your investment, according to experts), enticing pictures on the Internet (since that is where most research begins – think of it like a dating site! – 11 to 14 attractive pictures seem to be the "sweet spot"), and a clean, clean-smelling, and depersonalized house (people want to feel it's "their" home). Consider staging to increase the speed of the sale and get a higher sale price. The national average cost is $1,500 to stage; it's estimated that investing 1% of the home's value in staging results in a higher home sales price of up to 15%. If your house is empty, consider "virtual staging" for online potential homebuyers. Check out the garage – for Jana F. it's the litmus test – it should be neat, tidy and painted, and have it empty when showing so it looks larger. Nice views? Include an online drone tour of the house and its surroundings. Display pictures of how the house and yard look during each season. Get a home inspection before you list so there are no surprises that could derail a sale. Unless you can carry two mortgages, sell your home first before purchasing a new home.

Recognize that women are the decision makers when deciding to purchase a home, influencing the choice more than 90% of the time. Women look for security, low maintenance, flow of the floor plan, storage, and a place to retreat. Keep this in mind when preparing your house for sale. And, single women now make up about 20% of home purchasers. Remember that selling your home is a business transaction; take the emotion out of the process.

And, avoid words that can be giveaways to potential buyers: cozy (this place is tiny!), classic (it's really old), great opportunity (it's a dump), up-and-coming neighborhood (lots of crime).

- **The tax bite.** A study by Self, a financial technology company, found that the average U.S. citizen will pay $525,037 in taxes (primarily on earnings, but also property, cars, and other purchases) over his/her lifetime (New Jersey had the highest tax burden/Alabama the lowest.) More about taxes in Chapter 8.

- **Golf courses.** If you're considering a home on a golf course, you'll generally have gorgeous views from the windows facing onto the course. Choose your location carefully, as a home near a tee box, green, or cart path will have more people and more noise associated with it than one on a fairway. Make sure you watch some foursomes play through to get a sense of how close people will be to your home, or the potential for errant balls to come too close to your property. Courses are groomed early in the morning, so noise could be an issue. The last caution is that overall golf participation/number of golf rounds are decreasing. Golf courses may be turned into a park or preserve area, or in some cases there have been contentious lawsuits about developing the land into additional homesites or commercial areas. A house on a golf course adds a premium to the lot, but its closure could be an issue.

- **Medicare.** Doctors can refuse to accept Medicare. Be sure to ask when checking out physicians. Lydia was under 65 when she moved to Georgia, and her primary care physician accepted her as a patient (she had private insurance at the time), but the physician did not accept her significant other who was over 65 and on Medicare (unless he was willing to pay the difference). However, Lydia was allowed to "stay" as a Medicare patient with her physician after transitioning to Medicare. A doctor refusing to accept Medicare's typically lower reimbursements is a big (and unwelcome) surprise to some people. As an example, for the same service, private insurance may pay the provider $180, but Medicare would only pay $130. The site www.medicare.gov will help you find providers.

- **Natural disasters.** Is the area you're considering susceptible to tornadoes, hurricanes, floods, earthquakes, wildfires, sink-holes (caused by the dissolution of rock such as limestone by rain and surface water – most prevalent in Texas, Florida, Alabama, Kentucky, Pennsylvania, and Tennessee), or red tide (periodic harmful algae blooms that can produce toxins, found mostly in SW Florida, the Texas coast, and the Gulf of Maine) in any area you are considering? See the "Wicked Weather and Deadly Disaster" link for FEMA (Federal Emergency Management Agency) and the link to the United States Geological Survey (USGS) at the end of this chapter to see if an area you're considering may be prone to these unwanted events.

- **Other potential negatives.** What's the proximity to airplane flight paths, smelly paper or turpentine plants, nuclear power plants, Superfund sites, or the sound of traffic from nearby roads/highways/ballparks, and so forth? If choosing a building lot, be sure that the headlights of approaching cars won't shine into your house because of the way the home is or will be situated on the street (a friend learned that one the hard way after building in a new community).

- **Short-term rentals.** These are a controversial issue within many areas of the country. If you don't want to live next to a short-term rental, or if you want to rent your home short-term or purchase a home/condo as a short-term investment, check to see if it's allowed, and if so, find out the specific rules for your prospective community.
- **HOAs/COAs/POAs.** Does the community you're considering have a homeowner's or condo or property owner's association? These associations, run by volunteers who live in the community, have many rules – people tend to love them or hate them (I like my HOA, but my friend Paula F. moved out of the same community because she couldn't stand someone making decisions affecting her own property). HOAs/COAs/POAs can control street parking, how long your trash cans can remain outside, how many dogs you may own, have a say about your house color, landscaping, etc. There are about 350,000 of these associations in the United States, and about a fourth of Americans live in a community with some kind of a community association. Be sure to familiarize yourself with the covenants, conditions and restrictions (CC&Rs) of any community you're considering. If you don't like not having complete control over what you can do with your home, avoid community associations. But, remember that your neighbors could be parking boats, trailers, and RVs in their driveway or on empty lots, letting their dogs run wild, running businesses out of their homes, or not maintaining the lawn.

And, it's worth emphasizing, after what happened with the condo collapse in Champlain Towers South, in Surfside, Florida, to closely examine condo documents. Condos should have reserve funds for repairing, replacing, and maintaining the buildings. Don't consider low homeowners' fees something that is necessarily a great thing. Read the minutes of the past few years' worth of board minutes to see what the issues are, and ask to see the reserve documents to ensure money is being set aside for important issues that could arise. Ask people if they have had special assessments, and why they were necessary.

- **Purchasing a lot?** Some communities have a timeframe by which you must start building; others do not. Be sure to ask. You may not want a timetable from purchasing to building, or you may not want empty lots next to the house you build/ buy for several years – or more.
- **What about caregiving?** Besides potentially babysitting your grandchildren, what about caring for your *own* parents? The Center for Retirement Research at Boston College reports that around 17% of adult children will care for their parents at some point. With longer lifespans, 60-year-old retirees may be responsible for caring for their 80–90-year-old parents. Something to consider as you contemplate relocation (and check out multigenerational living in the next chapter).
- **New(er) or Established Community?** This is kind of a "Goldi-locks" situation. You want one that is "just right" – enough development so that you know the community is viable, but early enough into its creation that residents are eager to make new friends. Although an established community will have more landscaping and fewer disruptions from construc-tion and trucks rumbling through the streets, many prefer to go for the newer community (and remember that the age usually skews younger in a newer community). Just be sure the basic infrastructure is in place.
- **Bring your posse with you.** If you have like-minded friends, get them to move, too! When I relocated, so did a co-author of one of my books as well as another friend . . . along with their spouses. Michael M. and Anthony L. were work colleagues and friends for decades, and both purchased a second home in the same community in Arizona when they retired.

95

- **Envision your future self.** We tend to think like Peter Pan – we'll never grow up/grow old. The larger community should be welcoming to older adults. Think larger street signage, longer crosswalk times, complete streets (roads that accommodate bikes, cars, and pedestrians), walking paths with benches, free shuttle service and/or excellent public transportation, good health care, and options for other living arrangements in the area if you can no longer live without assistance.

- **LGBTQ+ friendly communities.** It's estimated that there are 2.4 million LGBTQ+ adults over 50 in the United States, and that self-reported number is expected to double by 2030, according to the UCLA Williams Institute. Of course, the LBGTQ+ community wants the same things everyone wants – good transportation, low crime/tax rates, scenic beauty, and so forth. And, they want to live in places that are tolerant and accepting. Chapter 5 will provide specific examples of not only cities that fit the bill, but communities that are designed specifically for the LGBTQ+ population.

- **Extrovert or introvert.** Are you more of an extrovert – talkative, friendly, life-of-the-party kind of person who gets energized being around others, or are you more of an introvert – you enjoy smaller groups, need time to recharge, and are more reflective and self-aware? Research has shown that your personality type may affect where you choose to live. Extroverts tend to prefer wide flat spaces (think the beach or walkable cities), while introverts are attracted to mountains or wooded areas because seclusion rejuvenates them. Have a significant other who is your opposite? Find a mountain town with a big lake or consider Santa Cruz, California, Bar Harbor, Maine, or Oahu, Hawaii.

- **Purchasing materials for your new (or current) home.** Think about the warranty on some of your purchases. For example, I have replaced faucets, locks, door handles, and other assorted parts on my sinks and doors from companies such as

Kwikset, Moen, and Grohe that offer lifetime warranties. I've saved a lot of money by calling for replacements.

- **Universal Design.** Whether you stay put, buy new, buy a resale, rent, or remodel, you need to know about – and implement – a concept called "universal design." When it comes to housing, universal design makes living arrangements more usable by as many people as possible at little or no extra cost. It benefits people of all ages and abilities. Specifically (I love specifics!), it means higher electrical outlets to minimize bending, "comfort-height or "right-height" toilets (two to four inches higher than a regular height toilet), rocker switches to make turning lights on and off easier, non-slip flooring, wider hallways to accommodate a wheelchair (if necessary), and so forth. For a terrific list of exterior and interior universal design ideas, see the Aging-in-Place Checklist from the National Association of Home Builders of the United States at the end of this chapter.

Most of us recall Dorothy clicking those ruby slippers and chanting: "There's no place like home." We want to live in a place that encourages positive relationships, healthy living, growth in mind and spirit, and the opportunity to live our best lives. The next chapter will suggest specific locations and communities you may want to call home.

## Checklist: Retire Close to Family . . . or Not Too Close!

(With permission from TopRetirements.com)

*Please take some time to answer these questions and discuss them with whomever you think you should.*

**Do you get along well on a daily basis with these family members?**
- Yes___
- No___
- Yes, but . . . __

**Are you a person who really needs to be around family members on a close basis to be happy?**
- Yes ___
- No ___
- Not sure ___

**Do you have some good reasons to move away from where you live now (expense, taxes, climate, lifestyle, type of home)?**
- Yes ___
- No ___
- Some ___

**Could you be happy living in the new area/region/town where your relatives live?**
- Look forward to it ___
- Have some concerns ___
- Not at all ___

**Can you afford to move near these relatives?**
- Yes ___
- No ___
- Not sure ___

**Are you concerned you might be taken advantage of?**
- Yes ___
- No ___
- Maybe ___

**What is the likelihood that the family member you are living near might move or be transferred?**
- Very small ___
- Considerable ___
- Not sure ___

**Would you consider renting in the new area for a time, just to check things out?**
- Yes ___
- No ___
- Not sure ___

**If part of a couple, are you both on the same page about moving there?**
- Yes ___
- No ___
- Haven't discussed it ___

**Do you have a situation where no one else can help a family member who really needs help?**
- Yes ___
- No ___
- Maybe ___

**Do you have a plan for where you want to live in the last decade or two of your life (if so, does that involve being near family)?**
- ■ Yes ___
- ■ No ___
- ■ Partially ___

**Are you being pressured to move near family?**
- ■ Yes ___
- ■ No ___
- ■ Somewhat ___

**Is there a more creative way to solve the problem of being near family? (We know several people who spend the winter or summer near their children, but they rent)**
- ■ Yes ___
- ■ No ___
- ■ Wouldn't consider it ___

## So How Did You Do?

There is no passing grade on this checklist. The point is that if you (and your significant other, if you have one) spend some time on these questions, it will get you started with an assessment of whether it is a good idea to move near your relatives. If many of your answers suggest drawbacks, maybe you should put up the caution light and think of another plan.

(With permission from TopRetirements.com)

# Aging-in-Place Checklist

### Exterior

- Low-maintenance exterior (vinyl, brick)
- Low-maintenance shrubs and plants
- Deck, patio, or balcony surfaces are no more than ½ inch below interior floor level if made of wood

### Overall Floor Plan

- Main living on a single story, including full bath
- No steps between rooms/areas on the same level
- 5-foot by 5-foot clear/turn space in living area, kitchen, a bedroom, and a bathroom

### Hallways

- Minimum of 36 inches wide, wider preferred
- Well lit

### Entry

- Accessible path of travel to the home
- At least one no-step entry with a cover
- Sensor light at exterior no-step entry focusing on the front-door lock
- There needs to be 32 inches of clear width, which requires a 36-inch door
- Nonslip flooring in foyer
- Entry door sidelight or high/low peephole viewer; sidelight should provide both privacy and safety
- Doorbell in accessible location
- Surface to place packages on when opening door

### Thresholds

- Flush preferable
- Exterior maximum of ½ inch beveled
- Interior maximum of ¼ inch

### Interior Doors

- There needs to be 32 inches of clear width, which requires a 36-inch door
- Levered door hardware

## Windows

- Plenty of windows for natural light
- Lowered windows or taller windows with lower sill height
- Low-maintenance exterior and interior finishes
- Easy-to-operate hardware

## Garage or Carport

- Covered carports and boarding spaces
- Wider-than-average carports to accommodate lifts on vans
- Door heights may need to be 9 feet to accommodate some raised roof vans
- 5-foot minimum access aisle between accessible van and car in garage
- If code requires floor to be several inches below entrance to house for fume protection, you can slope entire floor from front to back to eliminate need for ramp or step
- Ramp to doorway if needed
- Handrail if there are steps

## Faucets

- Lever handles or pedal-controlled
- Thermostatic or anti-scald controls
- Pressure-balanced faucets

## Kitchen and Laundry

Counters

- Wall support and provision for adjustable and/or varied height counters and removable base cabinets
- Upper wall cabinetry – 3 inches lower than conventional height
- Accented stripes on edge of countertops to provide visual orientation to the workspace
- Counter space for dish landing adjacent to or opposite all appliances

- Base cabinet with roll-out trays and lazy susans
- Pull-down shelving
- Glass-front cabinet doors
- Open shelving for easy access to frequently used items and appliances
- Easy-to-read controls
- Washing machine and dryer raised 12 to 15 inches above floor
- Front loading laundry machines
- Microwave oven at counter height or in wall
- Side-by-side refrigerator/freezer
- Side-swing or wall oven
- Raised dishwasher with pushbutton controls
- Electric cooktop with level burners for safety in transferring between the burners, front controls and downdraft feature to pull heat away from user; light to indicate when surface is hot

## Miscellaneous

- 30-inch by 48-inch clear space at appliances or 60-inch diameter clear space for turns
- Multilevel work areas to accommodate cooks of different heights
- Open undercounter seated work areas
- Placement of task lighting in appropriate work areas
- Loop handles for easy grip and pull
- Pull-out spray faucet; levered handles
- In multistory homes, laundry chute or laundry facilities in master bedroom

## Bathroom

- Wall support and provision for adjustable and/or varied height counters and removable base cabinets
- Contrasting color edge border at countertops
- At least one wheelchair maneuverable bath on main level with 60-inch turning radius or acceptable T-turn space and 36-inch by 36-inch or 30-inch by 48-inch clear space

- Bracing in walls around tub, shower, shower seat, and toilet for installation of grab bars to support 250–300 pounds
- If stand-up shower is used in main bath, it is curbless and minimum of 36 inches wide
- Bathtub – lower for easier access
- Fold-down seat in the shower
- Adjustable/handheld showerheads, 6-foot hose
- Tub/shower controls offset from center
- Shower stall with built-in antibacterial protection
- Light in shower stall
- Toilet 2½ inches higher than standard toilet (17 to 19 inches) or height-adjustable
- Design of the toilet paper holder allows rolls to be changed with one hand
- Wall-hung sink with knee space and panel to protect user from pipes
- Slip-resistant flooring in bathroom and shower

## Stairways, Lifts, and Elevators

- Adequate handrails on both sides of stairway, 1¼-inch diameter
- Increased visibility of stairs through contrast strip on top and bottom stairs, color contrast between treads and risers on stairs and use of lighting
- Multistory homes may provide either preframed shaft (i.e., stacked closets) for future elevator, or stairway width must be minimum of 4 feet to allow space for lift
- Residential elevator or lift

## Ramps

- Slope no greater than 1 inch rise for each 12 inches in length, adequate handrails
- 5-foot landing provided at entrance
- 2-inch curbs for safety

## Storage

- Adjustable closet rods and shelves
- Lighting in closets
- Easy-open doors that do not obstruct access

## Electrical, Lighting, Safety, and Security

- Light switches by each entrance to halls and rooms
- Light receptacles with at least 2 bulbs in vital places (exits, bathroom)
- Light switches, thermostats and other environmental controls placed in accessible locations no higher than 48 inches from floor
- Electrical outlets 15 inches on center from floor; may need to be closer than 12 feet apart
- Clear access space of 30 inches by 48 inches in front of switches and controls
- Rocker or touch light switches
- Audible and visual strobe light system to indicate when the doorbell, telephone, or smoke or $CO_2$ detectors have been activated
- High-tech security/intercom system that can be monitored, with the heating, air conditioning, and lighting, from any TV in the house
- Easy-to-see and read thermostats
- Preprogrammed thermostats
- Flashing porch light or 911 switch
- Direct wired to police, fire, and EMS (as option)
- Home wired for security
- Home wired for computers

## Flooring

- Smooth, nonglare, slip-resistant surfaces, interior and exterior
- If carpeted, use low (less than ½ inch high pile) density, with firm pad
- Color/texture contrast to indicate change in surface levels

### Heating, Ventilation, and Air Conditioning

- HVAC should be designed so filters are easily accessible
- Energy efficient units
- Windows that can be opened for cross-ventilation, fresh air

### Energy Efficient Features

- In-line framing with 2-by-6 studs spaced 24-inch on center
- Air-barrier installation and sealing of ductwork with mastic
- Reduced-size air conditioning units with gas furnaces
- Mechanical fresh-air ventilation, installation of air returns in all bedrooms and use of carbon monoxide detectors
- Installation of energy efficient windows with Low-E glass

### Reduced Maintenance/Convenience Features

- Easy-to-clean surfaces
- Central vacuum
- Built-in pet feeding system
- Built-in recycling system
- Videophones
- Intercom system

### Other Ideas

- Separate apartment for rental income or future caregiver
- Flex room that can be used as a nursery or playroom when the children are young and as a home office later; if combined with a full bath, room could also be used for an aging parent/aging in place

# More Resources

## *Books*

Bray, Ilona. *Selling Your House* (4th ed.). Nolo, 2021.
Frederick, Ryan. *Right Place, Right Time: The Ultimate Guide to Choosing a Home for the Second Half of Life.* Johns Hopkins University Press, 2021.
Jameson, Marni. *Downsizing the Family Home: What to Save, What to Let Go.* Sterling, 2016.

## *Websites (Where Should You Retire?)*

Free online quizzes, but you may need to enter your email or register to get your results:

> https://www.bestplaces.net/fybp/
> https://www.best-place-to-retire.com/places-to-retire-quiz
> https://www.topretirements.com/retirementranger.html
> https://money.cnn.com/quizzes/2012/pf/retirement/best-places-to-retire-quiz/
> https://internationalliving.com/take-the-45-second-quiz-and-find-your-perfect-place-to-live-overseas/
> https://www.liveandinvestoverseas.com/your-ideal-retirement-destination-quiz/
> https://internationalliving.com/the-best-places-to-retire/ (international relocation)

## *Websites (General)*

> TopRetirements: www.Topretirements.com free registration/ very interactive member-driven discussion forum
> Best Places: www.bestplaces.net from demographer Bert Sperling; compare two cities on more than a dozen categories including crime rate, cost of living, climate, etc.
> AARP's Livability Index: https://livabilityindex.aarp.org/compare

AARP's site rates "livability" based on housing, neighborhood, transportation, environment, health, engagement, and opportunity.

"Wicked Weather and Deadly Disasters": https://www.washingtonpost.com/graphics/2019/national/mapping-disasters/

https://msc.fema.gov/portal/search (see if you're in a flood zone – just enter an address at this Federal Emergency Management Agency website)

Sinkholes: https://www.usgs.gov (put in "earthquakes," "sinkholes," "hurricanes," and so forth into the search bar of the National Geographic Survey to find links where these disasters are most common)

CHAPTER 5

# Locations, Locations, Locations

■ ■ ■

From *Alice in Wonderland* by Lewis Carroll: Coming to a fork in the road, Alice asks the Cheshire Cat: "Which road should I take?" The cat replies: "Where are you going?" Alice says: "I don't know." "Then it doesn't matter which road you take," the Cheshire Cat responds.

Perhaps you're like Alice, and uncertain which path to choose when it comes to where to live in retirement, especially when a home may have taken on additional functions such as an office, a gym, a restaurant, and even a classroom. That's entirely understandable, and it's the focus of this chapter: specific possibilities for relocation. In previous chapters, we discussed what makes retirement successful, what to do with your 168 hours a week, options for working after leaving your primary career, what you might want/need in an ideal retirement location, and "should you stay or should you go."

It's surprising how many different varieties of living are possible: developments that are cities, master-planned communities that have a club component so you can easily meet people, places that are walkable or bikeable where you can ditch your car, communities designed for the LGBTQ+ population, multigenerational homes, living on luxurious cruise ships, aging in place within a community, homesharing, and so forth. As we explore some possibilities, keep in mind the "Food for Thought" list in the previous chapter, and this handy **PERFECT** acronym when evaluating a place:

**PERFECT:**

P = Property (politics; proximity to healthcare, grocery stores and other shopping)

E = Environment (climate, air quality, natural disasters, safety)

R = Real Estate (cost of living/taxes; housing that fits your needs, wants, and wallet)

F = Fitness (healthcare; opportunities to optimize health in mind, spirit, and body)

E = Engagement (things to do/employment if desired or necessary)

C = Connections (friends and family; feeling like you "belong")

T = Transportation (airports/public transit/getting around via foot or bike); check out www.walkscore.com to see how walkable a potential place is if you want to hoof it; the walkscore site also shows you how bikeable a place is.

No location is truly perfect, but narrowing your criteria to what's most important to *you* is a good start for finding your happy place. Let's start with some "best of" lists, and then delve into specific communities/ways of living that could be your nirvana.

## Low Cost of Living (U.S.)

"Low cost" is a subjective word. The National Association of Realtors reported that the median home price in the United States hit $363,300 for the first time in July 2021. For some, the retirement that people want is the one they can afford. Locations that are desirable yet offer a low cost of living could be your number-one requirement. If this is you, there are a number of places that may fit the bill. "The Penny Hoarder" crunched numbers involving not only cost of living, but access to medical care, opportunities for community engagement, reasonable home values, low crime rates, and the health and number of retirees. They created a list of 11 places, along with enticing nuggets about each location (the link with additional info on each city is found at the end of this chapter in the "More Resources" section). Here is a sampling (I have visited all of these places and recommend them):

- St. George, Utah (city is experiencing rising wages if you plan to work; close to Zion National Park)
- Palm Coast, Florida (you can live as close as five minutes from the ocean; lots of nature trails and bike paths). Aside – this is where I live, on the barrier island in a master-planned community on the ocean.
- Loveland, Colorado (many cultural activities, less than an hour's drive from Denver)
- Cape Coral, Florida (spring training for the Red Sox and Twins nearby; about 400 miles of man-made canals: "a third of your backyard is water")
- Santa Fe, New Mexico (mountain scenery; more than 300 days of sunshine; known for its history and art – including, of course, artist Georgia O'Keefe)
- Asheville, North Carolina (art, food, and nature in the Blue Ridge Mountains)

Additional info about the financial issues affecting where you live in retirement is included in Chapters 7 and 8.

## Low Cost of Living on Steroids: Places That Pay You to Move There

How about free land? Some areas, predominantly small U.S. towns looking for full-time residents and an increased tax base, are providing free or virtually free building lots for those who want to relocate. There are restrictions on the offers, such as building time-frames, but if you meet the requirements, and you think it's something you might be interested in doing, it's worth investigating. If you take this approach, do your homework before making any decisions.

Examples (links at end of this chapter):

- Lincoln, Kansas, population of about 3,500, is offering a free lot from 14,000 to 35,000 square feet in a residential neighborhood (water, sewers, and streets are in place). Homes must be a minimum of 1,300 square feet, and must meet certain design standards and building timeframes.
- Mankato, Kansas, population of about 900, is offering a free lot with construction of a house with a minimum of 1,200 square feet, not including garages, basement, and porches; completion within two years of receiving the lot.
- Internationally, there can be low-cost homes in other countries such as Italy and Japan, but some tend to be vacant residences that require a lot of renovations, may have quite a bit of "red tape," and are located far from major cities. One city in Italy, Latronico, offers homes in much better shape, but for a bit higher price. (It might be easier to get a job teaching English overseas and enjoy living in a foreign country that way.)

## Best Places for Active Retirees (2021)

The United Health Foundation does a yearly ranking of states based on activity levels of adults 65+ who are in self-reported good health. The top five states in 2021 with the most active adults 65+: Colorado, Washington, Minnesota, Utah, and California. States with the most sedentary adults: South Dakota, West Virginia, Oklahoma, Kentucky, and Mississippi. Mississippi is ranked last, with 46% of those surveyed reporting "no physical activity or exercise other than their regular job in the previous 30 days."

If you're looking for places that beg you to walk or hike because of their inviting natural beauty, here are "10 Great Outdoor Towns for Retirement" from TopRetirements: Bend, Oregon; Burlington, Vermont; Eagle, Colorado; Reno, Nevada; St. George, Utah; Boone, North Carolina; Traverse City, Michigan; Dahlonega, Georgia; Morgantown, West Virginia; Arkadelphia, Arkansas. The last two locations, Morgantown and Arkadelphia, also enjoy a lower cost of living than the national average. (I can attest that Bend and St. George are great.)

If biking is your preferred mode of transportation, consider these top-biking city recommendations from the Travel Channel, which include: Boulder, Colorado ("hundreds of miles of bike paths" and "over 300 days of sunshine a year"); Portland, Oregon ("no other city in the United States has more cyclists per capita. . .or coffee shops"); Chicago, Illinois ("be in a major US metropolis or sitting on the beach within 3 minutes of each other"); Minneapolis, Minnesota ("enjoy 120 miles of bikeways, bike-pedestrian bridges like the Stone Arch Bridge, and the city's bike share program"); or Seattle, Washington ("Mountain views? Check. Beach biking? Check. Forests and parks? Check. City trails? Check."). See link at the end of this chapter for the complete list. (I rank Boulder, Portland, and Seattle very highly.)

If you're looking for specific communities designed to be active for all ages or for those 55+, we'll address master-planned and active-adult communities later in this chapter.

## Best Places to Retire Lists 2021 (U.S.)

Here are several recent holistic "best places" lists from well-regarded sources (websites for each are listed at the end of this chapter):

- **TopRetirements.** Why I like this site: This online site began in 2007 and has more than 200,000 unique visitors/month. It's free to join, and very member-driven. Lots of wonderful discussions by real people moving to real places. TopRetirement's 2021 best-places list is based primarily on members' feedback: Flagstaff, Arizona; Prescott, Arizona; Pensacola, Florida; Beaufort, South Carolina; Chattanooga, Tennessee; Asheville, North Carolina; Del Webb North Myrtle Beach, South Carolina; Lost Lakes in Cocoa, Florida, and Riverside Club Golf and Marina in Ruskin, Florida (these are manufactured home communities with most homes under $150,000); Sun City Center, Sun City, Florida; Las Cruces, New Mexico; Santa Fe, New Mexico; Sarasota, Florida; and Charlottesville, Virginia.

- *Forbes.* Why I like this site: *Forbes* analyzed almost 800 U.S. locations to determine their 2021 top 25 cities for retirees. *Forbes* evaluated locations based on the qualities in the PERFECT acronym, listed near the beginning of this chapter. The Forbes list of 80 cities is in alphabetical order, but here are several that are not duplicated by TopRetirements that I particularly like: Charlotte, North Carolina; Clearwater, Florida; Jacksonville, Florida; Knoxville, Tennessee; San Antonio, Texas; Virginia Beach, Virginia, and Wenatchee, Washington. Link to the full list is at the end of this chapter.
- **SeniorLiving.org Research.** Why I like this site: Rankings of all 50 states are based on 15 weighted factors that the site's readers "consider crucial to living a long and happy life" including weather, cost of living, active physicians per 100,000 people, relative tax burden, monthly housing cost, and life expectancy at birth. The *worst* states, using the same criteria, are also listed. The 10 *highest* ranked states: Florida, Oklahoma, Mississippi, Delaware, Massachusetts, Maryland, North Dakota, California, North Carolina, and South Carolina. The 10 *lowest* ranked states: Oregon, Kentucky, New Mexico, Kansas, Alabama, West Virginia, Washington, Indiana, Connecticut, and Montana. Of course, if some of these factors don't matter to you, such as the monthly housing cost, their rankings would be less meaningful to you.

## Best Places to Retire Internationally (2021)

- *U.S. News & World Report.* Why I like this site: Kathleen Peddicord writes for *U.S. News & World Report,* is the author of many books about international living, and has been involved in international retirement and relocation for more than 30 years. Her recommendations for considering "affordable and exotic places" abroad include cost, safety, healthcare, how much English is spoken, and advice on establishing residency. Peddicord's 2021 picks: Tavira, Portugal; Mazatlan, Mexico; Lisbon, Portugal; Cuenca, Ecuador; Northern Belize; Pedasi, Panama; St. Chinian, France; Gozo, Malta, and Ambergris Caye, Belize.

    At the end of this chapter, under "More Resources," there is a list of thoughtful and important questions Peddicord suggests you ask yourself if considering retiring abroad. I mentioned previously that 13% of those still working/ already retired in the United States have expressed an interest in living abroad. And, in 2019, almost 432,000 retired U.S. workers were drawing Social Security benefits from outside the United States.

Lists of best places to retire can be helpful, but, as the saying goes, "One person's treasure is another person's trash." Only *you* can decide what's *your* best place, based on *your* criteria.

## "Niche" Lifestyles

In this section, let's explore communities or lifestyles with one major overriding theme. These communities may include similar amenities that other communities offer, such as pools, tennis/ pickleball courts, walking paths or parks, etc., but there is "something" about the community that is the driving force for relocation. Use the PERFECT acronym near the beginning of the chapter to ensure you're okay with the other important parameters, such as cost of living, climate, health care, transportation, and so forth. Here are a dozen or so niche communities. (Warning: Some of these types of communities are affordable for only a very small segment of the population, but it's still fun and informative to know what's out there – even if it's out of reach.)

- **Golden Oak at Walt Disney World Resort, Lake Buena Vista, Florida** (www.disneygoldenoak.com). If you're an affluent die-hard Disney fan, you can live in a gated, Disney-themed community within the Walt Disney World property. Golden Oak is comprised of several neighborhoods as well as private Four Seasons Residences. Disney themes run throughout – from Disney carvings in the beautiful wooden staircases within the homes to Disney-themed benches and whimsical Disney statuary as you stroll around the community. Summerhouse is the private clubhouse where you can eat, meet, swim, and enjoy community activities. HOA fees run approximately $25,000/year, and some Disney perks are included. At build-out, there will be approximately 300 homes on 980 acres. Homes start around $3 million and go up, up, up. It's a bunny-hop 8-minute drive to the Magic Kingdom, 7 minutes to EPCOT, 15 minutes to Disney's Animal Kingdom, and 11 minutes to Disney's Hollywood Studio. When I toured this community, I was told a number of people bought a second home for extended family. Truly a niche location!
- **NALCREST** (National Association of Letter Carriers, Retirement, Education, Security and Training) (www.nalc.org/member-benefits/nalcrest). This 55+ community, located in Lake Wales, Florida, about an hour south of Orlando, was founded in 1964 by the National Association of Letter Carriers President William Doherty for retired letter carriers of the United States Postal Service (and their spouses). There are 500 ground-level efficiency/one bedroom/two bedroom apartments starting around $400 month. And, perhaps not surprisingly. . . no pets allowed!
- **Ave Maria** (https://www.avemaria.com/). When you think of Italy, you may think of churches and piazzas (in addition to

wonderful people, historic ruins, and delicious food). There is a unique community in Florida, Ave Maria, located about an hour's drive east of Naples, with an impressive Catholic church in the town center. Founded in 2005, this community was developed by Tom Monaghan of Domino Pizza's fame. In addition to the church, there is Ave Maria University, Ave Maria Law School, and a private K–12 school. The downtown is designed to be walkable, with apartment and condos above the shops, single-family homes, and a Del Webb active-adult community with a golf course (opened in 2021) within this 5,000-acre planned community with a current population of about 31,000. Other amenities, such as a water park, playgrounds, tennis, and sports fields are offered. Pricing is from the low $200,000s. And, in case you were wondering, people of all faiths (or no religion) are welcome in Ave Maria. I have visited this community, and it's an attractive, interesting place.

- **Margaritaville(s)** (https://www.latitudemargaritaville.com/). Are you a Jimmy Buffett fan, aka a Parrothead? Do you subscribe to the Margaritaville philosophy of "Growing older – not up?" Are you "55 or better"? If so, Margaritaville might be for you. There are currently three Margaritaville locations: Margaritaville Hilton Head (it's actually in Bluffton, about 20 miles away from Hilton Head); Margaritaville Watersound on Florida's panhandle (the community's town center overlooks the Intracoastal Waterway); and Margaritaville Daytona Beach, Florida (this location has a shuttle that will drive you to its beach club on the Atlantic Ocean, which is 11 miles from the community). These communities are developing, and the Daytona Beach and Hilton Head locations will each have about 3,000 homes, and about 3,500 in Watersound's initial phase. Residences start in the mid-$200,000s and include single-family residences, cottages, and paired villas. If you're looking for sports, fitness, and lots of social amenities and opportunities to meet and interact with your neighbors, a town square with a theater and bandshell, and places to eat and drink, this could be – excuse the pun – your "(cheese-burger in) paradise." There are no golf courses within the communities, but there are some close by you could join. HOA fees are determined by the type of home and range from around $230–$317/month. By the way . . . A *Wheel of Fortune* contestant won a home in one of the Margarita-villes – a $375,000 value. I visited these popular communities in Daytona Beach and Hilton Head, and they are fun, busy, in-demand, and growing fast. Fins Up!

---

*True Life: Jeannie L. relocated to Margaritaville, Daytona Beach. Jeannie's thoughts on choosing a place, and liking it so much she works there, too!*

I spent 30 years as a middle school and high school band director in Texas. I was retiring from teaching and started looking for communities in Florida that were close to the beach. After teaching for so long, I wanted to look at communities that were adult-oriented. I wasn't a huge fan of Jimmy Buffett, but I had been to some of his concerts and really enjoyed them.

Rumors were flying that Buffett was going to be a partner in some retirement communities, and the first one would be in Daytona Beach, so I started doing my research. There was no sales center, but a Facebook page was created by a local businessman to gather information from people who were interested in Latitude Margaritaville Daytona Beach (LMDB). We quickly got to know one another on social media before we ever met in person. I soon realized that this community was exactly what I was looking for!

The first residents moved into LMDB in March of 2018. I visited the community in April of the same year. I was touring the model homes when I noticed a small group of residents having a Bloody Mary get-together at the tiki hut near the models. I started talking to them and they were so kind, fun, and welcoming. I purchased my villa lot within three hours of my visit. I knew immediately that this community was going to attract active, fun, and young-at-heart people. I moved in on August 1, 2018.

There weren't a lot of residents, nor were the amenities in place, so it didn't take long to figure out how to entertain ourselves until our town center was built. We would take turns hosting residents in our homes. Bonds and lifelong friendships soon developed, which reassured all of us that we were embarking on the time of our lives! After amenities were built, we were blessed with an amazing resort pool, restaurant, and bar, a fitness center with an indoor lap pool, a work and play center that has a fully outfitted pottery center, a dog spa, a woodworking room, and a beautiful theater that is available for banquets, shows and other events. Our most prized amenity is our private beach club that is about a dozen miles from our community. We have a daily charter that transports residents back and forth to the beach. When we arrive we have chairs and umbrellas ready for us to use.

This place is above and beyond anything I imagined. I recently decided to go back to work because, believe it or not, it is exhausting going to so many activities! I am now a guest experience coordinator for Latitude Margaritaville Daytona Beach. I love meeting potential future residents. Yes, I both live and work (and usually eat, too!) in my community.

My advice for those looking into new communities is to be diligent in your research. You will know when you have found the right place. If you leave unsure if that is the place for you, then that is *not* the place. Ask lots of questions about the lifestyle and the average age group of the residents. Find out if they have open social media pages where you can ask questions of current residents. You get the best information by talking to the people who live there.

- **Co-housing.** This living style, also called collaborative housing, originated in Denmark in the 1960s and migrated to the United States in the 1980s. Community, caring, connection, and common interests are at the heart of this lifestyle choice. Some of the hallmarks: a "Common House" with a kitchen and dining area and other resources surrounded by individually owned homes, management by residents, community meals, equality among residents, nonideological, decision-making based on consensus, and a reduced environmental impact. There are more than 260 of these communities in the United States, including 55+ co-housing communities. A "how-to" for creating one of these communities is also included in the co-housing link at the end of the chapter. Co-housing could be a great option for anyone, single or coupled, looking to live in a small community with lots of social support.

---

*True Life: Pam J. moved to the senior co-housing community of Wolf Creek Lodge in Grass Valley, California, in 2013. Pam's story:*

As a "lonely only" (no siblings) I knew from an early age I needed to expand a sense of family in other ways. So I went looking for "community." For years it was a spiritual one in the hills of Northern California. When that experience came to an end, I was again on the lookout. In the early 2000s I learned about the concept of co-housing, ultimately ending up with a group interested in not just co-housing, but senior co-housing.

In January 2013 I moved into Wolf Creek Lodge in Grass Valley, California . . . into my own 650-square foot condo at 70 years of age. It turns out I had truly come home. Now, I am happily integrated into the extended family I had always wanted, enjoying the camaraderie of 36 neighbors, mostly retired, who dine, play, and do the work of our community together and, most importantly, support one another. It is an amazing experience that has helped me grow as a person. I highly recommend it.

---

- **LGBTQ+ communities**. I noted earlier in the book that there is a growing population of older adults who identify as LGBTQ+. A number of cities are known for being

LGBTQ+-friendly, and what is even more exciting is that communities dedicated to this population are in place/being developed. According to SeniorLiving.org and Senioradvice.com, examples of cities that are particularly welcoming, as well as offering a high quality of life, include West Palm Beach, Orlando, and Tampa, Florida; Phoenix and Tucson, Arizona; Atlanta, Georgia; Buffalo, New York; Eugene, Oregon, New Orleans, Louisiana; and Austin, Texas (see "More Resources" at the end of this chapter for ranking rationale and websites). A desire to feel welcome, less likely to have children, and wanting social support and services as they age are driving forces fueling the development of LGBTQ+ communities. Here are several examples (websites at the end of the chapter have additional communities and details/pricing along with a link to community centers throughout the United States ):

**Fountaingrove Lodge** in Santa Rosa, California describes itself as "the nation's first lesbian, gay, bisexual, transgender (LGBTQ+), and Friends focused independent senior community with the option of continuing care services." Their 10-acre campus opened in 2013.

**The Resort on Carefree Boulevard** (Fort Myers, Florida). Founded in 1996, this women-only community has about 280 homes/RV sites on 50 acres. About half the residents are full-time.

**Stonewall Gardens** is a 24-unit assisted living facility in Palm Springs, California. It opened in 2014. And it's pet-friendly "because your pets are your family."

**A Place for Us**, situated at the border of Cleveland and Lakewood, Ohio, "is the first LGBTQ+-friendly senior-housing community in the state of Ohio." This 55+ pet-friendly community offers one- and two-bedroom apartments and caters to lower-income renters.

**Rainbow Vista** is 15 miles from Portland in Grisham, Oregon. It's for those 55+ who can live independently, is pet-friendly (limit of one), and offers studios, and one-bedroom units along with amenities including a laundry room, exercise room, and a billiard/game room.

**Village Hearth Cohousing** began development in 2020 (see earlier section on "co-housing" for a description of this lifestyle option) and describes itself as "the first LGBTQ+-focused 55+ co-housing community in North America." Located 15 minutes from Durham, North Carolina, there will be 11–40 units on a total of 11–20 acres.

- **Indo-Americans**. There are approximately 360,000 retired Indian-Americans in the United States, according to the National Indo-American Association for Senior Citizens. Although a good number live with extended family, there are retirement communities that have been built specifically for Indo-Americans. Two examples: Nalanda ("no stopping of the gift of knowledge") Estates near Tampa, Florida, a 55+ community (sold out, but may have resales), and ShantiKiketan ("abode of peace" in Tavares, Florida, also 55+). There are presently four Priya Living communities in California, with apartments starting around $2,400/month, and offering community spaces and amenities. As their advertising says, "Sip chai on the patio." More are in the planning stages. Websites are at the end of the chapter.

- **Black Americans**. Close to 24% of Black Americans live in intergenerational households, so a housing type designed for more than one family (check out multigenerational living, later) could be a popular option.

"Black ExcelList," a YouTube Channel with more than 260,000 subscribers, lists "The Top 12 Retirement Cities for African Americans." There were close to 475,000 views on this post, with some respondents strongly agreeing and others strongly disagreeing with the list, which is in keeping with most recommendations; where you retire is a very personal decision. Rankings were based on things to do, cost of living, climate, livability, percentage of the population that is black, and size of the city. Here is the list, beginning with their top-ranked city: Jacksonville, Florida; Winston-Salem, North Carolina; Chattanooga, Tennessee; Harrisburg, Pennsylvania; Raleigh-Durham-Chapel Hill, North Carolina (aka The Triangle because of the location of North Carolina State, Duke, and the University of North Carolina); Philadelphia, Pennsylvania; Charlotte, North Carolina; Washington, DC; Greensboro, North Carolina; Atlanta, Georgia; Augusta, Georgia; and Rochester, New York. Links at end of chapter.

One approach for some Black Americans is to move abroad to places that are diverse and welcoming, with a lower or reasonable cost of living, lots to do, a pleasant climate, other Black expats and/or populations of African descent, and good health care. A 2021 article by Parker Diakite in *Travel Noire*, "The Ten Best Places for African Americans to Move Abroad," suggests these locations: Medellin, Columbia; Lisbon, Portugal; Belize City, Belize; Dakar, Senegal; Limon, Costa Rica; Accra, Ghana; Panama City, Panama; Bangkok, Thailand; Barcelona, Spain, Montreal, Canada; and Tulum, Mexico. (See end of chapter for link.)

I asked Kathleen Peddicord, author, journalist, and founder of "Live and Invest Overseas" for her recommendations. Kathleen is considered to be the foremost authority on living, retiring, and investing overseas. She graciously contributed this:

## The Best Places to Retire Overseas—Three Beautiful, Welcoming Options That Are Budget Friendly and Color Blind by Kathleen Peddicord

No question, your retirement savings can stretch much further many places overseas than they might anywhere in the United States. It's possible to retire in dozens of beautiful, safe, good-weather, and culturally rich places across the globe on a budget of as little as $1,500 a month. Right now, that's less than the average monthly Social Security check.

However, a lower cost of living is only a place to start this conversation. Retiring abroad, even part-time, opens the door to adventure and reinvention. Ours is a great big beautiful world bursting with opportunity. The retirement lifestyle you want is out there. You just need to get up, get moving, and go seize it.

If you're a retiree of color, the upside to choosing to spend your retirement beyond U.S. borders can be greater. It could be possible for you to retire to a place where the color of your skin plays no role in how accepted and welcomed you are by the local community – either because the people of the local community look like you or because they're enlightened enough not to care one way or the other. Retiring overseas could give you the chance to be not a retiree of color but simply a retiree taking full advantage of this stage of your life.

After World War I, when Black Americans experienced life overseas for the first time, many chose to remain in France, where they felt more respected, and Paris remains a good option for an American of color looking to retire well. Home to a large community of expatriates from every part of the world, Paris is one of the most diverse points on our planet.

On the other hand, Paris isn't a top budget choice.

Following are my three picks for the best places to think about reinventing your life in retirement overseas that are budget-friendly and also color-blind.

## Belize—Part Caribbean, Part Central American, English Speaking, and a World Apart

No single race or ethnic group stands out in Belize, making it easy to find common ground and assimilate. Belizeans refer to their country as a "Boil Up." That's a Belizean Kriol gumbo made with yams, cassava, tomatoes, onions, sweet potatoes, fish, pig's tail, plantains, and bananas. An exotic mix of diverse ingredients. That's Belize.

Land, water, gold, timber, and oil have been bringing people to Belize since the Maya settled in the region more than 4,000 years ago. At one time, the forests, coastlines, and rivers of this country supported an agrarian Maya population of nearly 500,000, about 150,000 more people than live in Belize today.

The country's official language is English. Everyone you meet speaks it, but that belies the stories of their origins. The 350,000 people populating Belize today are descendants of migrants from Britain, yes, but also and more so the surrounding Central American countries. You've got Mexicans, Guatemalans, Hondurans, and Nicaraguans mixing with current-day generations of the Maya who originally inhabited this land, the pirates who came later, the Mennonite farmers who began arriving on the scene in the sixteenth century, and the British who ruled until 1981.

124

Belize is a country of freedom-seekers. The pirates came to ply their pirate trading out of view. The Mennonites came from Germany and the Netherlands so they could be Mennonites without anyone bothering them. The British came so they could bank in private. And the folks from the surrounding countries who've sought out Belize over the past few decades typically have made their way across this country's borders in search of safety and a chance to start over.

Today a new population of freedom-seekers is finding its way to these shores—American retirees. And they're as welcome as was every group that came before them.

Belize is perhaps best known and loved for its islands, especially Ambergris Caye, the largest and most developed, boasting both long beaches of soft, white sand and an established and growing community of expats and foreign retirees. This is the Caribbean at its best.

Inland is the Cayo District, a dramatically different region where life revolves not around the sea but the rivers. For some, river views don't substitute for ocean vistas; others prefer them. The main appeal of Cayo, thanks to its abundance of fertile land, water, and year-round sunshine, is the opportunity it offers for a healthy, fulfilling, back-to-basics, self-sufficient lifestyle. This can be the best place on earth to leave the troubles of our age behind. Cayo is also Belize's most affordable lifestyle choice and, in part because of this, the fastest-growing region in the country.

The greatest challenge to living in Belize can be its undeveloped infrastructure. The country has but four highways, one international airport, and limited but improving facilities for medical care.

## Portugal – Open Minded and Forward Thinking With Europe's Best Weather and Excellent Health Care

In the more than 30 years I've been covering the retire-overseas beat, I've had the chance to meet and speak with untold numbers of expats and readers. Each one has his or her own ideas about what, for them, would constitute the ideal quality of life in a new country. Many love the proximity, the regular sunshine, and the affordability of the Americas. Some prefer the exotic, adventure lifestyle and drop-dead low cost of living of Asia. But, for some, nothing but Europe will do. One energetic would-be retiree summed it up to me succinctly: "Forget the developing world. I'll take low hassle and easy living, please!"

Many retirees take Europe off their wish list because they can't imagine that they could actually afford to retire to the Continent. In fact, certain spots in the Old World are as budget-friendly as some Central American options.

One country in this part of the world stands out. Home to more than 100,000 expat retirees, Portugal is a land of superlatives. This little nation boasts arguably the best beaches in Europe, along with the best weather, the best golf, and, thanks to decades as an expat hotspot, the most welcoming locals in Europe, many of whom speak English. The classic Mediterranean diet typical here is one of the healthiest.

Portugal isn't the world's cheapest place to live, but it is a bargain compared with elsewhere in Europe. It's also the third-safest country in the world (after Iceland and New Zealand). Violent crime is unheard of, and street crime is limited to the tourist spots.

Everyone is welcome. As a Portuguese friend told me, "Portugal is not a country of several groups or peoples. We are all just Portuguese. Being black in this country is not a novelty, and it attracts no attention."

Capital city Lisbon is one of the oldest in Western Europe. Originally settled as a Phoenician trading post, Lisbon flourished in the fifteenth and sixteenth centuries, the Golden Age of Discovery. If you like places with long pasts, you'll love it here.

The country's southern coastal Algarve region is a land of medieval towns, traditional fishing villages, open-air markets, cobblestoned streets, and whitewashed houses with lace-patterned chimneys surrounded by fig, olive, almond, and carob trees, all fringed by a 100-mile-long coastline. The Algarve offers a one-of-a-kind lifestyle that could be described as quintessential Old World meets twenty-first-century resort to deliver one of the Continent's best values.

## Mexico—Easy, Accessible, Affordable, Familiar, and Diverse

More than 9 million Americans live overseas, nearly 2 million of them in Mexico. Our neighbor to the south is far and away America's most popular overseas retirement haven. From world-class beaches along its Pacific and Caribbean rivieras to sixteenth-century Spanish-colonial towns oozing charm, Mexico offers up some of the best of Latin America.

And it's all so accessible. You could move to Mexico with a pick-up truck and a credit card, receiving your residency visa in one day if you qualify and you can qualify simply by showing sufficient funds in a bank or IRA account. Retiring overseas doesn't get easier.

The U.S. dollar's strength against the Mexican peso makes the low cost of living an even greater bargain. English-speaking professionals, service providers, and residents are easy to find, especially in the touristed areas, though you'll have a fuller experience of life here if you learn at least a little Spanish.

Mexico isn't a backwater. Its GDP is more than double that of Argentina, its nearest competitor. The country has a good energy supply and a solid manufacturing base, and its high-end manufacturing sector, including aerospace, is growing at record levels. This kind of active economy translates into a fully appointed retirement experience.

Although you can't use your Medicare coverage outside the United States, retired in Mexico you could drive or fly north for qualifying care if you needed it. You wouldn't necessarily. The medical care available in Mexico is international standard and a fraction the cost of healthcare in the United States.

Mazatlán, on Mexico's Pacific coast, offers the unique opportunity to enjoy the conveniences of a cosmopolitan lifestyle while having the beach literally on your doorstep. Living here, you could start each day with a walk on the sand at sunrise then spend the afternoon shopping in the historic city center.

Founded in 1531, Mazatlán's heart is an impressive collection of Spanish-colonial structures that today house restaurants, cafés, galleries, and shops . . . with the ocean as backdrop. Mazatlán boasts all the conveniences of home, including big-footprint shopping from Walmart to Home Depot, making it possible to embrace the best of traditional Mexican life without giving up much of anything from back home.

This is one of the most affordable beachfront property markets in the world and a bargain compared with other top coastal options in Mexico including Cancún, Playa del Carmen, Puerto Vallarta, or Tulum. You could own a beach home in Mazatlán with a frontline view of the water for less than $200,000.

- **Built-to-Rent Housing Communities.** This is a newer, interesting trend; only about 6% of homes in the United States are built solely for rental and managed by real-estate companies. But, that number is increasing, because some retirees don't want to rent an apartment or purchase a home or condo, are unable to come up with the down payment to purchase a residence, don't want the associated hassles of homeownership, don't want a big investment, but *do* want the extra space, want a garage, want a free-standing residence, and want the perks of living in a single-family neighborhood, perhaps gated, with a professional management company to deal with the maintenance, repairs, and landscaping. About 30 states now have these communities. Some have look-alike houses, others look quite varied. "Rents like an Apartment. Lives like a Home" is the catchy tagline of NexMetro, with communities in Arizona, Texas, Colorado, and Florida. Another major player is Christopher Todd Communities in Arizona and Texas.

I visited the single-family community Coastal Run at Heritage Shores, a 55+ development within the larger Heritage Shores community in Bridgeville, Delaware (note – only an hour's drive to the ocean). The master-planned community of Heritage Shores offers one-to-three-year rentals managed by Allen & Rocks, Inc. Built-to-rent communities reminds me of "Rent the Runway" – some people only want limited use of a designer outfit without purchasing it, so why not the same for a single-family home? See links at the end of this chapter for pricing and more details.

- **Live on a Residential or Cruise Ship.** Want to literally cruise through retirement? Estimates of how many people "live aboard" range from 50,000 to 100,000, according to the editors of magazines dedicated to this lifestyle. However, there are only a few luxury ships/yachts that are built/being built as residences. *The World,* launched in 2002, is touted as "the largest private residential ship on the planet." It offers 136 studios or one-, two-, or three-bedroom residences. Amenities include a spa, a wellness team, dining, a nondenominational house of worship, and a variety of leisure activities, not to mention traveling the globe. The residents plan the ship's itinerary (as this is being composed, The World is in the Persian Gulf). Residences are priced from $600,000 to $13,000,000, and there are additional ship services fees. Passenger ships have a lifespan of about 30–40 years, so it's more a lease than a purchase. There are some rentals available.

  *Somnio,* meaning "to dream" in Latin, will be launched in 2024. At 728 feet, it will replace *The World* as the longest residential vessel; this "residential superyacht" has 39 apartments that start at more than $11 million and are "by invitation or referral" only. See the More Resources section at the end of the chapter for links for *The World* and *Somnio*. Of course, they are beyond reach for most of us, but still interesting to know this option exists.

How about a second home without purchasing a second home? Some people cruise so frequently that a cruise ship functions as their second part-time home. Assuming a cruise to the Caribbean on a mainstream line like Royal Caribbean, with pricing often around $2,000 (or less) a week per person, which includes food, gratuities, housekeeping, entertainment, and unending people to meet, a couple could conceivably live on a cruise ship for 10 weeks out of the year for about $40,000, like Edmund and Rosalind G., who string together many back-to-back-to-back sailings. A few people have lived on cruise ships for long periods of time, such as Beatrice Miller, who resided full time on the *Queen Elizabeth 2* for nine years, and Ms. Lee Wachtstetter, who took up residence on the *Crystal Serenity* more than a dozen years ago. No house payments, no shopping/no preparing meals/no doing dishes/no cleaning. All Aboard?

• **Introvert/Extrovert.** Dictionary definition of an introvert: "a person who prefers calm environments, limits social engagement, or embraces a greater than average preference for solitude." Dictionary definition of an extrovert: "an outgoing, gregarious person who thrives in dynamic environments and seeks to maximize social engagement." Or, are you a person who is extroverted or introverted depending on the situation, and thus consider yourself an "ambivert"? If you're thinking of relocating, and you define yourself as either an introvert or extrovert, there is research on this topic that could be helpful. Studies have shown that introverts generally prefer wooded, secluded, and mountainous terrain, while extroverts generally prefer flat, open, beachy areas. (I guess the person who coined the phrase "Life is better at the beach" is an extrovert.) Examples of desirable mountain cities for introverts from Livability.com: Salt Lake City,

Utah; Boulder, Colorado; Asheville, North Carolina; and Los Alamos, New Mexico. Examples of great cities for extroverts ranked by Livability.com: New York City, New York (no surprise there, right?); Boston, Massachusetts; Miami, Florida; Dallas, Texas; and Scottsdale, Arizona.

If city living isn't your thing, two other suggested lifestyles that are good for introverts and extroverts are master-planned communities and active-adult (55+) communities (both discussed later). Why? Because there is *choice*. You can be as involved – or uninvolved – as you'd like. Nancy L. is the personification of an extrovert; she lives in a master-planned community and is involved in the group activities of tennis, golf, and exercise classes, eats out often with others, and is always ready to talk or text or meet up to play cards or go bike riding. Michael L. is a widowed introvert who is still working from home, and likes his 55+ community for exactly the same reasons – he can choose which activities to participate in, and they are organized by someone else – he just needs to show up. So, he will attend his community book club meetings if he has read the book (and may or may not join the discussion), goes to group exercise classes or works out alone at the gym, plays golf at the community course with the same group of men once a week, swims laps on occasion in the community pool, and attends some lectures/socials offered by his community. He has a small but close group of friends, and socializes with them, often at events organized by his community, or Michael will invite his few close friends over to his condo to play poker. Both extroverts and introverts can thrive in master-planned communities.

- **Master-Planned and Active-Adult Communities.** A master-planned community, referenced earlier, is an all-ages residential community, usually with a variety of housing options that offer a large number of amenities, frequently including golf courses, tennis, pickleball, pools, hiking trails, gyms, and perhaps restaurants and other types of commercial amenities.

Master-planned communities are frequently gated with security and homeowners associations (HOAs) that can dictate what you can plant in your yard, the color of your house, when you can put out your trash, the model of your mailbox, and so forth. These communities provide great opportunities for social interaction, often with a "lifestyle director" hired for just that role – coordinating socials, book clubs, lectures, exercise classes, tennis clinics, and so forth. These communities may stretch over several thousand acres. And yes, you will pay additional fees for having this amenity-rich lifestyle – someone has to pay for the pools and such!

Full disclosure: My husband and I have lived in a master-planned community for the past 14 years – and love it. We moved in when the streets and some amenities were in place, and enjoy the club atmosphere and the ease of meeting others through social activities. We were new to the state (Florida) and knew only two couples.

Another variation of a master-planned community is an active-adult community. If you're tired of hearing the pitter-patter of little feet or teenagers gunning their cars, and want to be surrounded by hopefully like-minded (and like-aged) neighbors, consider an active-adult community, which is a master-planned community where the resident(s) must (usually) be 55 or older (Margaritaville, discussed earlier, is an example of an active-adult community.) In some cases active-adult communities may allow a lower minimum age (such as a younger spouse) if 80% of households have someone 55 or older. The emphasis is on engagement, activity, and being as social as you'd like. Yes, grandchildren can visit, but perhaps with time limits – and they are expected to follow the rules. Jean M. is single and lives in the active-adult community of Leisure World, in Silver Spring, Maryland. Jean loves the proximity to Washington, DC, and the fact that the community provides transportation, security, and a medical center, as well as a host of amenities for its 8,000 residents. Her community is older, founded in 1997, and she has lived there for more than

20 years, staying on after caring for her mom for five years as she succumbed to Alzheimer's. Jean's mom willed the condo to Jean, who was over 55, in her will. One small caution about active-adult communities – you don't want to end up in a "silo" where everyone is close to the same age. It's important to have friendships and relationships with people of all ages, and enjoy multiple perspectives.

Generally, if you purchase in a still-growing master-planned or still-growing active-adult community – one in which the basic infrastructure is in place, but it's still developing – it's much easier to integrate and meet people. Of course, as with Jean, there are always exceptions, since she met many people while caring for her mother and was happy to remain in Leisure World.

Where are some popular master-planned communities? These are the 10 top-selling ones in 2021 according to the Real Estate Consulting Group RCLO, although because some of these are so large, they will of course have more sales: Lakewood Ranch (Sarasota, Florida . . . if you want to live next to Rock Star royalty, Mick Jagger bought a home, along with his girlfriend, in The Lake Club, a community within Lakewood Ranch); The Villages (The Villages, Florida); Summerlin (Las Vegas, Nevada); Cane Bay Plantation (Charleston, South Carolina); Wellen Park (Venice, Florida); Valley Vista (North Las Vegas, Nevada); Ontario Ranch (Ontario, California); Great Parks Neighborhood (Irvine, California); Mission Ridge (El Paso, Texas); Rain Dance (Windsor, Colorado). Bigger isn't always better, but bigger usually correlates with more amenities. See the website at the end of the chapter for the entire top-50 list. And, according to Investopedia, these are the best 2020 active-adult communities, based on "amenities, access to shopping and entertainment areas, cost of living, and suitability of housing": The Villages (Florida); Sun City Hilton Head (Bluffton, South Carolina); Sun City Summerlin (Las Vegas); Sun City Huntley (Huntley, Illinois); Laguna Woods Village (Laguna Woods, California); Lake Providence (Nashville, Tennessee); Village at Deaton Creek (Hoschton, Georgia); Del Webb Sweetgrass (Richmond, Texas); Solvita (Kissimmee, Florida); and Stone Creek (Ocala, Florida).

A reminder: If it's important to you, be sure to consider politics along with other factors such as average temperature, crime, and cost of living. For example, BestPlaces.net rates The Villages as "strongly conservative."

The more than 2,000 active-adult communities in the United States is a testament to this popular retirement lifestyle. Big players include Del Webb (owned by Pulte), Hovnanian, Lennar, and Robson Communities. Links to these developers, with their locations, amenities, and pricing, are at the end of this chapter. I have visited master-planned communities built by all these companies, and these people are having *fun*.

- **Multigenerational Living.** Have an aging parent who needs to move in with you? A divorced adult child with her own child who needs someplace to live? Single and want to share a home with a friend or friends? Rebecca Y. has an architect son who designed a casita for Rebecca's elderly mom so her mom had privacy, yet could be in close proximity. When her mom died, and Rebecca and her spouse relocated, the new owners turned the casita into a sizable work-from-home office with its own kitchenette and bathroom. Brian and Dianne S. purchased a three-story/five bedroom home in a community that can accommodate three generations: Brian and Dianne use the master bedroom on the third floor (with its own washer/dryer), the second floor is the communal living area, and the first floor has four bedrooms, one of which is used by Brian and Dianne's son and daughter-in-law, and the other two by the son and daughter-in-law's son and daughter. This floor also has an additional washer/dryer, and a small kitchenette.

  It's estimated that 25% (close to 70 million American adults) live in multigenerational homes – homes with three or more generations living under one roof. If you're interested in this "hive" or "home within a home" arrangement, where you may be able to share the mortgage/utilities/

childcare/transportation and other costs, consider a "next-gen" house. Builders are getting into the act, with homes that can be designed with a separate entrance, single-car garage, kitchenette, bedroom, bathroom, and living area. Builders such as Lennar, K. Hovnanian, and D. R. Horton are examples of builders who have tapped into this popular and growing lifestyle. Links are at the end of this chapter.

- **CCRCs (Continuing Care Retirement Communities), aka Life Plan Communities.** CCRCs can provide one-stop shopping – that is, you can transition from independent living, to assisted-living, to complete nursing care, all on one "campus." There are usually a variety of housing options, such as condos, apartments, single-family homes, and/or duplexes, and generally shared dining is available, along with gyms, pools, art rooms, tennis courts, walking paths, lifelong learning opportunities (some are affiliated with universities), and other community amenities, allowing you to segue to more support as your needs change. There are approximately 2,000 CCRCs in the United States (interestingly, about the same number as there are master-planned communities).

  A five-year analysis, "The Age Well Study" by Mather Institute and Northwest University, is underway, and preliminary results of this study demonstrate that almost 70% of those in CCRCs self-report more optimism, social connections, and satisfaction with life; higher levels of volunteering and physical activity; better health; fewer chronic conditions; and greater life purpose.

  I know three couples and a single woman who have put down deposits at a lovely CCRC, in northeast Florida, Fleet Landing. Differing reasons: For one couple, in their early 80s, the wife has Alzheimer's and cancer, and her husband wants to provide care for her as her condition progresses while having a place to live where he can age in place. Another couple, in their mid-70s, though hale and hearty now, don't want their care to become the responsibility of their three adult children who live in another state, so they want to be proactive with their living arrangements. This couple also decided to sell their single-family home before they "have to," so they can make friends in their new community and enjoy the amenities while they are still in good health. They were tired of contacting servicepeople, replacing old appliances, and didn't want to be forced to make a big decision under pressure. The third couple, who are in their early 70s, don't have any children, and they want to feel settled and secure in the last decades of their lives. They have put down a deposit to hold their place in line for the type of residence they want when they decide to move, but are in no hurry. The fourth, a single woman, has no dependents and wants to live in a community that will address her changing social and medical needs. She is hoping her sister and another close friend will also decide to move there, so they can "age in place" together. The attitude is "live for today, but have a plan for tomorrow."

Sandy and Sam H. spent several years investigating and visiting CCRCs, and chose Shell Point in Fort Myers, Florida. Shell Point is the largest CCRC in Florida, and second largest CCRC in the country. The location, surrounded by water, impressed Sandy and Sam (they are avid kayakers), as did the residents, amenities, healthcare, continuing educational opportunities, proximity to culture, variety of housing styles and the food (very important). They have been very happy with their choice. I have visited both Shell Point and Fleet Landing, and liked both of them very much.

Because there are about 2,000 CCRCs in the United States, if your goal is to stay close to where you presently live or be near friends or adult children, there's a good chance you'll find a CCRC not too far away. About 80% of CCRCs are not-for-profit, and generally no one is "kicked out" if they run out of money, assuming the community is operating on a sound financial basis. Most CCRCs charge an entry fee plus

135

a monthly fee, although some CCRCs forgo the entry fee and charge a higher monthly fee. The fees vary based on the type of contract, size of accommodation, and the number of occupants. The highest entry fees, naturally, will be for a contract providing care for life, and the lowest for a fee-for-service contract.

For example, Fleet Landing offers a plan that includes it all: your residence, dining options, health services with an on-site physician, short-term rehabilitation services, assisted living, memory care, and skilled nursing care. In 2021, the upfront fee for independent living in a two-bedroom single family home starts at $306,800 for a single person and $329,800 per couple, with a monthly fee of $3,455 for a single and $4,791 for a couple. A one-bedroom apartment for a single starts at $174,300, plus a monthly fee of $2,546. The upfront fee becomes nonrefundable after 52½ months, with the refundable amount being generally 95% refundable for the first five months, and then being reduced by 2% per month thereafter. Although residents can choose to pay a higher initial fee (significantly higher) to receive a more generous refund if they later decide to move, it's not a popular option.

The entry cost to "buy into" a CCRC in the United States ranges from about $300,000 to $1 million, with varying monthly fees depending on desired level of care ranging from $2,000 to $5,000. The previous examples of people who chose a CCRC will use/did use the sale proceeds from their present single-family home to pay their CCRC buy-in, and for them, the peace of mind is worth it. With CCRCs, there are many alternatives and choices; the contracts can be complex, and it's obviously a big decision, personally, financially, and emotionally. For more information, and for a handy printable checklist if/when you visit this kind of living option, see the CCRC checklist at the end of this chapter.

- **Green House Project.** We've heard of "nursing homes," but many people are not familiar with an alternative called the "Green House Project." This is an initiative created in 2003 by Dr. William H. Thomas, and there are now more than 300 of these nontraditional nursing home models in more than 30 states. Single-family homes within a community generally have 6–12 residents along with a nursing staff that provides a family-style atmosphere. Gloria M.'s husband suffered from Lewy body dementia, and when Gloria could no longer care for Dimitri within their home, she was able to find a Green House in a residential neighborhood that was a 20-minute drive from her house. Studies have shown Green House caregivers spend more time with the residents by a factor of four. (Perhaps not surprisingly, this model had much lower rates of Covid-related deaths per 100 residents compared to traditional nursing homes – 2.98 vs. up to 27.) Pay is through Medicare, Medicaid or private pay, with private pay ranging from $250 to $500/day. See the end of this chapter for the website related to this innovative style of nursing care.

- **Tiny Homes/Micro Communities.** Could you live in a tiny home or microcommunity of tiny homes? Although there isn't a formal definition, to be called a "tiny house" we're talking an average of 400–800 square feet (contrast that with an average of approximately 2,300 square feet for a house in the United States). Some of these tiny homes are built on a trailer that can be moved from place to place, while others are built off-site and moved onto permanent foundations. Tiny homes can be appealing to minimalists, singles, or couples who need something cost-effective, or people wanting to leave a smaller footprint on our planet. How much are they? At the cute planned community I visited (Lakeshore in Oxford, Florida, tagline "Live Large. Carry Less."), lot leases start at $265/month. You do not own the land, there's a $90 monthly lifestyle fee (there were lots of amenities, including a pool, a club house, a garden, pickleball, fitness classes, and a dog park), and a $340/month utilities and maintenance fee – water, trash, Internet, landscaping, security etc.. The homes started a bit under $200,000 (with front and back porches), and went up from there. One of the residents had purchased a home for herself, and another for visitors!

Some tiny home communities are comprised of all tiny homes, and others include RVs or vans. A few other examples of tiny home communities that are viable or in development: Cedar Springs Tiny Village in Paris, Ohio; The Village and The Hamlet, both in Flat Rock, North Carolina; and Village Farm in Austin, Texas ("Live big while going tiny.").

Did you know you can buy tiny house kits on Amazon? And Netflix even did a series, "Tiny House Nation." See the end of this chapter for links for this style of living.

Besides discrete communities, some jurisdictions allow tiny homes to be built in a backyard as "accessory dwelling units" (ADUs), perhaps as a "granny flat" built by adult children for their elderly parent(s), or by a parent for a child who had to move back home for financial reasons. And, some companies (primarily in California) are willing to place a tiny home in your backyard for free in order to create affordable housing – you pay a portion of your rental income from the tiny home to the builder. These accessory dwelling units, whether built for income or not, or for family or not, usually require permitting before they can be built, and not all places allow them.

- **RV Home Yet?** More than 11 million Americans own an RV, and about one million live in them full-time, according to the RV Industry Association. The allure? As their site states: "The comforts of home and the office with the benefits of the outdoors." Take your pets with you, provide your own guest quarters when visiting others, and meet lots of new people. You can rough it or live in the lap of luxury, with some RV parks offering spas, hot tubs, pools, casinos, and other amenities. The reality can be quite different than that portrayed in the film (based on the book) *Nomadland*. If you're on the road a lot, you may find it more challenging to develop a strong social support system. (Recall the anecdote in Chapter 2 by Carol and Phil White, who lived and traveled in their RV for a year.)

- **Homesharing.** Multigenerational living was discussed earlier, but what about two or more *unrelated* people sharing a home, but each having his or her private space? Two (or three) *can* live more cheaply than one, and this is a growing trend for those who wish to save money, perhaps benefit from some built-in social support, or for one person to be able to remain in his/her home with the help of another person living there and helping out. For example, Doris and Lydia, both widows – and sisters – decided to homeshare, moving into Doris's two-bedroom apartment. Doris didn't drive and had some health issues, so Lydia would drive her to her appointments and do some light housekeeping and shopping and pay Doris a very modest rent in exchange for living in the second bedroom. A win-win for both.

  Michael, a retired chemist, lived within walking distance to a university. A grad student, Kyle, lived in Michael's home and did some home maintenance chores and yard work in exchange for living there (along with a small monthly payment). They connected through Craigslist. A bonus – Kyle shared stories of his exciting research in evolutionary biology, a topic Michael loved.

  On a formal basis, there are homesharing companies that will help match people. Of course, the upfront vetting of a potential roommate is very important. It's not always happily-ever-after, but major issues can often be avoided by asking the right questions about things such as smoking, drinking, drugs, visitors, early riser or night owl, ability to maneuver steps, feelings about pets, references, willingness to perform chores/errands if it would reduce the amount of the rent, and so forth. If you're interested in pursuing homesharing as a cost-saving measure and perhaps a potential opportunity for social engagement – either looking to use your home or to move into someone else's place – see the links at the end of this chapter. A third of adults in an AARP survey, and 44% of adults in a 2021 Silvernest survey said they would be willing to consider homesharing (although only 10% had actually done so). Are you one of them?

- **College Towns/University-Based Retirement Communities (UBRCs).** Where can you find plenty of cultural and lifelong-learning opportunities, stimulating intergenerational discussions, walkability, sports, restaurants, bookstores, often top-notch medical care, lots of opportunities to work and volunteer, and, of course, cheap beer and lots of bars? Yup, college towns. The availability of lifelong-learning opportunities should be considered when contemplating a place to relocate, such as taking/auditing college/community college courses at free or reduced rates, and OLLI (Osher Lifelong Learning Institute) in Chapter 2. If college days were the best days of your life – and even if they weren't or you never attended college – moving to a college town is popular choice. And, with nearly 4,000 colleges/universities in the United States, according to the National Center for Education Statistics, there are plenty of places to consider. As an example, Greg H. graduated from Princeton – and when he retired, Greg and his wife, Allison, moved to the town of Princeton where Greg audits classes at his alma mater year-round. See the 2021 list of "The 10 Best College Towns for Retirement" from the *College Gazette* at the end of this chapter.

  As an alternative to relocating to a regular house, apartment, or condo near a campus, there are specifically designed University-Based Retirement Communities (UBRCs), sometimes also referred to as College-Linked

Retirement Communities. There are a hundred or so of these kinds of communities in the United States, according to PBS News Hour. Their hallmarks include locations in close proximity to the campus; minimal travel time and often walkable; access to all levels of health care (most are CCRCs/Life Plan Communities, discussed earlier); coordination with the university or college to ensure access to classes and other cultural and recreational campus opportunities; and a financial relationship between the UBRC and the college/university. One big player is Kendal, which has a number of affiliate UBRCs. As with CCRCs, the perks of this fun and engaging lifestyle don't come cheaply. Entry fees to a university-based retirement community can range from $10,000 to several million, along with monthly fees.

A few specific UBRCs:

- Lasell Village (Lasell University, Newton, Massachusetts)
- Mirabella at ASU (on the urban campus of Arizona State University, Tempe, Arizona)
- Oak Hammock at the University of Florida (Gainesville, Florida)
- Capstone Village at the University of Alabama (Tuscaloosa, Alabama)
- The Village at Penn State (State College, Pennsylvania)
- Kendal at Granville (a mile from Denison University, in Denison, Ohio)
- Kendal at Hanover (Dartmouth College, Hanover, New Hampshire). Penn State's UBRC site has this terrific tagline: "Live like a senior. Feel like a freshman." That sums it up perfectly!

• **NORCs/Village-to-Village Networks.** Naturally Occurring Retirement Communities (NORCs) and Village-to-Village Networks happen "organically" – people age in place over time. A NORC can be a condo, an apartment building, or a single-family neighborhood, where a large percentage of residents (at least 50%) are 60 or older.

141

*The Village Network* is a term for a situation in which the residents, volunteers, government, or philanthropic groups organize services for their NORC. This may include coordinating access to healthcare, fitness and wellness programs, meals, home-sharing, educational and social activities and services, and transportation. Members of a Village Network typically pay a fee or annual dues for these services. It's estimated there are approximately 5,000 urban NORCS (most NORCS are in cities), according to the National Institutes of Health, and more than 400 village-to-village networks. With people looking out for one another and/or organized services, NORCS and village-to-village networks can be a cost-effective alternative – or at least the ability to stave off long-term care in a facility. See the end of this chapter for helpful websites.

- **New Urbanism or Traditional Neighborhood Developments (TNDs).** Have you been to Capri, Italy? Or wandered around Annapolis, Maryland; Alexandria, Virginia; or St. Augustine, Florida? These are examples of walkable older places where you can live, work, shop, and play. Beginning in the early 1980s, developers got into the game and started building brand-new, well-defined towns based on this model, called new urbanism or traditional neighborhood developments. You never have to leave if you don't want to do so – these communities are self-contained. (If you saw the 1998 film *The Truman Show* with Jim Carrey, it was filmed in Seaside, Florida, one of the first new urbanism communities.) Hallmarks of this type of community include: walkability (a 10- to 15-minute walk should get you pretty much anywhere you want to go); increased density; variety of housing designs and pricing (with residences close to the street to invite neighbor interaction – garages located in the rear); mixed use, including shops and offices; access to health resources; narrow roads for traffic calming; sidewalks for bikes and walking; natural landscaping, public places . . . the emphasis

142

is on living a healthy, socially-connected, and happy life. It's estimated there are more than 600 New Urbanism communities in the United States. I have personally visited a number of these, including several in Maryland (Kentlands, Silver Spring Downtown, Rockville Town Square); Oregon (North-West Crossing); Florida (Baldwin Park, Celebration, Haile Village), and South Carolina (Habersham, I'On). Want a brand-spanking-new-urbanism town on 3,000 acres that is slated to break ground soon? Check out Avalon Park in Daytona Beach, Florida – designed to have more than 10,000 residents at build-out (www.avalonparkdaytonabeach.com) with homes and apartments at a wide range of pricing. This is the same developer as Baldwin Park in Orlando, mentioned earlier.

- **"15-Minute Cities."** Andres Duany and Robert Steuteville are two big names in the new urbanism movement. The previous section discussed creating *new* walkable communities, but if you're interested in city living in the United States and want accessibility to goods and services within a 10- to 15-minute bike ride or walk, MoveBuddha.com compiled a list of cities that meet the "ideal geography where all of a family's daily and weekly needs are located within a 15-minute walk or bike ride." Their top five cities: Miami, Florida; San Francisco, California; Pittsburgh, Pennsylvania; Boston, Massachusetts; and Washington, DC. For the entire 25-city list and an explanation of the weighting of factors, go to: https://www.cnu.org/publicsquare/2021/08/09/top-10-15-minute-city-list-headed-miami. I've been to all these cities, and this is an attractive option if the other parameters (cost, climate, politics, etc.) meet your criteria.

- Have a desire for a very particular lifestyle? There really is something for everyone:

  **The Artist.** Burbank Senior Artists Colony (Burbank, CA). Rental apartments with a theater, club house, art studio, writing classes, a choir, and lifelong learning programs

143

(https://www.seniorartistscolony.com/). One bedroom/ one bath starting around $1,900/month.

**The Pilot.** Spruce Creek Country Club (Port Orange, Florida) is the largest fly-in community in the country, boasting a 4,000-foot lighted runway. A number of homes have hangars (they look like giant garages) attached to their houses. Not all people own planes. I play tennis here sometimes – great gated/master-planned community with a semi-private club component (https://www.sprucecreekclub.com/). Trivia: John Travolta owned a home and housed his Gulfstream II Jet here. Houses from under $200,000 to $2 million plus.

**The Astronomy Lover.** Arizona Sky Village (four-acre lots; re-sales only) in Portal, Arizona. Ideal because it is away from everything. With streets named Milky Way and Newton Way, you know this is for hard-core star-gazers only. A number of residents have their own observatories. Turn off your lights! A 4.6 acre lot is available for $42,000 (https://www.newscientist.com/article/dn12352-arizona-sky-village-a-town-built-for-astronomy-lovers/).

**The Naturist.** Looking for clothing-optional communities? Paradise Lakes, north of Tampa in Lutz, Florida, is one of the best-known. It's a gated community that has single-family homes, townhomes, condos, an RV park, and a resort component (https://paradiselakesresort.com). Example: A two bedroom/two bath condo offered at $169,900. Bring lots of sunscreen. See the end of the chapter for additional links for this style of living.

**Welcome to the Agrihood.** There's a surge of interest in communities that promote health and wellness. Although many communities offer the requisite pools, tennis/pickleball/gyms, some have gone further – incorporating farms into their communities. Three examples: Chicahominy Falls, a 55+ community in Glen Allen (near Richmond), Virginia with a fully functioning farm (https://

chickahominyfalls.com) and homes starting around $400,000; the almost 400-acre Olivette Riverside Community with its four-acre farm and lots starting around $215,000, located seven miles from Asheville, North Carolina (https://www.olivettenc.com/); and Agritopia (https://agritopia.com/), a planned community in Gilbert, Arizona (about 16% of the community's 160 acres is the organic farm). A five-bedrom/three-bath 2,907 square foot resale in Agritopia is offered at $790,000. "Generations at Agritopia" is within Agritopia and offers luxury independent living, assisted living, and memory care. Pricing dependent on services (https://livgenerationsagritopia.com/). If you want to get "back to the land," see the link at the end of this chapter.

**Ecologically conscious.** Babcock Ranch (www.babcockranch .com), in southwest Florida near Punta Gorda, is the first solar-powered town in the United States (the 650,000 solar panels are in huge fields about five miles away). This developing community on 17,000 acres is also a new urbanism community, described previously. Pricing starts in the upper $200,000s, and Babcock Ranch will have about 50,000 residents when it's built out. It's non-gated and an interesting place if you want to get into a brand-new community with a range of prices, lots of amenities (including a golf course), and be part of a city with a terrific ecological approach. Half the community is comprised of greenways, parks, and lakes, and it's surrounded by a 73,000-acre nature preserve. I visited Babcock Ranch on a Sunday, and the place was hopping, with people strolling around the town square, an active Farmer's market, and lots of activity on the golf course. Prior to becoming Babcock Ranch, the land was used for "cattle ranching, tree farming, rock mining, vegetable growing, alligator farming and even experimental ostrich breeding."

**Equestrian.** If, like Richard III, you're willing to give "My kingdom for a horse," you'll be happy to know there are lots of communities with the ability to keep, ride, groom – or just enjoy being around – horses. Aiken, South Carolina is known as horse country, and a developing community called Anderson Farms (https://www.andersonfarmsaiken.com/) could be worth checking out. Lots range from two to five acres at around $30,000/acre. Or, you could live in Woodside (https://woodside-communities.com/), a nice and more moderately priced community with a variety of neighborhoods that accommodate all ages (it used to be called Woodside Plantation, but I am happy they changed the name to just "Woodside"). No horse facilities, but you're in Aiken, so plenty of access to horses. The median listing for a home is about $300,000. Having toured Woodside and the cute community of Aiken, it's understandable why *Southern Living Magazine* has ranked Aiken among the South's best small towns.

**Oenophiles.** Do you live by the W.C. Fields quote "I cook with wine, sometimes I even add it to the food"? If so, you may want to consider a community that has its own vineyard, or is in close proximity to vineyards.

Two examples: Viniterra (http://www.viniterra.com/location/) in New Kent, Virginia, is located within the master-planned community of New Kent Vineyards, and is within 25 miles of Richmond and Williamsburg. Like a very fine wine, this lifestyle does not come cheaply – the median home price is $800,000. Wolf Ranch in Georgetown, Texas has lower prices than Viniterra, good weather, is surrounded by the lovely Texas Hill Country, is a half-hour drive to Austin, and is close to a number of area wineries. Priced from the mid-$400,000s. Check out www.wolfranchbyhillwood.com.

**Military.** There are approximately 2.2 million military retirees in the United States; this number will grow to about 2.3 million by 2031. People often seek out people with similar interests, so it's no surprise that there are communities for retired military, or communities that are open to all but attract a lot of retired military, or areas of the country that retired military gravitate to because of a military base nearby. In some cases, retired military can live on an Army or Air Force Base. Examples of actual retirement communities: Indian River Colony Club (https://colonyclub.com/), a true 55+ military community located in Viera, Florida. Packed with amenities, close to lots of services, healthcare, shopping, the beach, and only an hour from the Orlando airport. Homes starting in the $200,000s. Sun City Grand in Surprise, Arizona (www.suncitygrand.com), is an active-adult community that sponsors at least four military-related specialty groups, although it's not a dedicated military community. Residences start in the high $100,000s (resales only). Army Residence Community in San Antonio, Texas (https://armyresidence.com) is a "life plan" or CCRC (Continuing Care Retirement Community) that allows residents to segue from independent living to assisted living to skilled nursing care. Minimum age of 62, and it "welcomes all officers, retired or honorably discharged from all branches of service, warrant officers, as well as senior level GS 14 and above federal employees, to include spouses and surviving spouses." We discussed CCRCs earlier; the financial structure can be fairly complicated.

There are Military Relocation Professionals (MRPs) who can help you in your search – MRP is a certification from the National Association of Realtors (http://www.militaryrelocationpro.org/find-mrp). Thank you for your service!

*True Life: Laurie N.'s husband served in the United States Navy for 20 years. Chuck's birthplace and military career shaped their choice of a retirement location. Laurie's story:*

I grew up in Maryland. After earning a BS and a master's degree, I worked for the Food and Drug Administration, developing more sensitive and reliable vaccines and working as a regulatory scientist. My husband of 30 years is seven years older than I am, and he was pursuing a second career as a cyber security engineer for a defense contractor after serving our country for two decades. As a native Floridian, Chuck was pushing for retirement in Florida where we would not have to shovel snow, pay state income tax, and we could enjoy the proximity to a military base for benefits including medical, commissary, exchange privileges, and military associations. In addition, we wanted to be close to a beach, be able to exercise outside year-round, have access to good healthcare, and be able to access programs that focus on the elderly (for my mom, who has Alzheimer's). We purchased a piece of property from one of my husband's Navy buds on Amelia Island. We thought of it as either an investment or a place we would eventually build our retirement dream home.

By 2018, my two sons were out of college and the stress of my job and caring for my mother became more than two full-time jobs. Hence, the "when" decision of timing for retirement. Intellectually, I was not ready to retire, but emotionally, I was exhausted and knew I needed a change of pace. We began the dreaded task of purging some of our belongings to prepare for the sale of our house, and retired in 2019. We rented a house in Fernandina Beach, Florida and oversaw the building of our dream home on the Amelia Island lot. I was able to enroll my mother in an amazing adult daycare memory program close-by, and started my own consulting company. As my mother's caregiver and running my part-time business, I still have time to ride bikes, take long walks on the beach with my husband, and read books for pleasure. We moved into our wonderful new home in April 2021 and love it! We are taking advantage of what our little island has to offer and also all the historic cities to the north and south of us. We are close to several Navy bases and a plethora of good healthcare options in Jacksonville, FL, and love the amazing weather that allows us to explore all the state parks and catch a sunrise or sunset.

Getting to this point was a journey, with hiccups and some not-so-easy decisions, but now that I have made the transition, I am experiencing more of what this area has to offer along with meeting new people and forging new friendships. It's an exciting time of discovery and personal growth.

---

**Commune Living.** The Farm Community (https://thefarmcommunity.com/) in Summertown, Tennessee, was formerly called Rocinante (named after Don Quixote's trustworthy horse). It's sometimes described as a "retirement commune for aging hippies." It started in 1971 with a convoy from San Francisco with about 300 of founder Stephen Gaskin's followers.

The Farm Community's website describes it as: ". . .an intentional community of families and friends living on three square miles in southern middle Tennessee, founded on the principles of nonviolence and respect for the earth." There is even a TED talk about The Farm Community (TED Talk link: https://www.youtube.com/watch?v=kUy1eIwXwNU). Love, Peace, Freedom!

**Intentional Communities.** Interested in starting your own community, or joining one that is forming? Well, there's a site for that, too: The Foundation for Intentional Communities lists more than 230 forming (or re-forming) communities, mainly communes, co-living (where unrelated individuals share a dwelling), and eco-villages (emphasis on sustainability), both nationally and internationally, as well as offering an online class that explains how to start your own intentional community. With a nod to *Field of Dreams* – build it and they will come?

Is your head spinning? Are you suffering from analysis paralysis after contemplating the myriad lifestyles and places to live? Many questions don't have just one correct answer, yet we often approach decision-making as though that is the case. And, our answers about the best places to live often change as our circumstances change.

There are many locations that are wonderful for retirement, and once you determine your "nonnegotiables" and narrow your list to several "must-haves," the task of choosing a place becomes simpler. The best answer to where you should live when you retire might be where you live now. . .just don't take that approach because it's easier to do nothing than to do something. You could be missing out on a great adventure. As Yogi Berra famously said, "When you come to a fork in the road, take it!"

Regardless of where you decide to live, you want to be healthy in mind, spirit, and body. We mentioned earlier the emphasis is to enjoy a long "healthspan," not just a long "lifespan." The next chapter, "Forever Young," will provide a roadmap for doing just that.

## Considering Overseas Retirement?

Questions to consider/discuss from Kathleen Peddicord, adapted from her book, *How to Retire Overseas: Everything You Need to Know to Live Well (for Less) Abroad* (2018, Penguin/Random House). Your responses can help guide you to the best overseas places to consider. As you'll see, some of the questions are oriented toward places that may be less developed than the United States. (With permission from Kathleen Peddicord):

**Climate.** Do you enjoy a change of seasons? Do you need regular sunshine? Do you mind rain? Can you handle heat? Humidity? Do you prefer a varying length of day? Are you okay living in a place that is at risk for hurricanes?

**Health Care.** Do you have preexisting conditions? How old are you? These are the two most important factors when it comes to qualifying for international health insurance. Would you be uncomfortable seeing a physician whose first language is not English?

**Infrastructure.** Do you lose your cool if you can't send an email the first time every time you try? Would you mind living on a dirt road? Would you mind your road access being temporarily cut off during the rainy season? Do you need American television? Are you afraid of the dark?

In much of the world, electricity isn't 100% reliable. Would you be comfortable owning a car and driving yourself around in a new country? Would you be unhappy without your favorite comfort foods?

**Accessibility to the United States.** Do you have children or grandchildren you want to see regularly? Do you have a health condition that could necessitate a quick return stateside?

**Language.** Do you speak a second language? Are you terrified at the idea of learning one?

**Culture, Recreation, and Entertainment.** What's your favorite thing to do on a Friday night? How would you rather spend a free Sunday afternoon – in a museum or taking a long walk in the woods? How regularly do you want to be able to dine out? To watch a first-run movie in English? To visit an art gallery or attend the theater? What would you like to see from your bedroom window? The ocean? A mountainside covered with wildflowers? A vineyard? A busy street scene?

**Residency.** Would you like to be able to live full time and to stick around indefinitely in the country you have your eye on? If so, you need to understand the options available in that country for establishing legal residency.

**Environment.** Would you be okay seeing litter and poor children every day? Garbage and poverty can be two of the toughest things to take in any third-world country. Some visit a developing country and see unrealized potential; others see struggle.

**Taxes.** From where will you be deriving your income while living overseas? The source of your income will have a lot to do with your ultimate tax liability, both in the United States and in your new jurisdiction. If your only income will be from Social Security or a retirement pension, moving overseas should be a tax-neutral experience for you (though you should confirm this).

## CCRC Checklist

### 10 Questions to Bring on Your Senior Housing Tour

By Clare Absher RN, BSN

1. **What is your first impression of the facility during your tour?** Don't get wrapped up in elaborate décor or distracted by needless bells and whistles. Instead, focus your attention on basic cleanliness, necessary amenities, and staff.

   - Did the facility accommodate your family with making tour arrangements?

- Are you greeted by warm and friendly staff who are eager to show you around?
- Is the facility location convenient for visiting, shopping, and healthcare?
- Do you notice residents socializing among each other and do they seem content?
- Are the common areas clean, free of odors, and adequately heated/cooled?
- Is the facility floor plan easy to navigate and does it feel "warm and cozy"?
- Does the staff address residents and their family in a friendly and respectful manner?

2. **How is the dining experience?** Don't overlook the importance of a good meal and a pleasant dining experience. It should also come as no surprise that good food really matters a great deal to your parent.

- Is your family invited and encouraged to stay for a meal during your visit?
- Do you observe residents and staff interacting during mealtimes in the dining area?
- Can you view daily/weekly menus offering variety and good nutritional meals?
- Is the food presented in an appetizing manner with adequate selections?
- Does the food taste good? Did your senior genuinely enjoy the meal?
- Does a qualified dietitian plan or approve menus? How are special diets accommodated?
- Does the dining room environment encourage residents to relax and socialize?
- How many meals are served daily and is tray service to rooms available when ill?
- Do more dependent residents receive extra help needed with eating?

3. **Are you free to visit and talk with staff, residents, and other families?** Expect to have private, unsupervised conversations with whomever you choose. Staff should encourage communications, surprise visits, and not tolerate any "hush-hush" nonsense.

- Do visitors seem welcome and are they comfortable with the staff?
- Are you able to meet the DON (Director of Nursing) and talk with staff freely during your visit?
- Are visiting hours flexible to accommodate your schedule?
- Are you free to talk openly with residents and families in an unsupervised setting?

- Are you allowed to make an unscheduled visit and do you feel welcome when popping in?
- Do staff interact with residents and each other politely when unaware of your presence?

4. **What social and recreational activities are of interest to your parent?** Socializing is often a big reason for moving into a senior facility. Explore which activities offered might spark some interest for your mom or dad.

   - Is a "Daily Events and Activities" calendar posted and is the facility following this schedule?
   - Are there classes and supplies for arts and crafts, music, games, computers, gardening, and cooking?
   - Is there pet therapy or are residents allowed to bring their pets to stay with them?
   - Are there special events with guest speakers, social dances, and holiday celebrations?
   - Does the facility schedule trips and provide transportation to events off premises?
   - Are religious services held on the premises or are arrangements available to attend nearby services?
   - Are there fitness facilities as well as regularly scheduled exercise classes?
   - Are there outdoor common areas for gatherings?

5. **Does the facility feel safe and secure?** Many seniors, including your parents, may be afraid and feel unsafe living alone. Safety and security are often big motives for relocating to a facility.

   - Does the facility provide ample security in the way of guards, locked doors, and alarms?
   - What is the facility's means of security if a resident should wander?
   - Is there an emergency evacuation plan in place?
   - Is the facility well-lit with emergency devices throughout if help is needed?
   - Is a 24-hour emergency response system accessible from the units with its own lockable door?
   - Do all the bathrooms have an emergency pull-cord in event of an accident?

6. **What are your parents' choices for living accommodations?** Facilities range from spacious apartments to single rooms. Your parents will want to have a say in their living space.

   - Are there different sizes and types of units to pick from with optional floor plans?
   - Are single units available or are there cheaper double units for sharing with another resident?
   - Does the facility have furnished/unfurnished rooms and what can be brought from home?
   - May your senior decorate his or her own room and is there adequate storage space?
   - Are bathrooms private with handicapped accommodations for wheelchairs and walkers?
   - Do all the units have a telephone, cable TV, and Internet access?
   - Does kitchen unit have refrigerator/sink/cooking element for preparing food in the room?

7. **How much does it cost and what's involved with the moving in and out?** The needs assessment determines whether your loved one is a good match for the facility. Affordability may ultimately be the deciding factor of the facility being a good match for your loved one.

   - Does the assessment process include the potential resident, family, facility staff, along with the physician?
   - Is there a written plan of care for each resident and a process for assessing changes in needs?
   - Will the room be held/reserved should your loved one require a hospital/nursing home stay?
   - Is there a written statement available of the resident rights and responsibilities?
   - Does contractual agreement disclose all services, accommodations, and associated fees?
   - What is the basic monthly fee and what are specific costs for various levels of services?
   - What additional services and staff are not included but available if needs change?
   - When may a contract be terminated and what are the policies for refunds and transfers?
   - Is the unit rented or owned by the resident and who is responsible for utilities, Internet, cable, and phone?

8. **Does the facility offer the personal care and health services needed?** It's a deal breaker if the facility can't provide the help your mom or dad require. Make certain the care offered can meet your parent's needs now as well as in the future, to avoid relocation as their needs evolve.

   - Is staff available to assist with activities of daily living (ADLs include bathing, dressing, grooming, eating, and help with walking)? Is staff available to assist with ADLs 24 hours a day if needed?
   - Does the facility have programs for Alzheimer's and other dementia needs? Are there specialized areas dedicated to memory care residents?
   - How are medical emergencies handled and what is protocol for responding to them?
   - May a resident take his or her own medications or get assistance should need arise?
   - Does the facility have a pharmacy; if so, does it review medicines regularly?
   - Does staff assist in arrangements to provide nursing and/or other medical care?
   - What wellness care and medical services are provided onsite?
   - Are physical, occupational, or speech therapy services available onsite or via an agency?
   - Are housekeeping, linen service, and personal laundry included?
   - Does the facility provide transportation to doctor appointments and shopping?
   - Is there a hair salon and barber onsite or is transport provided to outside shops?

9. **Is the staff professional, kind, and qualified to care for your parents?** Make no mistake that it is the caregivers that matter most when it comes to deciding where your parents will be happy. Look for caregivers that seem genuinely content with their jobs.

   - What are the facility's practices and philosophy regarding staffing?
   - What are the hiring procedures and requirements for employment?
   - Are criminal background checks, references, and certifications required on all employees?
   - Is there a staff-training program in place and what does it entail?
   - Is the staff courteous to each other as well as to residents and their families?
   - Do you observe if requests for assistance by residents are responded to in a timely and respectful manner?

- Is the appropriate staff or supervisor available to answer questions or discuss problems?
- Would you be comfortable dealing with current administrators and staff daily?

10. **Investigate the facility licensure, certifications, and reputation in the community.** Be sure the facility meets your state requirements as they vary a lot. Word of mouth is always a good way to find out first-hand about the reputation of the facility in your community.

   - If your state requires the facility and its director to be licensed and/or certified, does it have a current license/certification displayed?
   - Is the facility accredited by the Joint Commission and what professional associations do they voluntarily belong to?
   - What do community health professionals, church members, and family caregivers say about the facility's reputation?
   - How long has facility been in business to determine stability and financial health?
   - Who or what corporation manages the facility and is it a for-profit or nonprofit organization?
   - Is there a resident council for residents/family to have a means of voicing their views on the management of the community?
   (With permission from Clare Absher RN, BSN)

# More Resources

## *Books/Magazines*

DePaulo, Bella. *How We Live Now: Home and Family in the 21st Century.* Atria Books, 2015.

Erisman, Ryan. *The 2022 Florida Retirement Handbook.* Ryan Erisman, Inc., 2021.

Frederick, Ryan. *Right Place, Right Time: The Ultimate Guide to Choosing a Home for the Second Half of Life.* Johns Hopkins University Press, 2021.

Padgett, Alyssa. *A Beginner's Guide to Living in an RV: Everything I Wish I Knew Before Full-Time RVing Across America*(Kindle Edition), 2020.

Peddicord, Kathleen. *How to Retire Overseas: Everything You Need to Know to Live Well (for Less) Abroad.* Plume, 2018.

*Where to Retire* magazine (https://www.wheretoretire.com/) Magazine production was suspended due to the pandemic; check periodically to see if it's back in production.

## *Websites*

Search for communities by amenity: www.privatecommunities.com (click on"select an amenity" and explore some great possibilities).

General "where to retire" sites: https://ideal-living.com/; https://www.bestplaces.net/; https://www.aarp.org/home-family/your-home/best-places-to-live/

Walkscore (site will also calculate a bikescore): www.walkscore.com

Pennyhoarder list of affordable places to retire: https://www.thepennyhoarder.com/retirement/best-places-to-retire/

Free Land in Lincoln, Kansas: http://www.lincolnks.org/; free Land in Mankato, Kansas: www.mankatoks.com; additional free land link: https://www.wideopencountry.com/free-land-in-the-us/

Top Retirements: 10 Great Outdoor Towns for Retirement https://www.topretirements.com/blog/great-towns/10-great-outdoor-towns-for-retirement.html/

Travel Channel: Top 13 Cycling Cities in the U.S.: https://www.travelchannel.com/interests/outdoors-and-adventure/photos/top-cycling-cities-in-the-us

LGBTQ+ cities and communities: https://www.seniorliving.org/retirement/lgbt/

U.S. LGBTQ+ community centers in the United States: https://en.wikipedia.org/wiki/List_of_LGBT_community_centers_in_the_United_States

Cohousing: https://www.cohousing.org

Cohousing communities (list): https://www.cohousing.org/directory/

Village Hearth Co-housing Community (LGBTQ+ friendly): https://www.cohousing.org/directory/village-hearth-cohousing/

Indian-American Communities (Nalanda, Shantikeketan, and Priya Living): https://www.nalandaestates.com/ (sold out but may have re-sales) and http://florida.shantiniketan.us/; https://www.priyaliving.com/

"Ten Best Places for Black Americans to Move Abroad": https://travelnoire.com/the-10-best-places-for-black-americans-to-move-abroad

157

"Top 12 Retirement Cities for African Americans": https://www
.youtube.com/watch?v=0pfz9YUovMo

Build-to-Rent Communities:

NexMetro (Texas, Colorado, Florida, Arizona): https://nex-
metro.com/about.php

Christopher Dodd (Arizona and Texas): https://www.christo-
phertodd.com/;

Coastal Run at Heritage Shores: https://homes.heritageshores.
com/for-rent

Living on a Cruise Ship:

The World: www.aboardtheworld.com

Somnio "superyacht": https://somniosuperyachts.com/

Most extroverted and introverted states:

http://introvertdaily.com/the-most-introverted-places-in-the-
united-states/

Top-Selling Master-Planned Communities:

https://www.rclco.com/publication/the-top-selling-master-
planned-communities-of-mid-year-2021/

Well-known active-adult developers (housing starts from the
$200,000s): Del Webb:

(www.delwebb.com); Hovnanian (www.khov.com); Lennar
(www.lennar.com); Robson (www.robson.com)

Multigenerational Living: Hovnanian (https://www.khov.com/
blog/what-is-a- multigenerational-home/ ); Lennar (www.lennar.com
click on "Next Gen";

D.R. Horton (https://www.drhorton.com/multigen)

Green House Project: https://thegreenhouseproject.org/
resources/research

Tiny Homes:

Cedar Springs Tiny Village (New Paris, Ohio): https://cedar-
springstinyvillage.info/

Village Farm (Austin, Texas): https://villagefarmaustin.com;

Lakeshore Community (Oxford, Florida): https://www
.simple-life.com/lakeshore-community/ (Simple Life has two

additional communities in Flat Rock, North Carolina, both close to Hendersonville and Asheville.)

RV Living: "Top 75 RV Parks in American with the Most Amenities": https://www.theactivetimes.com/travel/top-rv-parks-america-most-amenities

Homesharing (some of these have fees associated with their services):

https://nationalsharedhousing.org/ (a clearinghouse for U.S. non-profit homesharing programs)

https://www.silvernest.com/

https://www.seniorhomeshares.com/ (free)

https://helpmelaw.org/sites/default/files/homeshare-interview-questions.pdf (good example of interview questions for a prospective roommate)

College Towns:

General list of best college towns for retirement, *College Gazette* (2021):

https://collegegazette.com/the-10-best-college-towns-for-retirement/ UBRCs (University-based retirement communities):

Lasell Village (https://lasellvillage.com)

Mirabella at ASU: https://www.retirement.org/mirabella-asu/

Oak Hammock at the University of Florida: https://www.oak-hammock.org/

Capstone Village at the University of Alabama: https://capstonevillage.ua.edu

The Village at Penn State: https://www.retireatpennstate.org/

Kendal at Granville: https://kag.kendal.org/

Kendal at Hanover: https://kah.kendal.org/

NORCs (Naturally Occurring Retirement Communities: There is no centralized database; call the Eldercare Locator at 800-677-1116 and ask for the number of your local Area Agency on Aging.) An example: https://aging.ny.gov/naturally-occurring-retirement-community-norc

Village to Village Network: https://www.vtvnetwork.org/

Congress for the New Urbanism: https://www.cnu.org/resources/what-new-urbanism

Traditional Neighborhood Communities by town and state:

Links to TND and New Urban Neighborhoods (no longer in business, but useful):

https://www.tndtownpaper.com/neighborhoods.htm

Where to be naked in the United States:

http://www.naturistplace.com/nudeusa.htm#fl

https://www.sunbathersclubs.com/retirement-living-34back-to-nature34

Agrihoods:

https://agrihoodliving.com/featured-communities/

# CHAPTER 6

# Forever Young

■　■　■

The title of this chapter is a song by Rod Stewart. I used *Forever Young* for the mother/groom dance at the wedding of both of my sons. Although we cannot be "forever young," we can cultivate healthy behaviors and mindsets that can extend our physical and mental healthspan, and, like the clever title of the book by Dr. Roger Landry, we can aspire to "Live Long, Die Short." Okay, enough with the song/book allusions. Let's see how to do it.

Life expectancy in the United States recently took a dip, primarily due to Covid-19. Overall life expectancy was 78.8 years in 2019, and fell to 77.3 years in 2020. For women, life expectancy dropped from 81.4 years to 80.2 years from 2019 to 2020; for men it decreased from 76.3 to 74.5 from 2019 to 2020, according to the CDC. The Stanford Center on Longevity did a survey of more than 2,300 adults, and 77% said they wanted to live to 100, and more than a third believed they'd reach 90 or beyond. Unfortunately, hope is triumphing over reality by our actions and habits when it comes to living a longer and healthier life. But, there is hope. Dr. David Sinclair, Professor of Genetics, Harvard Medical School, found that we can add almost 15 good years to our lives through healthy habits. Let's see how we can accomplish that, and get older without getting old. By the way, the longest documented human lifespan? So far, it's a French woman, Jeanne Calment, who lived 122 years, 164 days.

## Nature (Genetics) versus Nurture (Environment)

Most scientists feel about 30% of our lifespan is beyond our control. This percent was determined using studies of identical twins separated at birth and raised by different families – same DNA/genes, different environments. Through inheritance, our genes can directly cause diseases that may affect how long we'll live (such as inheriting genes for Tay-Sachs disease, cystic fibrosis, sickle cell anemia, or mutations in the breast cancer genes BRACA1 and/or BRACA2), although many advances have been made in prolonging the lives of those born with genetic diseases/issues. And, of course, our genes may also protect us from disease.

It's encouraging and empowering to know that around 70% of our healthspan is somewhat under our control. According to the United Nations, out of 193 countries, Hong Kong has the highest average lifespan at 85.29, and the Central African Republic is last at 54.36. The United States? We're a mediocre 46 out of 193 countries. We could and should be doing better. As Jim Morrison of the Doors said, "No one here gets out alive," but we should be able to stay around longer – and be healthier.

What's the difference between Hong Kong and the United States? A study that followed more than 100,000 health professionals over almost 30 years in the United States is telling. The researchers looked at several desirable behaviors: being a non-smoker, maintaining a healthy weight, moderate alcohol intake, regular exercise, and healthy eating patterns. Subjects in the study who practiced most of those healthy behaviors at age 50 tended to live a decade longer – and were healthier, too – than those who did not. Guess what? Most people in Hong Kong can check most or all of those "healthy behavior" boxes, and in addition, enjoy accessible, excellent, reasonable healthcare, as well as having a culture of honoring, caring for, and respecting their elders. A good model to follow! In the United States we pay significantly more for health-care than other "rich" countries, yet our life expectancy is less than most other high-wealth countries. Why? Reasons include more uninsured people (we do not have universal healthcare), we eat more calories/person (easy access to tasty but unhealthy food), we have higher rates of substance-use disorders, our country has large wealth disparities, and we have more auto accidents (as we know, the United States is very car reliant). But, don't get me wrong – I am very happy I live in the United States.

Our personality also affects our longevity. Psychologists and scientists have confirmed that humans have five basic and stable traits: conscientiousness, extraversion, openness, agreeableness, and neuroticism. Numerous studies demonstrate that *conscientious* people tend to live longer. Conscientious people practice self-control; they are industrious, disciplined, and responsible. Thus, they tend to be nonsmokers, take fewer risks, eat healthier, and exercise more – all behaviors that affect longevity. Being conscientious has as much effect on our longevity as intelligence and socioeconomic level. The good news is that people tend to become more conscientious as they age. And, let's not forget the environment. Air and water pollution, smoke/fires, environmental toxins, food deserts, lack of safe places to live/walk/exercise; our surroundings also affect how healthy we are and how long we'll live.

It's important to recognize that the only person we can really change is ourselves. We know intellectually it's important to exercise, eat well, and practice other healthy behaviors. So, let's approach it a bit differently; let's look at three words that may not be familiar, but may drive a change in behavior when we know what's going on inside our bodies.

## Epigenetics

We cannot change our genes, but can we influence their behavior? Recent studies show the answer to that question is a surprising "yes." This is called "epigenetics." One way it works at the cellular level is by adding a group of atoms (a carbon atom and three hydrogen atoms called a methyl group) to certain places on DNA that then alters how a gene behaves or is "expressed." As an example, with negative consequences, an alcoholic pregnant woman who is bathing the fetus in alcohol can change the way the fetus's brain develops by altering how the fetal genes are expressed, resulting in possible mental and physical defects called "fetal alcohol spectrum disorder." As a positive example, a study in Stockholm used subjects who exercised only one of their legs on an exercise bike for several times a week, 45 minutes each time, over a three-month period. The scientists did biopsies comparing the leg muscles – the exercised leg showed the DNA was altered on those genes that control insulin metabolism and genes for lowering inflammation in our body; the unexercised leg was not affected. Evidence that reinforces one of the reasons exercise is good for us; it can change how our genes function. Powerful stuff.

## Telomeres

Visualize shoelaces, and the little plastic pieces at the ends of them. Our chromosomes, comprised of DNA, have little caps at the end that protect them. These caps are called telomeres. When the cells within our body divide, the telomeres shorten a tiny bit. After repeated cell divisions, without the telomeres to protect them, the cells die. Telomeres are involved in aging, and a Nobel Prize in Medicine was awarded to three scientists in 2009 for their discovery of the role of telomeres in aging.

The good news is that we can strengthen and lengthen our telomeres through exercise and eating well. One study that illustrated this involved identical twins, with one set of twins exercising more than the other – the twins who exercised more had longer telomeres. In fact, identical twins and NASA astronauts Scott and Mark Kelly were used as subjects in telomere studies. Scott, who went to space, had a significant increase in the length of his telomeres, while

Mark, who remained earthbound, had telomeres that remained pretty much the same (the scientists took samples from both brothers prior to, during, and after the mission). The assumption is that Scott Kelly's increased time exercising while in space, combined with healthier food choices during the year he lived on the International Space Station, were responsible for his increased telomere length (most, but not all of Scott's telomeres returned to their pre-flight length soon after he returned to terra firma). Another study involved women (all living on the earth!) who exercised to alleviate stress and compared them to a comparable group of women who did not exercise for stress relief. Those who did not exercise had shorter telomeres than those who did. Finally, studies show foods with high levels of omega-3 fatty acids, such tuna, wild salmon, Brazil nuts, cashews, and walnuts also lengthened telomeres.

## Mitochondria

Go waaaayyyy back to high school. Remember learning in biology class that mitochondria were "the powerhouses of the cell"? These tiny organelles turn food into energy. Some cells have a few thousand mitochondria per cell, some don't have any, and in some cells like muscle and heart – and recall that our heart is a muscle – mitochondria comprise about half of every heart cell. Turns out that exercising (think walking at a fairly rapid pace, riding a bike, tennis, jogging) for 20 minutes or so, several days a week, pumps up the number of mitochondria, makes them more effective at burning fat, and lowers the risk of diabetes by affecting insulin resistance. Studies have found that strength training in older adults boosts the number of mitochondria. But, you need to keep up the regimen to keep your mitochondria humming along – it's truly "use it or lose it."

This research about epigenetics, telomeres, and mitochondria is important because it demonstrates that our genes do not have to be our destiny. We have more control over our health and longevity than we think.

## SHIELD for Our Bodies, Minds, and Spirits

I love acronyms. Acronyms help us remember important ideas, and they are handy little devices for summarizing concepts. For example, you can use the acronym MET to remember what we just discussed – how research about **m**itochondria, **e**pigenetics, and **t**elomeres has hopefully convinced you that moving your body and eating foods with high levels of omega-3 fatty acids are vital to becoming healthy, remaining healthy, and altering, in a positive way, our genes. You knew there were benefits to eating well and exercising, but you may not have realized that those two behaviors can actually change how our genes function, which is *huge and important.* But, before we proceed to a discussion of other behaviors that will hopefully make us "live long and die short," what is most likely to kill us? (Quite the buzzkill, huh?)

According to the CDC's National Vital Statistics System (NVSS), these are the most updated statistics for 2020 for the "leading, underlying causes of death" (females and males combined):

1. Heart disease
2. Cancer
3. Covid-19
4. Unintentional injury
5. Stroke
6. Chronic lower respiratory disease
7. Alzheimer's disease
8. Diabetes
9. Influenza and pneumonia
10. Kidney disease

(Yes, number 3 is a shocker, and hopefully will soon be removed from this list.)

So, let's use another acronym, SHIELD, to expand and reinforce behaviors for a healthy body and mind, and see how we can postpone, for a very long time, being put into one of the preceding causes-of-death categories. Consider the following points a kind of maintenance manual for our bodies.

- **S: Sleep.** Forget "Sleepless in Seattle." We are "Sleepless in the United States." The CDC estimates that one in three adults in our country has sleep issues, a frightening and scary statistic. In 1910, people slept an average of 9 hours a night; in 1942, it was 7.9 hours, and today, more than a third of adults report sleeping fewer than seven hours a night. The CDC recommends that adults up to age 64 get 7–9 hours of shut-eye, and those 65 and over should strive for 7–8 hours.

What caused this sleep crisis? A combination of factors, including aging, which lower levels of vasopressin, the hormone that helps us retain fluid, resulting in the urge to get up to urinate more often; enlarged prostates in men that press against the urethra and thicken the bladder wall which weakens bladder muscles; longer commuting times and working more hours (many Boomers were/are "workaholics"); higher stress and worry levels; less time spent outdoors, resulting in less natural light, which helps regulate our sleep cycles; more sedentary lifestyles, which can contribute to weight gain and sleep apnea; and a steady stream of blue light from smartphones and other electronic devices at night that affect our circadian rhythms (biological clocks) by suppressing melatonin, the hormone that regulates our wake-sleep cycle. During the pandemic, studies showed some people slept more, particularly because of curtailed social schedules and cutting commuting time by working from home, and some slept less because of additional stress, illness, and worry.

The negative effects of lack of sleep range from irritating to deadly: We're less alert; we're less productive; our ability to process information is impaired; we may become moodier and more unpleasant to be around; we feel sluggish and thus less likely to exercise and/or fight off unhealthy food/drink temptations; we're more likely to be in workplace, home, or auto accidents; and we're at greater risk for Alzheimer's as well as physical diseases such as elevated blood pressure, heart disease, diabetes, obesity, and stroke, along with mood disorders including depression and anxiety; and we have lowered immunity and a decreased sex drive. We also make less leptin, a hormone made by our fat cells that *decreases* our appetite, and more ghrelin, a hormone produced primarily in the stomach that tells us to *eat.* As the final insult, sleep deprivation can cause an increase in the stress hormone cortisol, which can cause wrinkles by breaking down the skin protein collagen. Yikes, that list is scary enough to make us unable to *ever* fall asleep!

But, being optimists, how can we nudge our sleep closer to the 7-, 8-, or 9-hour ideal, and make it quality sleep?

Some suggestions:

1. Assess your bedroom environment. You've probably heard that the bedroom should only be used for sleeping and sex. Sex causes the release of chemicals called endorphins that lower anxiety, along with the hormone oxytocin, which acts as a sedative. So, "getting it on" might translate to getting more and better sleep. A room that is cool (around 65 degrees), dark, quiet, and free of distractions is also recommended. For room colors, many find blue or earth tones relaxing, and red and bright purple energizing, so note how color affects *your* mood. Hard as it is, leave your phone in another room (did you know there is a term, nomophobia – "no-mobile phobia" – to describe the anxiety people feel when they are away from their phone?). Don't watch TV to fall asleep. Try to keep your going-to-bed and getting-up times the same every day. Keep the room neat and uncluttered, smelling nice (vanilla and lavender are good), and make sure your pillows, sheets, and mattress are comfortable. Quite a list . . . but the good thing is that all these are under our control. Try introducing one of these changes per week.
2. Consider your sleeping position. The best sleeping position depends on your circumstances. Sleeping on your back with

the head slightly elevated is frequently recommended for postnasal drip and acid reflux, and it also helps avoid creasing your face over time (yes, that can happen if you sleep on your front or side). But, if you're a back sleeper, don't make your pillow too thick or it could cause neck pain. If you have lower back pain, consider side sleeping in the fetal position or side sleep with your legs pulled up slightly toward your chest, and a pillow between your legs. Sleeping on your right side can help minimize reflux or heartburn; side or stomach sleeping can help keep airways open; using an adjustable bed or a wedge pillow may help you find that elusive perfect night of sleeping. It's trial and error to figure out what works best for *you*. Each position has its pros and cons depending on your individual, if any, medical conditions.

During my three pregnancies, sleeping on the left side (which improves circulation and decreases the pressure of your increasing body weight on your liver) with a pillow between your legs (to relieve the pressure on your back) was considered the best position. My youngest is now in his 30s, and I still find this the most comfortable position for me.

3. Medical issues. Address any of these that you can; for example, get a CPAP (Continuous Positive Airway Pressure) machine for sleep apnea: exercise, eat better, and lose weight for obesity and joint pain; do Kegel exercises for lax pelvic floor muscles. My favorite explanation of how to do Kegels is from the Mayo Clinic: "Imagine you are sitting on a marble and tighten your pelvic muscles as if you're lifting the marble. Try it for three seconds at a time, then relax for a count of three." Aim for three sets of 10 daily. Take appropriate medications for other issues that cannot be treated through lifestyle changes.

4. Naps. The common wisdom is that naps are good for us. After all, babies must be on to something, and the siesta (a short nap that is taken in the early afternoon, usually after the midday meal), is a mainstay in some cultures. But there are some dos and don'ts when it comes to napping.

Keep it relatively short – you want enough sleep to increase alertness, mood, and energy levels, but not enough to make going to sleep at night an issue. The Sleep Foundation recommends that a 10- to 20-minute nap will give you enough time to feel refreshed, without feeling groggy upon waking. Try not to sleep past 3 p.m. so it doesn't interfere with your night's sleep. Besides the repair to our body and brain while we sleep, it's thought that *when* we sleep evolved to coincide with the time when predators were most active – at night. As a consequence, those who work night shifts are more likely to develop atrial fibrillation (an abnormally fast and irregular heart rhythm) and heart disease, and working night shifts increases the risks of an earlier death, because those workers are fighting against their bodies' natural rhythms.

5. Food and drink. Try to avoid solid foods for at least two hours prior to bedtime, to lower the chances of indigestion or acid reflux. Do the same with liquids, to make it less likely you'll have to get up to urinate. But, if you want to eat/drink something closer to bedtime, here are a few suggestions, and why they are a good choice: Eggs, turkey, almonds, and bananas are all good sources of tryptophan, which helps produce serotonin; and/or try a cup of chamomile tea, which contains apigenin, an antioxidant that can make you sleepy. What to avoid: Abstain from alcohol for at least four hours prior to sleeping, since alcohol interferes with our restorative REM (rapid-eye-movement) sleep. Alcohol does make us fall asleep faster, but it can suppress or cause pauses in breathing. And, it's best to avoid foods and drinks with caffeine such as coffee, energy drinks, and even chocolate ice cream (darn) that may keep us awake, and spicy foods that can do a number on our digestive system.

Sleep issues, which affect about a third of the adult population, are serious stuff. Use the preceding suggestions to change where you sleep from a bed of thorns to a bed of roses. Sweet dreams!

- **H: Handle Stress.** "H" is the second letter of our SHIELD for a healthy body and mind. Stress can get a bad rap. There's a good kind of stress, called "eustress" ("eu" means "good" in Greek, and was coined by endocrinologist Hans Selye in the 1970s). This could be the exhilarating stress of sky-diving, of performing in a play, of stressing your bones and muscles to make them stronger, of speaking up for yourself when you've been wronged. Unfortunately, though, about a third of Americans live with what they perceive to be negative stress, according to the American Psychological Association. The circumstances retirement can foist upon us – fearing we don't have enough money, loneliness, perhaps the responsibilities of being a caregiver, maybe changes in relationships, or working on a new definition of who we are – can all be negative stressors (distress).

When we experience physical or psychological stress, our bodies churn out the stress hormones cortisol, epinephrine, and norepinephrine, which help regulate insulin; our blood pressure increases, along with our heart rate and blood sugar levels; and we have increased blood flow to our large muscles to prepare us for the "fight or flight" response. Ideally, this is short term, we deal with the issue, and our levels of stress hormones return to normal. This response was a beneficial evolutionary advantage that helped our ancestors escape predators. However, with repeated negative stressors, the body is bathed in these chemicals often and for prolonged periods, resulting in depression, anxiety, irritability, fatigue, and physical and mental distress.

An ongoing study by the National Institute of Aging found that there is a 40% increased risk of heart attack or stroke within the first year of retirement, compared to those still working. Although some of the retirees in this study were downsized, or left their job because they were ill, when you start following thousands upon thousands of people in an ongoing study, as does this one, individual factors like being ill before retiring or being downsized start to have less overall effect, and we see a broader trend. There is stress at the beginning of retirement for many because it's a change and unfamiliar.

In Chapter 1, I discussed the Holmes-Rahe Stress Inventory, and noted that retirement ranked tenth among more than 40 stressful life events. A 2013 JAMA (*Journal of the American Medical Association*) internal medicine paper reports: "The prevalence of stress in primary care is high; 60% to 80% of visits may have a stress-related component." Wow.

**Although we may not be able to control what happens to us, we *can* control how we react.** That is such a powerful statement. Let's look at several strategies for controlling or lowering stress:

1. Be assertive. Say "no thank you" to demands on your time that you don't want/need.
2. Exercise. This "free" wonder drug lowers stress hormones, and helps you sleep better so you can better deal with stress. For me, playing tennis, walking, or riding my bike helps; others use Yoga, Pilates, or t'ai chi. And, it doesn't have to be a big time suck. Twelve minutes of walking can boost feelings of positivity, according to researchers at Iowa State University.
3. Take deep breaths. Visualize relaxation flowing into you when you inhale, and stress flowing out of you when you exhale.
4. Sleep better – see earlier section. A rested body and mind are better prepared to handle stress, and will lower stress hormones.
5. Change the way you think. For example, instead of feeling overwhelmed by all the work of moving to a new home, relish downsizing your no-longer-needed material things and bask in the joy you feel as you donate to those who can use them.
6. Be proactive. Get a massage, listen to soothing music (in Karla's case, old rock-n-roll songs make her feel more energized and ready to tackle unpleasant tasks); laugh; surround yourself with positive people; stretch; take time for yourself each

day, reconnect with your spiritual side, play with a pet (even watching fish swimming in an aquarium reduces stress and lowers our blood pressure); and/or make a list of 10 things for which you are grateful.

7. Practice mindfulness (a term coined by Dr. Jon Kabat-Zinn) and be "fully present" – give your full attention to what you're involved with in that moment. It's a tough one, with texts and emails and to-do-lists swirling through our brain as we chat with a friend or listen to a grandchild tell a long story about what happened at school, or knowing we need to check in with elderly parents. We tend to be more future or even past oriented rather than present oriented – often waiting to jump in and tell *our* story at the first opportunity. Being fully mindful has great benefits, including lowering stress, increasing working memory and focus, and improving relationships, as well as improving the functioning of our immune system and making us more resilient.

8. Practice gratitude and be optimistic. According to *Harvard Health*, "Gratitude helps people feel more positive emotions, relish good experiences, improve their health, deal with adversity, and build strong relationships." Talk about a terrific, no-cost way to reduce stress! And research by psychologist Lewina Lee found a link between optimism, which can lower stress, and longevity. Although being optimistic is thought to be about 25% inherited, it can be cultivated.

9. Replace "musts" with "prefers": Remember that we are responsible for our own feelings; we can choose how we respond. Change "I must be perfect in everything I do" to "I prefer not to make mistakes, but if I do, I know I'm still an okay person." Treat yourself like you'd treat a good friend. You don't mercilessly beat up on them; don't beat up on yourself.

Let's face it – a life that is completely stress free would be boring, but too much negative stress is unhealthy. Work for a balance that works for you.

- **I: (Interact). Our third SHIELD letter for health is "I."** The importance of friends and family was addressed in Chapters 1 and 2, and recall that secret 3 for a successful retirement is "Have strong social support." Studies were cited that show how vital social connections are to our health, happiness, and longevity. Social support cannot be overstated. As John Donne so eloquently stated, "No man is an island." The statistics about loneliness in the United States are frightening. According to a Kaiser Family Foundation/Economist Survey, about 25% of Americans over 65 report that they "often or always feel lonely, feel that they lack companionship, feel left out, or feel isolated from others." Connection to others is vital for physical and mental health and happiness. It's more than just *having* friends and family; we need to interact and engage with them on a regular basis. Research shows loving, long-term relationships are a key component for a long, healthy life.

Where you live; your hobbies/sports/travel; your volunteer activities; second (or third) careers; your postretirement work; family, friends, and pets can all play a role in making connections. Reach out to those you were close to where you grew up, or to high school or college friends. In planning a 40-year high school reunion, Claudia Y. reconnected, through the alumnae coordinator at her alma mater, with several men and women she was close to in high school, but the group had slowly drifted apart. This group now plans several "happy hours" a year at different area bars/restaurants, and they have rekindled their friendships. Mitch found and reconnected with an old college buddy, who was also an environmental science major, and Mitch and his wife and Mitch's friend and his wife have taken trips to Antarctica and the Galapagos Islands together.

The research about "first loves" finding one another and reuniting after years or decades apart is compelling. If your first love is unattached, and you are, too try to track him or her down.

You may be surprised at the outcome. Nancy Kalish, PhD (she died in 2019 from a heart attack) did a survey of 1001 "lost loves" who reunited after at least five years of being apart before reconnecting again. The statistics were astounding: 78% of those who were first loves at age 17 or younger, and apart for five or more years, were still together when she tracked them down. The book Kalish published about her survey is listed at the end of this chapter. Compelling.

If you took a psychology class in high school or college, or just enjoy the subject matter, you may have come across a fascinating classic experiment by researcher Harry Harlow, PhD, published in 1965. The prevailing idea in the 1950s and 1960s was that babies become attached to their mothers because they are a food source, but Harlow thought this view "overlooked the importance of comfort, companionship, and love in promoting healthy development." Harlow raised monkeys in isolation that had been taken away from their mothers at birth; these isolated monkeys engaged in self-mutilation and displayed antisocial behavior. When introduced to the group, these isolated monkeys would not interact with the group; some would refuse to eat and died.

In addition, Harlow did studies where he removed the baby monkeys from their mother and provided them with two "surrogate mothers" – one made of wood and wire, and another made with soft rubber and terry cloth (for Harlow, the terry-cloth mother simulated "the comfort provided by a mother's touch"). In one experimental set-up with the baby monkeys, the wire mother had a milk bottle, but the terry cloth mother did not. In another set-up, the cloth mother had the bottle and the wire mother did not. The baby monkeys preferred the soft mother, with or without food, and would go to the wire mother only to feed. Those monkeys without any type of surrogate mother would "cower in fear" in a new situation; those with a surrogate mother would explore and then return to the surrogate. Harlow's studies demonstrated the importance of connection for normal development. Connection is vital – whether you're a monkey or a human.

For many, religion or spirituality is another way to connect and interact with others or with a higher power. According to the Pew Research Center, 64% of Boomers say that religion/spirituality is very or somewhat important, with women more likely to say it's "extremely important." The difference between religion and spirituality: Religion generally emphasizes rituals, teachings, and practices (such as going to a mosque, church, temple, etc.), whereas spirituality is a connection to something bigger than we are, and is associated with nonorganized religious activity. Since religion or spirituality can provide meaning to peoples' lives, they can be a great comfort during times of illness, financial hardship, or difficult end-of-life situations for themselves and their loved ones.

People who are part of religious or spiritual communities live longer and are more positive, according to studies by the Mayo Clinic and Merck, and they spent fewer days in the hospital, as well as in long-term care. A sampling of 500 patients with heart disease reported higher quality of life if there was a religious/spiritual connection compared to those without any type of religious or spiritual community. And, a study of 1,700 adults found those who regularly attend religious services live longer than those who don't; and those who regularly attended religious services had half the levels of an inflammatory substance that is associated with disease called interleukin-6, compared to those who didn't attend. Being part of a religious or spiritual group can also provide vital social support and better ways of coping with illness by having a belief in a "higher power." Although we acknowledge there can be negatives – if you think you're going to Hell, for example, or if you're so rigid in your thinking that you isolate yourself from others with different perspectives, religion or spirituality could be a detriment rather than a "blessing."

Remember Three Dog Night's "One (is the Loneliest Number)"? The band really nailed it when it comes to the importance of interaction with others.

- **E: (Exercise).** *"The single best predictor of the need to go into a nursing home is how strong your legs are."* Dr. Walter M. Bortz, geriatrician, Professor of Medicine, Stanford University. How's that for a shocking statement? Ah, yes. We know (at least intellectually) that exercise is good for us. There have been *so* many studies reinforcing the benefits for our body and mind that it goes without saying it's vital – why it's the very important "E" in our SHIELD acronym. But I am saying it anyway, because the statistics about who is exercising and how much are pretty daunting. According to the CDC, 28% of adults 50 or older report *no* physical activity (other than exercise from their job); this statistic was 27% among those aged 65–74, and 35% among adults 75 or older. And, the CDC reports women are less active than men, and those with chronic diseases are also less active (perhaps not surprisingly) than those without chronic diseases. There is also a correlation with education and body mass – the lower the education level and the higher the body mass, the less exercise.

Recent research shows that exercising is more important than dieting for health. The emphasis has traditionally been about how much we eat/weigh rather than how much we move, yet in the United States there has been an average increase of 15 pounds among men and women since the late 1980s-early 1990s . . . and we're not getting any taller. We also know that "yo-yo" dieting is associated with health risks. So, the latest approach is a "weight-neutral" approach, emphasizing being active and improving our cardiac and respiratory health.

If persuasion and facts can change behavior, here's a list of the benefits of exercise (and don't forget Dr. Bortz's quote about going into a nursing home and the strength of your legs . . .):

1. It creates more connections (synapses) between and among our nerve cells, improving our brain's ability to process information.

2. It lengthens our telomeres and pumps up our mitochondria, resulting in anti-aging effects (discussed earlier in "epigenetics").
3. It improves lung function by making our respiratory muscles work more efficiently, resulting in a lower requirement for oxygen, and decreases the production of carbon dioxide (less huffing and puffing).
4. It eases the pain of arthritis (this seems counterintuitive, but it does so by causing increased joint lubrication), decreases the chance of a fall/trip, improves our range of motion, strengthens muscles, increases flexibility, enhances our immune system, and improves sleep.
5. It lowers levels of mild to moderate depression (studies demonstrate lower levels of depression within a month of starting an exercise routine), elevates our mood, increases our energy level, and raises endorphin levels (chemicals that block feelings of pain).
6. It builds up bone cells (osteocytes), and decreases the risk of osteoporosis and osteopenia, which causes our bones to become brittle and weak.
7. It ups our production of nitric acid, which dilates our blood vessels, increasing blood flow (and can also play a role in improving erectile dysfunction, resulting in better or more sex), and lowers blood pressure.
8. It lowers our "bad" LDL and increases our "good" HDL.
9. It decreases our chance of getting certain diseases, including adult-onset diabetes; obesity; strokes; heart disease; gallstones; and breast, endometrial, and colon cancer.

   And, a 2021 study in the *Journal of Clinical Oncology* found that women who stayed physically active before, during, and after chemo had fewer issues with memory and thinking, commonly called "chemo brain."
10. It can help reduce and help relieve the unpleasant symptoms of menopause, including sleep quality, depression and insomnia, and perhaps help tame the midlife

"menopot," – the accumulation of midriff belly fat with falling female estrogen levels.

11. It can improve bladder control through Kegel exercises (described earlier). Where exactly are the pelvic muscles, anyway? If you're a woman, pretend you are squeezing a tampon in your vagina; for men, pretend you are trying to stop the flow of urine. Congrats – you've just located your pelvic muscles.

12. It reduces the amount of fat stored in the liver as well as the fat that surrounds internal organs, particularly in the abdominal area.

13. It can counteract the evils of sitting. Sitting burns fewer calories per hour than standing (60–130 compared to 100–200), raises the risk for a number of diseases including diabetes, obesity, and heart disease, and sitting can stiffen the joints and cause lower back pain. I have been at my computer for the past several hours composing this section, so it's a "do as I say and not as I do," but in my defense I did ride my bike and walk first thing this morning, knowing I would be sitting for a long time today.

14. It can bolster our feelings of self-worth, and improve our appearance.

15. It has a beneficial effect on our biome (see later discussion of our biome), increasing the numbers and diversity of these important microorganisms.

Whew!!!! If there was a medicine that had these *incredibly* positive effects, we'd be rioting and clamoring for it, and we'd be willing to pay a hefty price for something with all these tremendous benefits. But, we already have it . . . *exercise*. It can be a no-cost fountain of youth. We just have to "drink" from it.

So now what? Hopefully you're convinced that exercise is important to living a long and healthy life. And, an easy way to remember the four important facets of exercise is . . .yup, another acronym, **FEBS**: **F**lexibility, **E**ndurance, **B**alance, **S**trength.

It's much easier to exercise if you're feeling (and looking) good; it *can* be a kind of a Catch-22. Sometimes it seems if you go to a commercial gym, it's filled with hard bodies and beautiful people using the machines. You just want to get out of there. Or, you start going to a dance/exercise class, but everyone knows the steps, and there you are, fumbling and bumbling through the routine. It can be tough on your psyche and tough on your ego. Some thoughts if you're in this situation, and you can't break free of feeling you're the center of (unwanted) attention (and of course, most people are concentrating on themselves, and many are feeling the same as you are):

1. Get a group together of like-minded people and hire a personal trainer (or do it solo if the cost isn't prohibitive). Karla I. has four women who come to her home each week. They defray the cost of the trainer that way, and use simple weights and their own body weight to do the exercises. It's fun, low-stress, and social.

2. Do activities you like that incorporate flexibility, endurance, balance, and strength. I bought a few weights (strength) and use them at home while playing the music I like on my iPhone ("All She Wants to Do Is Dance" by Don Henley is a great one). I started tennis in my late 40s, and play with friends several times a week, both socially and on two competitive teams (provides endurance and balance, plus a nice side dish of social connection). I'm not very flexible (my husband might say that applies to my personality, too, haha), and I do some stretching, but only half-heartedly. I tried yoga, but didn't like it – too slow for me (my flexibility needs work, but it's a process). I bought a bike with a basket and enjoy riding it for pleasure as well as using it for grocery shopping and errands (endurance).

Jeff and Dianne like gyms that are open 24 hours, such as Planet Fitness or Anytime Fitness. They know the slow times when they will basically be working out on their own, and like it that way. On the other hand, Kyle A. loves to go at peak times, and uses it as an opportunity to socialize as well. Scott and Jody L. have created a gym in their basement, and use their treadmill, weights, and mats to be sure they get their regular dose of FEBS. Carlton J. likes mall walking. Although the pandemic squelched this for a time, and he switched to walking outside, he lives in a cold-weather climate and is slowly getting back into his pre-pandemic mall walking . . . and enjoying his coffee at Starbucks when he's done. Lydia is single and volunteers at the library. She borrows exercise videos from the library to work out at home.

Kevin O. is into kayaking, and lives in a Continuing Care Retirement Community that backs up to a scenic canal – with dolphins! – where he kayaks (endurance/strength) several times a week. He walks (endurance), and goes to his community gym and works out (flexibility/strength) on his own, since he can get in with a passkey and can go when he knows it's empty or nearly so.

Become a fish. Miguel goes three times a week to his local YMCA. The water is kind to his arthritic joints, he knows his entire body is engaged as he does his laps, the water creates resistance that is good for his muscles, and Miguel says he feels his mental stress slip away while he is immersed in his watery world. He also has balance issues, and swimming removes the fear of falling while exercising.

3. Consider SilverSneakers. SilverSneakers is covered by a number of Medicare programs, and this program provides thousands of fitness classes at more than 15,000 U.S. locations for adults 65+, both in-person and online. You can check the cost (if not covered), the locations, and if you're eligible to participate at their site, www.silversneakers.com. A 2018 study in the *Journal of Applied Gerontology* found:

Members of SilverSneakers experienced better health through increased physical activity, reduced social isolation, and reduced loneliness.

There's the adage: "The best exercise is the one you'll actually do." The trick is to find something you enjoy, or at least tolerate, such as a sport; walking; biking – if you have a dog or get one, she/he will love you for it; skiing; rock climbing; or rollerblading. Like to dance? You're in luck! *The New England Journal of Medicine* published a study, "Leisure Activities and the Risk of Dementia in the Elderly." The results regarding active leisure activities: "Dancing was the only physical activity associated with a lower risk of dementia. Fewer than 10 subjects played golf or tennis, so the relation between these activities and dementia was not assessed."

When it comes to exercising, adding in a friend for social support makes it easier and more enjoyable, and makes it harder to back out once you've made a commitment. And, do it first thing in the morning before life gets in the way. If you're the competitive type, get a fitness tracker, and compete with your friends (or just compete with yourself). Carla C. has a FitBit and is in "competition" with several friends, and finds it motivating to get in those extra steps.

Research shows that up to about 7,500 steps a day decreases the risk of death, so take comfort that a moderate number of steps has a positive effect on longevity. It doesn't have to be 10,000 a day (most of us have read that was a marketing tool from a Japanese maker of a step-counter, not a scientific finding). Americans walk an average of 3,000–4,000 steps a day (about 1.5–2 miles), so pump it up.

To be a bit repetitive, walking checks so many boxes: it's free, can be done year-round, it's good for your muscles (including that vital muscle, your heart), good for your respiratory system, assuming you're not breathing polluted air and you're walking at a reasonable clip; you're carrying your own body weight, so it's good for your bones; it provides time to think or perhaps practice gratitude; it can be social if you go with a companion; it can be good for intellectual stimulation if you listen to a podcast, and it's a great goal-setting practice if you commit to doing it on a regular basis. If you're a swimmer, weightlifter, skier or involved in other "nonstep" exercises, aim for 30–45 minutes of exercise a day, which is the equivalent of roughly 7,000 – 8,000 steps.

Consider **HIIT**. There's exciting recent research about the benefits of **h**igh **i**ntensity **i**nterval **t**raining, or HIIT, for older adults. In fact, the benefit of this type of exercise is more dramatic for those 65 and older, bestowing the gifts of aerobic fitness, a decrease in abdominal fat, an increase in size of muscle cells, and the ability for muscle cells to produce more energy, compared to those who are younger. The premise of HIIT is fairly simple: Start out with a three-minute-or-so easy warm-up, such as walking, riding a bike, or using a rowing machine or a treadmill. Then, go "all out" – to the point you are more gasping than talking – for a period of up to three minutes on your feet, bike, and so forth. Then, return to a normal pace for three minutes.

Repeat this alternating high intensity/low intensity for 30 minutes and do it several times a week. And, don't forget Dr. Bortz's warning: *"**The single best predictor of the need to go into a nursing home is how strong your legs are.**"* That should get you moving!

**Here is Mary R.'s (very robust!) regimen, which puts most of us to shame:**

---

I'm 66, and coming back from not only a knee replacement (2018), but also a shoulder fix (rotator cuff and bicep repair in 2020). These are over-use injuries from decades of being active and, as an artist, from decades of carrying around heavy artwork and art stands. I was determined to get back to the sports that I love, and have added strength and functional strength training (strength training that helps with basic day-to-day living). I'm lucky to have two dogs that need twice-daily walks, so my day starts with about three miles with them, usually while watching the sunrise along our beach. I then either play golf (usually three times a week) or tennis (twice a week).

I often take a strength or conditioning class before playing tennis, which helps warm me up for the courts. On my couple "off" days, I swim and do cardio pool exercises. I was never a swimmer, but I'm finding that I'm getting stronger with this extra conditioning. Early afternoon, I do another shorter (two-mile) walk with the dogs. Recently, I've returned to Pickleball, which I thought my knee couldn't handle, but I've been pleasantly surprised. Guess you could say I love being outside (an understatement?) and find a way to spend four to five hours a day doing various sport activities. The more I move, the better I feel.

---

## Where to Exercise

If you can, exercise outside. Exercising in nature can reduce depression, anxiety, and increase energy levels and focus. Some trees give off compounds called phytoncides that support our "natural killer" cells that are part of our body's defense system. In the 1980s, a Japanese term, "shinrin-yoku," translated roughly as "forest bathing," became integral to Japanese healthcare. Even our National Institutes of Health has gotten into the "forest bathing" act, comparing outcomes for those walking in a forest to those walking in a city environment. The results showed that "forest environments promote lower concentrations of cortisol, lower pulse rate, lower blood pressure, greater parasympathetic nerve activity (our 'calming' system), and lower sympathetic nerve activity (our 'fight or flight' response) than do city environments. These results will contribute to the development of a research field dedicated to forest medicine, which may be used as a strategy for preventive medicine."

One final note (bit of a bummer): The preceding discussion didn't really include anything specific about losing lots of weight through exercise. Research has found our body tends to "hoard" our energy expenditures, perhaps harkening back to the days when food wasn't as plentiful, and hunting and gathering food wouldn't come at too enormous of an energy cost. It seems that when we exercise, we really only burn about 50–72% of the calories that we *think* we might be burning. So, that mile walk where we think we are burning 100 calories . . .we are probably actually burning more like 70. But, that's better than nothing, and console yourself with the fact that we burn calories just by being alive – it's called our basal energy expenditure or basal metabolic rate (BMR). Maintaining/ building muscle through exercise (muscle burns more calories than fat) is a great way to indirectly burn more calories. To calculate your BMR, go to https://www.calculator.net/bmr-calculator.html.

- **L: Learn New Things.** So, we are up to "L" in our "SHIELD" acronym for better mental and physical health. To recap: S: sleep; H: handle stress; I: interact, and E: exercise. "L" (learn new things) is vital. Our brains. Those three-pound dynamos that consume roughly 20% of our resting metabolic rate, or about 300 calories/day. Exercise and sleep help our brains function better, but the exciting news about our brains is neuroplasticity – our brains can change and create new nerve cells (neurons) and connections between/among them throughout our lives, a discovery that gained traction in the 1970s, although some scientists had proposed this possibility much earlier. (In high school, I was taught that we were born with all the brain cells we'd ever have . . . and that getting drunk would kill off 10,000 of them – they didn't know about neuroplasticity back then, and the teachers probably figured it would scare us away from drinking alcohol.) Neuroplasticity explains why children who have had one entire hemisphere (half) of their brain removed because of severe epilepsy often recoup most if not all of their brain function. One classic neuroplasticity study compared brain MRIs of London taxi drivers and London bus drivers. The hippocampus, an area of the brain that deals with spatial relationships, was much larger in the taxi drivers, who had to learn hundreds of routes, compared to London bus drivers, who drove the same route over and over. Moral: Do things to rev up those brain cells.

## Alzheimer's

Earlier in this chapter, Alzheimer's was listed as the seventh leading *cause* of death in the United States. But, what is it we're most *afraid* of? According to an Age Wave/Merrill Lynch survey of adults over 50, 54% said that Alzheimer's/dementia was the scariest disabling condition of later life, followed by cancer (22%), stroke (12%), and heart disease (5%). (Alzheimer's is the most common form of dementia.)

*Dementia* is an umbrella term that would include such dementias as Lewy body dementia, vascular dementia, and frontotemporal dementia. So, to paraphrase Steppenwolf, what do we need to do to keep/get our (mental) motor runnin' in an effort to dodge Alzheimer's and generally keep our brains young and functioning as long as we possibly can? Here's how:

1. Be active. Exercise, particularly aerobic exercise, such as brisk walking, swimming, running, or cycling, increases a protein (BDNF – brain-derived neurotrophic factor) that affects the survival, growth, and development of new nerve cells and strengthens the signals transmitted from neuron to neuron. The Chicago Health and Aging Project followed more than 10,000 people for more than a dozen years, and found that increased physical activity resulted in slower cognitive decline. So move it – for as long, for as often, and for as hard as you can. One of the best things for your brain is at the other end of your body – a good pair of sneakers.
2. Avoid stress/have friends. Chronic stress decreases connections among nerve cells. Antidepressant medicines or therapy for depression and anxiety can help increase connections. Supportive social connections and/or meditation can lower stress levels as well.
3. Get quality sleep. When we're in a deep sleep, scientists have discovered that certain cells help "sweep" our brains clean of plaque and other waste products, which coincides with the fact that those who have poor sleep (less time for

"sweeping") have higher incidences of Alzheimer's. Studies have shown more amyloid plaque in the spinal cord fluid of people who were sleep deprived compared to those who were not.

Also, growth-hormone production peaks during deep sleep, which is beneficial for our memory and the brain's working capacity. See earlier in this chapter (under "S") for sleep tips for better shut-eye.

4. Participate in novel activities. Try an escape room (I have done several – they really stretch the brain and most people do them with a group so you get the interaction benefit, as well); learn a new language or musical instrument; take up a new sport; read a book that transports you outside of yourself; travel to a place you've never visited before; join a community club or volunteer; listen to a podcast on a subject you know nothing about; watch or listen to news that espouses the *opposite* political persuasion that you have; strike up a conversation with a stranger; try a new game or puzzle; interact with people of many different generations; learn how to meditate; learn/play chess. As an added incentive to try new things, studies by Cornell University researcher Thomas Gilovich found we regret things we DIDN'T do twice as much as we regret things we DID do. So, go for it!

5. Laugh. When we laugh, we stimulate many different brain areas, and release the "feel good" hormone dopamine, which helps transmit information between nerve cells. Things that are counterintuitive are especially helpful keeping our brain sharp.

An example: Husband: Look at that drunk woman at the bar. Wife: Who is she? Husband: Twenty years ago, she proposed to me at this exact place, but I turned her down. Woman: Wow! She's still celebrating! (Did you see that punchline coming? – it's counterintuitive, which gives a little healthy jolt to the brain.) And, another, just for fun: "When I was a kid, my parents moved around a lot, but I always found them." Rodney Dangerfield.

6. Nourish your brain. Try the MIND Diet, which stands for **M**editerranean-DASH **I**ntervention for **N**eurodegenerative **D**elay. This is a combination of the Mediterranean Diet (see discussion in "Diet" section later) and the DASH (Dietary Approach to Stop Hypertension) diet. Recommended by researchers to lower your risk of Alzheimer's disease, the emphasis is on berries, green leafy vegetables, nuts, olive oil, whole grains (oatmeal, brown rice, quinoa), fish (salmon, tuna,), beans, poultry, and red wine in moderation.

Luckily, there *are* strategies and foods for teaching an old brain new tricks.

- **D: Diet.** The last letter of our SHIELD acronym for better health (**S**leep, **H**andle Stress, **I**nteract, **E**xercise, **L**earn new things) is **D** for diet. I am using the word "diet" to refer to food and drink that is regularly consumed, not "diet" in the sense of changing food intake to lose weight. Looking up the number and names of diets (ways to eat) on Wikipedia is enlightening . . . and frightening. You can truly find an A–Z listing of diets (from Atkins to Zone), totaling more than 150 different diets, and the rationale behind them. Some of them are really wild, such as the "Tongue Patch Diet" which involves stitching a patch to your tongue to make it painful to eat, and ingesting only 800 calories a day in liquid form to lose weight – just to be clear, *not* recommended.

For many of us, *diet* is a four-letter word. We're not getting taller, but we are definitely getting wider. Over the past 20 years, men have gained 15 pounds or more, according to the CDC and

National Center for Health Statistics, and for women it's 17 pounds. These additional pounds were *prior* to Covid-19, so it was sobering news when the American Psychological Association announced that about 40% of Americans gained weight the year after Covid-19 was declared a pandemic in March 2020. The average gain was 22 pounds for women and 37 pounds for men.

Reasons given for weight gain over the years include a combination of factors: too little exercise (exercising at robust levels can decrease appetite); too much food; extra sugars from energy drinks and sodas (which cause surges in insulin that make us feel hungrier sooner); overconsumption of easily-available fast foods, which tend to be heavy in fat, salt, and sugar, are low in nutrition, and have an addictive effect on our brain; larger portion sizes; electronics, including television, computers, phones; lack of access to fresh fruit and vegetables ("food deserts"), lack of safe places to exercise or walk; more time at work and less free time to make healthy meals at home and to exercise; higher levels of stress, which make us want to eat; and poor sleep, which wears down our self-control and increases levels of the hormone ghrelin, which stimulates our appetite. (Worth noting – nuts are often recommended as a healthy food, but it's usually accompanied with a warning about their caloric density. A 2021 review of 449 studies published in *Obesity Review* concluded: "Current evidence demonstrates the concern that nut consumption contributes to increased adiposity appears unwarranted.") So, munch away.

A slowing metabolism has also been blamed for weight gain; studies show that our metabolism stays steady from ages 20–60, although there is a slow decline after 60.

### Is There a "Best" Way to Eat?

Unfortunately, how we eat is frequently dictated more by how we want to *look* rather than how we want to *feel*. If the emphasis is on how we look, that's when we can get into crazy and unhealthy ways of eating like the "Tongue Patch Diet" or the "Prayer Diet" (you pray every day you'll lose weight). The MIND diet was suggested earlier as a specific way to hopefully prevent Alzheimer's disease. But in 2021, panels of nutrition experts at *Forbes, Health, U.S. News & World Report,* and *Good Housekeeping* evaluated the overall "best" ways of eating. The Mediterranean way of eating ranked number 1 with all of them. What makes the Mediterranean diet the "winner"?

**Aunt Lorraine.** First, a little story. My Aunt Lorraine lived a long, full life – until 101 – with a sharp mind and a trim, healthy body that was still able to walk up and down full flights of steps – to her basement, where the washer and dryer were located, and to the second floor, where her extended family (and at that age, there were *lots* of extended family members!) would stay when visiting. Almost every day, she climbed the steps of her local church to attend Mass. Was it luck or genetics? Some luck and good genes, yes, but there's more to it than that . . .

In 2004, researcher Dan Buettner partnered with National Geographic and the National Institute on Aging to try to determine if it's luck, our genes, and/or lifestyle behaviors under our control that are needed to live a long and healthy life. Buettner searched for groups of centenarians – those who reached the age of 100 but without suffering from lifestyle diseases such as diabetes, cancer, obesity, or heart disease. Although Buettner knew genetics account for up to 30% of our longevity, he was interested in finding out about lifestyle factors that could be adopted by others to help ensure a long and healthy life.

Buettner found five places that met his criteria – in Sardinia, Italy (allegedly, this area was circled on a map in blue, which gave rise to the term "Blue Zones"); Nicoya Peninsula, Costa Rica; Okinawa, Japan; Ikaria, Greece; and Loma Linda, California, which is the only Blue Zone in the United States. Over five years, Buettner delved into their lifestyle characteristics and identified what these centenarians shared that contributed to a long and healthy life:

1. Purpose and Attitude: Those in the "Blue Zones" felt they had a reason to wake up each day and had a good outlook on life. Aunt Lorraine met each day with the proverbial smile; and her family, comprised of seven children and lots of grandchildren and great-grandchildren, who live locally, gave her a sense of purpose, as did her strong and unwavering faith.

2. Food. Those in the Blue Zones ate moderate, healthy diets. Think nuts, beans, veggies, whole grains, minimal dairy and small portions of fish and meat. Drinks included water, tea, coffee, and wine. Many Blue Zoners unknowingly followed the Japanese phrase "Hara Hachi Bu," roughly translated as "Eat until your stomachs are 80% full." Aunt Lorraine ate her main meal early in the day, and pretty much just "nibbled" on nuts and fruits after that. And, she had to have her "cuppa tea" in the morning and the evening.

    The Blue Zoners in Loma Linda, California were Seventh-day Adventists, and were vegetarians. They don't smoke or drink alcohol, exercise regularly, and on average live 10 years longer than the rest of us in the United States. True story – my neighbors in Maryland were Seventh-day Adventists. Although they moved away, we kept in touch. Barbara F. died in her early 90s . . . while waterskiing on a lake (and slaloming – on one ski!).

3. Faith. Religion/spirituality/honoring their ancestors were an integral part of the Blue Zoners' lives. As Dan Buettner said, "To a certain extent, adherence to some sort of belief allows them to relinquish the stresses of everyday life to a higher power." We know chronic stress can negatively affect virtually every body system. Aunt Lorraine attended daily Mass for years, and felt her religion grounded her and brought her peace.

4. Activity. Movement was built into most Blue Zoners' lives. They were gardeners, shepherds, or took regular walks. It wasn't a case of scheduling time to go the gym; moving was

more an intrinsic part of their daily routine. Their environment often shaped their behavior, so over the course of the
day they moved . . . a lot. Aunt Lorraine had a beautiful backyard filled with plants and flowers that she tended to for
hours (with assistance as she moved up in years).

5. Wine. All the Blue Zoners (except those in Loma Linda, California, who abstained for religious reasons) drank an average of one to two glasses of wine a day, with meals, friends,
   or both. Did the resveratrol, the antioxidants, the tannins in
   the wine make a difference? Or was it the social aspect? Or
   both? Recent research proclaims that there is "no safe level
   of alcohol," but those in the Blue Zones might disagree. Aunt
   Lorraine occasionally indulged in a wee bit of the grape with
   food and family present.

6. Social Circle and Family. The Blue Zoners lived in communities of like-minded people who reinforced a healthy
   approach to living. Family was very important to them. Blue
   Zoners' social circle and family reinforced "good behavior."
   Although her peer group had pretty much disappeared,
   Aunt Lorraine had a daughter who lived with her in my
   aunt's home of more than 60 years, and her other children,
   grandchildren, and great-grandchildren lived close by and
   frequently visited.

Can we use Buettner's research to improve our own lives and
live more like Blue Zoners? Can we ride our bikes to the store, walk
in the forest, take the stairs instead of the elevator; eat more nuts
(assuming you're not allergic), whole grains, and veggies; relax,
meditate, or pray; look on the bright side, surround yourself with
those whose positive behaviors you'd like to mirror, create and
maintain strong family bonds, and have a vibrant social group?
I think we can.

Results of the Blue Zone research have been applied to cities. In 2009, the "Blue Zone Projects" partnered with AARP and
the United Health Foundation with Albert Lea, MN, a small town

of 18,000. The approach was to "optimize city streets, create bike lanes, sidewalks, improve public spaces such as parks and nature paths, and switch to healthier food choices in schools, restaurants, and grocery stores." Within a year, participants added 2.9 years to their average lifespan, had a 40% drop in city healthcare costs, and enjoyed a 90% increase in community satisfaction.

When I asked Aunt Lorraine her favorite thing about turning 100, she responded, with a twinkle in her eye, "There's no peer pressure." Sounds like something a Blue Zoner might say. So, yes, if you're looking for a "diet," I'd suggest you think "BLUE."

## Can We "Trick" Ourselves into Better Eating?

A jolting and dire statistic: About 74% of adults in the United States are either overweight (42.5%) or obese (31.1%), according to the National Center for Health Statistics. When we look at the most common New Year's Resolutions, the same ones top the list year after year after year: losing weight, eating better, and exercising more. We know, intellectually, what we *should* do, but for most of us, it can be so difficult.

"Portion distortion" is rampant (for example, a serving of ice cream is now 33% larger and a beverage serving is now 50% larger than it was in the 1980s); most serving sizes have doubled or tripled in size since the 1970s.

Psychologists, behavioral economists, and scientists provide some easy and effective "tricks" to tweak our environment to help us eat less and/or better:

## Easy "Food Hacks" for Eating Less/Better

1. Use smaller plates. Use salad plates for dinner instead of entrée plates, and purchase small bowls to control portions. We tend to eat what's in front of us, and our brain sees a full plate or bowl as more satisfying. The same amount of food on a smaller plate (the black circle represents the food and the white circle represents the plate in the figure) looks like

more food to us. It's an easy way to deceive our brain. The scientific name for this is the "Delboeuf Illusion" after Franz Delboeuf.

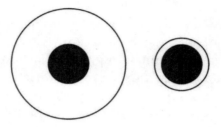

2.  Change your glassware. My husband and I received Lismore Waterford wine glasses when we were married (several decades ago). I can pour the equivalent of *four* glasses of wine from my Lismore glassware into *one* of my current wine glasses. Talk about portion distortion! And, according to Dr. Brian Wansink of Cornell University, we drink up to 30% *less* liquid from a tall and narrow glass compared to a short and wide one.

3.  Serving spoon size. People served themselves almost 15% more ice cream when they used a three-ounce scoop rather than a two-ounce scoop. And when given both a big bowl *and* a big scoop, they served themselves 57% more ice cream. Interestingly, the people were nutrition experts who thought they were attending a celebration for a colleague, and didn't know they were part of a study. So, even the best and brightest of us can be tricked.

4.  Use a big fork. Counterintuitively, a large fork can result in eating less. Customers at an Italian restaurant were given either large forks or smaller forks compared to the usual fork the restaurant used (about a 20% difference in size). The plates were weighed prior to being served and after the patron was finished eating. Diners using the small fork ate considerably *more*. Why? We know it takes awhile to feel full after we first start eating. The researchers concluded we

often use visual cues to know when to stop eating (unless we've been taught to *always* clean our plates, regardless!) and with the small forks, the food wasn't disappearing as quickly, so people just kept eating until the pile of remaining food looked small enough. With the large fork, the food disappeared quickly, so our eyes told our brain we were getting full.

5. Color and hunger. McDonald's, Pizza Hut, Wendy's, In-N-Out Burger. What do all these have in common? These fast-food chains all use red and yellow, and science has found these colors stimulate our appetite. Blue plates have been found to be more of an appetite suppressant. We also tend to eat more if there is low contrast between what we're eating and plate color. So, scientists found people eat more pasta with a white sauce on a white plate than they would eat on a red plate; and eat more pasta covered with marinara (red) sauce on a red plate than on a nonred plate.

6. Remove the "triggers" from your house. You may be a model of healthy eating all day, but for many of us, our willpower gets used up by around 8 p.m. What to do? Bart and Carol O. battled this for years, and finally realized they had to remove the junk food from the house – they simply could not resist its evening siren song. Twenty pounds lighter after two years (and realizing how good a juicy apple could taste at 8 p.m.), this one simple move made a huge difference. (They will often order a dessert when they go out to eat, though.) Changing your environment can change your health . . . for the better.

7. Watch what you say and with whom you eat. *Remove* weight. Don't *lose* weight. Dr. Pamela Peeke is a physician and nutrition scientist, and has an outstanding resume too long to list. But, one practical thing Peeke suggests is to use the word "remove" when it comes losing weight. "Remove" sounds permanent, right? Unlike "lose" weight, which sounds like something that could be found again (and is, unfortunately,

for most of us). A good psychological ploy. And, pick your
dining buddies carefully. Studies show we eat up to 48%
more when we eat socially among friends and family versus
eating alone or with those we don't know well. And, if we eat
with fit friends who order healthy meals, we tend to do the
same. Wear snug clothes when going out to eat. It can be a
subtle but effective reminder.

8. Try eating only during a 12-hour window. There is interesting research about the benefits of intermittent fasting,
and although there are many different intervals proposed
for eating/not eating, one that is doable for many is to eat
only between the hours of 6 a.m. to 6 p.m. or between 7
a.m. and 7 p.m. If you do this, you'll eliminate the common
post-dinner feeding frenzy, and may start burning fat for
energy because your glucose is depleted. Going longer
periods without eating seems to switch on "longevity genes,"
according to research using animal models.

9. Eat mindfully. We unconsciously eat more when watching
TV, using our phones, reading, talking to others, or eating
because of our emotions (sad/bored/lonely). Concentrate
on savoring each bite. Chewing at least 30 times before swallowing may help us eat less and give us time for our brain
to tell us we're no longer hungry. As Melissa Milne, author
of *The Naughty Diet*, says: "You don't feel bad about yourself
when you get fat. You get fat when you feel bad about yourself." The connection between eating and emotions is huge.
Be aware of this connection.

10. Make open-faced sandwiches, using only a single slice of
bread; fill half your plate with veggies and fruit; watch out
for the "halo effect" – just because a food is healthy doesn't
mean you can eat unlimited quantities.

11. Go natural. There are more than 10,000 food additives
approved by the Food and Drug Administration in the United
States to "preserve, package, or modify the taste, look, texture,
or nutrients in foods." Best advice: minimize processed foods.

## *Be Aware*

Many of us, although retiring or thinking about retiring, also have aging parents, and about 25% of Boomers are also caregivers to their aging parents. As we – and our parents – age, appetites and activity may decrease, we spend more time indoors, and we don't require as many calories as we once did. And, there are several vitamins and nutrients that become harder to absorb, make, ingest, or utilize. Although not all-inclusive, here are several important nutrient examples where older adults frequently fall short, and two additional considerations (your biome and exercise vs. eating to lose weight) for both you and your aging parents.

- B12. Tyler, 72, became acutely aware of the importance of B12 when he felt he had "brain fog" and couldn't concentrate. After a number of false starts, he was finally diagnosed with low Vitamin B12, which is vital for healthy nerve and DNA function. Low Vitamin B12 can mimic the symptoms of dementia. As we age, we don't absorb Vitamin B12 as well, and some meds, such as Metformin (for diabetes) and proton pump inhibitors for acid reflux can interfere with absorption. Good B12 sources: fish, meat, poultry, fortified breakfast cereals, and dairy. It's estimated about 20% of adults over 50 have low B12.
- B6. This vitamin (also called pyridoxine) becomes harder to absorb after we hit 50, and deficiencies are also found in chronic abusers of alcohol. B6 is necessary for our immune system and nervous system to function properly. Good sources: bananas, potatoes, fish, and fortified cereals.
- Vitamin D. We know our skin can make the "Sunshine Vitamin," but our skin gets less efficient producing Vitamin D as we age, which can result in symptoms including muscle weakness, fatigue, cognitive decline, and depression. Vitamin D also aids in the absorption of calcium, which we need for strong bones. According to the CDC, 20% of women aged 50

and over have osteoporosis (brittle, weak bones), and 27% of women 65 and over have it; for men, the percentages are 4% and 6%. But, 43% of men and women over 50 have low bone density, called osteopenia. Vitamin D sources: Consider salmon, eggs, tuna, and fortified cereal and milk. For many of us, 10 to 15 minutes of sun a few times a week on our arms and legs will do the trick, although pollution, the season, where you live and age all play a role in Vitamin D synthesis.

- Water. Our body is about 60% water. If your urine is dark yellow rather than pale yellow, or you frequently feel thirsty, you need more water. Water is necessary for just about everything involving our body, including proper kidney function, regulating temperature, pumping blood, lubricating joints, neurotransmitter production by our brain, preventing constipation, producing sweat that cools our body, and muscle contraction. Unfortunately, our sense of thirst decreases as we get older. Besides water itself, things like milk, juice, coffee and tea (although slightly diuretic in effect) count, as well as foods that have a lot of water in them, including cucumbers, watermelon, celery, and oranges. Weakness, headache, fatigue, and a rapid heart rate could all be signs of too little water. The 8×8 rule – eight 8-ounce glasses of water – is a good goal. Drink up!

- Fiber. When my mom was in her 80s, her doctor told her that for the elderly, it was often "all about the poop." As we age, our metabolism slows down, we have more sluggish intestines, and we're often less physically active. Fiber helps prevent constipation; it also helps to slow the absorption of sugar, thus lessening the chances of Type 2 diabetes; and fiber reduces the absorption of cholesterol into our bloodstream.

  Good fiber sources: bananas (and other whole fruits); beans, lentils, and peas. Add fiber gradually (for women over 50, shoot for a total of about 21 grams/day; for men over 50, about 30 grams/day). Too much fiber, though, can cause bloating, indigestion, and nausea.

- Protein. As we age, we lose muscle mass; this is called sarcopenia. Unfortunately, it's a natural part of aging, but the loss of muscle mass can become magnified with smaller appetites, swallowing issues, impaired taste/smell, dental issues, and limited financial resources. It's estimated that about a third of older adults don't eat enough protein, which of course also plays a role in body strength. Older adults should aim for about 25–30 grams of protein per meal (check with your doc – upping protein can be tough on your kidneys if you have kidney disease). Good sources: fish, poultry, lean beef/pork, eggs, nuts, and seeds. So, although loss of muscle mass is normal as we age (men lose about a third of muscle mass over their lifespan), we can work to slow down the loss.

  To repeat this quote a third and last time: *"The single best predictor of the need to go into a nursing home is how strong your legs are."*

- Our gut biome. We need to nourish the three to six pounds of microorganisms that live in our gastrointestinal tract (gut) called our biome (or flora or microbiota). These "friendly" microbes (bacteria, fungi, yeast, protozoa, and viruses) play a huge role in maintaining our health. Our biome started forming prior to birth, when we picked up microbes from our mother's placenta and vaginal canal, or from our mother's skin if born via C-section. We continue to populate our gut with microbes, with the "good" ones (such as *Lactobacillus* and species of *Bifidobacteria*), usually keeping the "bad" ones (such as some species of *Clostridium* and *Staphylococcus*) in check. Our biome helps digest fats, proteins, and carbohydrates; it aids in the absorption of minerals, including iron, calcium, and magnesium; it regulates our bowels; it makes Vitamin K and some of the "B" vitamins; it plays a role in longevity; and our biome produces substances such as dopamine and serotonin, which control many important bodily functions. Studies have found links with an unhealthy biome and weight gain, insulin resistance, sleep and anxiety issues.

"Fecal transplants" from healthy donors to those suffering from a bacterial infection called *C. diff* (*Clostridium difficile*) have cured infections from this nasty disease. Fascinating studies of immigrants to the United States found that those who adopted unhealthy dietary habits of American eating (more processed foods, more red meat, fewer high-fiber foods) changed their biomes very rapidly, particularly the diversity of microbes. We really are what we eat.

We can increase our beneficial microbes (called "probiotics") through eating them directly in various forms, including yogurt containing the phrase "contains live and active cultures"; from unpasteurized and refrigerated sauerkraut; and from buttermilk and sour pickles. And/or, you can eat *prebiotics*: plant fibers we can't digest, but provide food for our gut biome. Examples: bananas, beans (navy, white. black), lentils, raw asparagus, tomatoes, and oatmeal.

Exciting research from the University of Illinois demonstrated that exercise increases the number of good microbes in our gut without a change in diet; another study found that stool transplanted from young, healthy mice to older mice resulted in better memory in the older mice. More short-chain fatty acids, which are a nutrition source for our colon cells, were produced by the good gut microbes. We should, as the expression says, "go with our gut." A healthy gut biome is incredibly beneficial and important. A lot of new and exciting research in this area.

- Exercise vs. Eating. If you've struggled, like most people, to lose weight, it's worth noting the recent research by Dr. Glenn Gaesser from Arizona State University. He delved into more than 200 studies about exercise and dieting (and some of these studies were meta-analyses, which grouped and analyzed many combined studies), and found that exercise is more important for longevity than eating less. Losing weight by dieting drops our risk of dying by about 16%, but obese people who exercised can lower their risk of dying by 30%

or more, even if they don't lose weight. So, if you want to live longer, and you want to choose between exercise or eating less. . .take the stairs.

## Senior Exams (or, tests you can't study for. . .)

Nope, those medical evaluations never end. We should still get routine screenings, tests, immunizations, and boosters, but there have been several recent changes. In 2018, the U.S. Preventative Services Task Force recommended that **colonoscopy** screenings starting at the age of 45 rather than 50 offer a "moderate health benefit," due to an uptick in colon cancer cases among those younger than 50 years of age. The U.S. Preventative Services Task force is "an independent, volunteer panel of national experts in disease prevention and evidence-based medicine." See the end of this chapter for a link to this group's additional screening suggestions for older adults.

Concerns about **salt (sodium) level** intake in the United States have recently pushed the Food and Drug Administration (FDA) to try and lower the average 3,400 milligrams (mg) of sodium we consume per day, which is close to 50% more than the current 2,300 mg recommended limit for those 14 years and older. More than 45% of American adults have high blood pressure, and too much sodium raises blood pressure and is one of the top contributors to kidney disease, heart disease, stroke, and other cardiovascular diseases. The FDA is working with consumers and companies to lower the amount of sodium in processed and restaurant food.

A third fairly recent change concerns blood pressure. In 2017, the American Heart Association and the American College of Cardiology made the first changes to blood pressure standards since 2003. The old standard for normal blood pressure was 120/80; that is now considered elevated blood pressure, and normal blood pressure is less than 120 and less than 80. The old standard for high blood pressure was 140/90; high blood pressure is now defined as 130/80 for all adults. By the way, the higher number in a blood pressure reading represents the force of the blood on your arteries when your heart contracts; the lower number represents the force of the blood on your arteries when your heart is between beats. The pressure is measured in mm of mercury (Hg). The old standards – exercise, a healthy diet, weight loss, and medications (if necessary) can help control blood pressure. And, buy a blood pressure monitor – they are not expensive, and you can monitor your blood pressure at home.

You may remember the 2016 advice for middle agers to take a low-dose aspirin every day to prevent heart attacks (more specifically, it was recommended for adults 50–59 with a 10% or greater chance of cardiovascular disease over the next 10 years). In 2021, this recommendation was dropped for people in that specific category, based on the advice of the experts at the U.S. Preventative Services Task Force due to risks of internal bleeding (recall it's the same group, mentioned earlier, that said starting colonoscopies at age 45 instead of 50 offers a "moderate health benefit"). This is how science works – although people get annoyed with changing recommendations, knowledge evolves over time. Most of us today wouldn't be happy with heroin-laced aspirin for children, advertised by Bayer in 1898, targeted for children with colds and coughs.

The best advice is to discuss with your trusted health professional what you, as an individual, should do, based on your age, goals, and medical status. One size does not fit all.

### *A Somewhat Comforting Thought*

There's a term in psychology called "hedonic adaptation" that is a double-edged sword.

It describes how most of us react, over time, to a situation – a situation that could be dreadful or wonderful. It's the notion that after awhile, whether something good or bad happens to us, we return to our "baseline" or "set-point" of happiness (researchers estimate our "set-point" is about 50% genetic, 10% life circumstances, and 40% how we think and what we do). There have been tons of studies about hedonic adaptation – studying people who have lost limbs in car accidents, or interviewing and following those who have experienced the death of loved ones, or endured unwanted, messy divorces. It turns out, over a period of time, perhaps in a year or so, most of us return to our basic "set-point" of happiness. That can be very comforting news.

Then, there's the flipside. We purchase that new car or piece of expensive jewelry or big house or marry that person we think will make us deliriously happy forever, but after a while . . .yep, hedonic adaptation kicks in, and we also return to our happiness set-point. (This has been found to be true even of people who win big money prizes in a lottery.) It's because of hedonic adaptation that the idea of "buying experiences, not things" is popular advice. With each new experience, we enjoy a little bump of joy, and doing novel things that are pleasurable will help us counter hedonic adaptation. Also, being grateful, and frequently reminding ourselves how beautiful that view of the water is outside of our new house, or how quickly our car cools down when it's hot outside, or how much we appreciate the little things our loved ones do for us, or how lucky we are to be able to walk on a crisp autumn day, are ways to counter the downside of hedonic adaptation.

### The Financial Benefits of Becoming/Staying Healthy

Besides adding quality to your retirement years, staying healthy can add dollars to your retirement coffers. Yes, you'll need less money if you die at 50, but is that a good trade-off? Don't think so. Living longer by being healthy can pay off financially. Comparing fit and unfit people, fit individuals have fewer lifestyle diseases, including heart disease, atherosclerosis, diabetes, and fewer mental health issues. They are more likely to be offered a job compared to someone who is obese (yes, that is discrimination, but unfortunately it exists). If you're healthy, you could, if you wanted, work longer prior to retiring, allowing you to save more, or be able to work in retirement more easily after leaving your primary career.

Being healthy also translates into fewer dollars going into healthcare, and more money for enjoyable things, such as traveling to new places, visiting friends and family, or starting that small business you've dreamed about for years. Non-smokers and normal-weight individuals pay less for health insurance. Consider ditching unhealthy habits. A pack of cigarettes in 2021 averaged about $6.00. At a pack a day, that's a savings of $2,190 a year. Or save $3 a day usually spent on junk food or sodas, and save $1,095 (I have taken a week cruise, including food and entertainment, for less than that). And – let's face it – we feel so much better when we are healthy.

In an Age Wave/Merrill Lynch survey of more than 3,000 Americans, the overwhelming response for the most important ingredient of a successful retirement was *health*. The Roman poet Virgil got it right when he said, "The greatest wealth is health." But, it's important to have enough money to enjoy that health. That is the focus of the next chapter.

## More Resources

### Books

Chatztky, Jean, and Michael F. Roizen, M.D. *AgeProof: Living Longer Without Running Out of Money or Breaking a Hip*. Grand Central Publishing, 2019.

Christensen, Julie, and Dong-Seon Chang. *Dancing Is the Best Medicine: The Science of How Moving to a Beat Is Good for Body, Brain, and Soul*. Greystone Books, 2021.

Hurme, Sally Balch. *ABA/AARP Checklist for My Family: A Guide to My History, Financial Plans and Final Wishes*. American Bar Association, 2015.

Kalish, Nancy, PhD. *Lost & Found Lovers: Facts and Fantasies of Rekindled Romances*. iUniverse.com, 2005. (Originally published by William Morrow Inc. in 1997.)

Levitin, Daniel. *Successful Aging: A Neuroscientist Explores the Power and Potential of Our Lives*. Dutton, 2020.

Verburgh, Kris. *The Longevity Code: Secrets to Living Well for Longer from the Front Lines of Science*. The Experiment, 2018.

## *Websites*

CDC: https://www.cdc.gov/

National Institutes of Health: https://www.nih.gov/health-information

National Library of Medicine: https://medlineplus.gov/

U.S. Preventative Services Task Force: https://www.uspreventiveservicestaskforce.org/uspstf/topic_search_results?topic_status=P&age_group%5B%5D=66&searchterm=

# CHAPTER 7

# Dollars and Sense

■ ■ ■

Now that you know how to stay younger in body, mind, and spirit, it's time to focus on having enough money to enjoy your retirement years. Life expectancy has increased significantly over the past hundred years, so you will hopefully enjoy a longer retirement than your parents, and certainly longer than the retirement (if any) of your grandparents. According to the U.S. Centers for Disease Control and Prevention, life expectancy for all U.S. 65-year-olds is an additional 18.8 years. This was after dropping from 19.6 additional years in 2019, which was, hopefully, a temporary blip caused by Covid-19. So, assuming you are currently in good health, it would be wise to plan on funding a long retirement.

The 2021 Retirement Confidence Survey by the Employee Benefit Research Institute and Greenwald & Associates indicated that over 70% of those currently working are at least *somewhat confident* that they will be able to live comfortably in retirement, 80% of current retirees feel *confident* they have enough money to live in comfort, and 33% of retirees felt *very confident* of their money situation. But all that is really important is whether or not *you* feel currently, or will feel in the future, that *you* will be able to live comfortably in retirement.

## Retirement by the Numbers: Basic Cheat Sheet for Being Prepared

If you're looking for the quick-and-dirty CliffsNotes approach to not running out of money in retirement, here is a summary of certain things you need to do to prepare financially. And, of course, the earlier you start, the better:

1. *Save, save, save.* How much of your salary should you put aside? Experts recommend at least 10% to 15% of your annual income, and more if you're closer to retirement and haven't put much aside already. If you've hit your 40s or 50s and have not started saving, you may need to save two or three times as much from each paycheck.

2. *Establish an emergency fund of three to six months.* Remember, it's for an emergency . . . and the newest electronic gadget does not qualify as an emergency.

3. *Pay down debt.* If you're struggling with debt, personal finance guru Dave Ramsey suggests a technique called the "debt snowball." List your debts from lowest to highest. Pay the minimum balances on all debts except the smallest, and pay down the smallest debt first. Once you've rid yourself of the lowest debt, pay off the next lowest one. Continue until all debt is gone. Some experts suggest you tackle the debt with the highest interest rate first, but Ramsey's idea is that you'll feel better getting rid of the smallest debt first, and feel more motivated to continue to pay down the rest of your debts. Paying off the smallest debt is the beginning of your "snowball," and once it gets rolling, there's no stopping you! Once your debt is paid down, pay all your credit cards in full each month.

4. *Pay yourself first for retirement.* Put your retirement savings before your kids' or grandkids' college education. They have more time than you do to save for their own future, and can work, take out loans, or attend a community college for the

first two years. Of course, if you have the excess money to pay for their education, it's a great investment in their future.

5. *Contribute the maximum allowed to your retirement savings program at work.* At a minimum, contribute enough to get the maximum employer match available.

6. *Consider where and how you'll live.* Will you stay in place or do you want to move after retiring? Will you need to downsize or move to an area that costs less? And, think about how and where you eat. It can make a huge difference in your bottom line. In addition to eating healthier by preparing meals at home, recognize that the average cost of a home-cooked meal is about $4.30, while the average cost of a restaurant-served meal is about $20. Meal kit costs average about three times more than cooking at home, and delivery from a restaurant is about five times as expensive. Adjusting your eating costs can go a long way toward making your money stretch, both when saving for retirement and when you retire.

7. *Be flexible about work.* You may need to work in retirement, even if it's part-time (see Chapter 3 for ideas). Match your retirement lifestyle to your retirement income.

8. *Stay healthy.* Many healthcare costs are related to lifestyle, and we have control over them.

9. *Postpone taking Social Security, if you can.* Don't take Social Security until you reach your full retirement age (66 to 67 years old, depending on the year you were born). Wait until age 70, if possible, in order to maximize your monthly benefit.

10. *Review on a regular basis.* Review your financial status on a regular basis, getting professional help if necessary. Descriptions of the various financial specialties are included later in this chapter. Hiring a Certified Financial Planner (CFP) or a Certified Public Accountant (CPA) with a Personal Financial Specialist (PFS) designation will often be your best bet for all-around financial assistance.

## Expenses in Retirement

The first step in planning for your finances in retirement is to determine just how much money you will need to fund the lifestyle you want. Financial planners often estimate retirement expenses will be 70% to 80% of your preretirement expenses. The U.S. Bureau of Labor Statistics did a survey of Consumer Expenditures and determined the average retiree household (led by someone 65 or older) spends approximately $50,000 per year compared to the average of all households (retired or not) of approximately $63,000 per year (note that $50,000 is approximately 80% of the average preretirement expenses of $63,000, as mentioned above).

Even though ballpark estimates are interesting, and maybe even a starting point, *your* retirement expenses will be determined by the lifestyle you want to have in retirement. Are you going to sell your home and move? Will you be downsizing or maybe moving to a more expensive area – think beach areas, ski areas, or maybe other resort-type locations or expensive cities? Or will you be aging in place? Will you be taking up an expensive hobby, or possibly traveling the world? Do you plan on funding your grandchildren's education?

Your work-related expenses will surely disappear (unless you plan on working in retirement). Some of these expenses could be major, such as your contributions to a Section 401(k) plan, Social Security taxes, business clothes, commuting, and lunches (although as we know, Covid-19 has upended a number of the original working models). On the other hand, with 168 hours a week to do as you please, your non-work-related expenses will likely increase as you engage in activities that you previously did not have time to undertake. Your housing expenses will stay pretty static, unless you plan on moving, in which case many of your housing expenses will go up or down, and you will need to estimate your new mortgage payment, property taxes, insurance, utilities, landscaping, maintenance, repairs, etc. The worksheet at the end of this chapter titled "Compare Your Housing Costs" will be useful in this exercise.

Will you be eating out more, with a resulting increase in your food and entertainment expenses? Don't forget about healthcare, as you will no longer have employer-provided health insurance. You will likely be covered under Medicare, but that is not free, either, and you have to be at least 65 to qualify. There is a discussion of Medicare costs later in this chapter.

It may be easiest to estimate expenses on a monthly basis, and then add in large one-time costs, such as buying a new car, replacing your washer and dryer, repainting your house, annual vacations, and major travel costs.

You can start this planning process by preparing a summary of your current expenses category by category, and then make your best estimate of what they will be once you retire. The worksheet at the end of this chapter titled "How Much Do You Need for Retirement" will help you. There are other worksheets available online that can help you work through the estimate of your retirement expenses; a good one you might try is from Vanguard at https://personal.vanguard.com/us/insights/retirement/tool/retirement-expense-worksheet. Completing a worksheet envisioning your ideal retirement is a great way to really get a handle on what your finances will look like. You may be pleased with the results – that the costs are in line with your expected resources, or you might find you need to cut back some on your plans – possibly moving some of your "bucket list" items to a "chuck it" list.

If you are not happy with the results after completing the worksheet, go back and take a hard look at each of your expenses and separate them into needs versus wants. Needs are necessities such as shelter, food, healthcare, clothing – those things you must have. Wants are everything else that you can live without, including items such as vacations, a new car on a regular basis, a second home, designer clothes and jewelry, or maybe it is a bigger home or more expensive car than what you need. Before removing the wants, consider reducing the cost of your needs. You might downsize your home, or perhaps move to an area with a lower cost of living (how about a state with low taxes – see Chapter 8 for more about this), or consider home sharing, and then recalculate how the total costs match up with your projected resources. For a helpful chart of the cost-of-living indices by state for 2021, go to https://worldpopulationreview.com/state-rankings/cost-of-living-index-by-state.

Your projected assets and income at retirement will need to fund your expected lifestyle. If they don't, you will need to change your lifestyle to one that is more modest, or increase your projected assets and/or income. Assets might be increased by working longer before retiring (or if you're lucky, a nice inheritance from someone), and income might be increased by working part-time in retirement (perhaps refer back to Chapter 3, "Working in Retirement: It's not an Oxymoron").

### Don't Forget About Inflation

The cost of almost everything increases each year and, over time, the cumulative impact of this can be significant. If you plan your retirement based on your currently projected expenses and ignore the impact of the inflationary increases, you will surely be missing the boat. For example, $100 in purchasing power in 1979 would require approximately $375 in 2021, thus an overall price increase of approximately 275% over 42 years. During that period the annual inflation rates ranged from a high of 13.5% in 1980 to a low of −0.36% in 2020. It is hard to know what the rate will be in the future (and the rate in 2021 is looking like it will be close to 6%, although this is expected to be a temporary blip caused by Covid-19-related issues), but based on the historical rates in the United States an annual rate of around 3% may be realistic. If an item costs $200 in 2022, it would cost $361 in 2042 if the inflation rate was 3% each year. This is the rate I use in my personal retirement planning.

### Don't Ignore the Cost of Healthcare

Healthcare costs will be a major expense in retirement. So, it is not surprising that according to a Harris and Age Wave 2021 poll, healthcare costs, including long-term care, is the greatest worry of

52% of retirees and 66% of preretirees. According to the Fidelity Retiree Health Care Cost Estimate, a couple retiring at age 65 in 2021 may have $300,000 in healthcare costs during the balance of their lifetimes. Yes, a lot of your healthcare costs will be covered by insurance, but medical insurance is not cheap and it does not cover everything. (And, refer back to Chapter 6 to be sure you're doing all you can to remain healthy in mind, spirit, and body.)

Most of us will be eligible for Medicare once we turn 65, as long as we worked in Medicare-covered employment for at least 10 years and are a citizen or permanent resident of the United States. If you are not eligible, you may be able to purchase Medicare coverage if you are age 65 or older and a U.S. citizen or legal resident who has lived in the U.S. for at least five years. Medicare is not free, and it does not cover everything. Original Medicare has Part A (Hospital Insurance), Part B (Medical Insurance), and Part D (Medicare Prescription Drug Coverage). Most U.S. citizens and legal residents do not pay a monthly premium for Part A, while Part B has a standard monthly premium of $170.10 per person in 2022. Original Medicare Parts A and B are provided by the U.S. government. If you want drug coverage, you can purchase a Medicare Prescription Drug Plan from a number of insurance companies. The drug plans are different from one another in what drugs they cover and how much of the cost is covered. The monthly premium for these plans is set by the insurance companies with premiums ranging from under $10 a month to over $100 a month depending on where you live and how comprehensive a plan you buy. A good place to review the Medicare Part D plans available in your area, including their estimated costs based on both their monthly premium and the cost of the prescription drugs you are taking, is at www.medicare.gov.

Original Medicare plans have deductibles and copays. Although there are no out-of-pocket maximums, a lot of what would otherwise be out-of-pocket costs can be covered by purchasing Medicare Supplement Insurance (generally referred to as Medigap). The deductible for 2022 is $1,556 plus coinsurance for each benefit period for Part A Hospital Insurance. For Part B Medical Insurance, the annual deductible in 2022 is $233, after which there is a 20% coinsurance requirement. The annual deductible for Part D Drug coverage is $480 in 2022.

Many insurance companies offer Medigap plans to help cover the deductibles and copays of Medicare Parts A and B. There are a number of different plans, designated by alphabetic letters, starting with A (Basic) and going through the alphabet to letter N (Co-pay Plan). Each plan has different coverages, so it is important to look at the details of the various plans. A good place to see the individual plans, what they cover, and what they might cost is at www.medicare .gov. This site has a convenient chart comparing the coverage of the various plans, and you can also click on an individual plan to get the specific details of what is covered.

It is important to understand that the plans offered by the various insurance companies are the same – in other words Plan A at UnitedHealthcare would have the same coverage as Plan A at Anthem – but the monthly premiums can vary quite a bit, so it is worth shopping around once you decide which plan you want. The Medicare website shows the range of prices for each plan, with the current lowest starting price in 2022 of available plans starting at $193 per month for Plan C, and at $60 a month for Plan K for a 65-year-old nonsmoking male in my ZIP code.

A couple who selects a medium-priced drug plan costing $50 per month and a Medigap Plan C will pay a bit over $9,900 in premiums in 2022. If the same couple did not buy a Medigap Plan or a Drug Plan, they will pay about $4,100 in premiums in 2022 – but will be at risk for higher out-of-pocket costs for medical services and for drugs, because of the coverage limitations, deductibles, and copays of Medicare, as well as the absence of out-of-pocket maximums.

An alternative to having Original Medicare is to have a Medicare Advantage Plan, which is offered by a number of insurance companies. In 2021, 42% of Medicare participants used a Medicare Advantage Plan and it is expected that this percentage will continue to rise. These plans often offer coverage for medical costs that Original Medicare does not cover, and potentially at a lower cost. Examples of these extra coverages offered by some of the Medicare Advantage Plans are prescription drugs, gym memberships, vision, hearing, and dental services. Each Medicare Advantage Plan has its own rules about what is covered, as well as the out-of-pocket maximum costs. If you purchase a Medicare Advantage Plan, you will still pay the Original Medicare Part B premium of $170.10 per month in 2022 to Medicare, in addition to the premium for the Medicare Advantage Plan, which will vary from plan to plan and often can be zero. However, you will not need (and cannot purchase) Medigap, and generally not a Medicare Prescription Drug Plan (Part D), either, if you purchase a Medicare Advantage Plan.

A major difference between Original Medicare and Medicare Advantage Plans is that under Medicare you can go to any doctor or hospital in the United States that takes Medicare. This can be a significant issue when you, for example, need surgery and want to go to a specific surgeon based on reputation or recommendations from your friends. Medicare Advantage Plans generally require that you use doctors and other providers who are in the plan's network and service areas for the lowest costs, and some plans won't cover services from providers outside the plan's network and service area. Another major difference is that with Medicare you can go directly to a specialist for a specific medical issue, whereas with Medicare Advantage you would generally need to go to your primary care doctor first to get a referral to a specialist.

Medicare pays a fixed amount for your care each month to the companies offering Medicare Advantage Plans, and the plans must follow rules set by Medicare. The insurance company may also charge an additional premium, although interestingly enough, many insurance companies do not charge a premium and some plans (called Premium Reduction Giveback Plans) even offer a refund of some or all of the $170.10 Medicare monthly premium you pay to the government. In the end, however, the total cost to you will vary based on how comprehensive the plan is, what it covers, and what your out-of-pocket costs will be. By way of example, The Medicare site at www.medicare.gov shows thirty-four Medicare Advantage plans available in my area, many of which have no monthly premium, other than the $170.10 per month, which is actually paid to Medicare. Information on each plan is also provided. The plans that do have premiums charged from $18.50 per month to $105 per month. The plans showed a wide range of out-of-pocket maximums, starting as low as $2,500 (in network only) to a high of $7,550 in network and $10,000 for combined in and out of network. The plans have different coverages from each other, so you would have to look at each plan to see which one, if any, meets your needs. It can take some time to sift through the options, but it's worth it to get the best plan for you.

Two final cost issues with respect to Medicare are (1) the high-income premium adjustments, and (2) the need to sign up for coverage when you turn 65. The high-income premium adjustments, which are imposed for both Original Medicare and Medicare Advantage plans, apply in 2022 if your joint modified gross income (adjusted gross income shown on your income tax return for 2020 – note the one-year lag – plus interest income from municipal bonds) exceeds $182,000 ($91,000 if single). There are five brackets, each resulting in a higher premium adjustment for Medicare Parts B and D, with the top bracket applicable to incomes over $750,000 ($500,000 if single). The lowest bracket increases the monthly premium for Part B (Medical Insurance) in 2022 by $68.00 per person and for Part D by $12.40 per person. The highest bracket increases the monthly premium by $408.20 per person for Part B and for Part D by $77.90. So, worst case (not to imply that those income levels can be said to be worst cases), a couple with income over $750,000 have a total premium increase for Medical Insurance of approximately $9,800 and $1,870 for Prescription Drug Coverage. Assuming they selected a medium-priced Prescription Drug Coverage and Plan F Medigap coverage, their total premiums will be approximately $21,600 in 2022 for Original Medicare coverage – Ouch!

You should file for Medicare benefits three months before reaching age 65. If you are already receiving Social Security, you will be automatically signed up for Medicare Parts A and B (otherwise you have to apply); however, since Part B is not free, you have the option of turning it down. Unless you or your spouse are still working and have qualifying health insurance and/or drug insurance based on your job(s), you will generally have to pay a penalty if you wait beyond age 65 to apply for Medicare. The penalty for not getting Part B Medical Insurance when you're first eligible is an increase in your monthly premium of 10% for each 12-month period you could have had Part B, but didn't sign up. The penalty for late enrollment of Part D Drug Coverage is an extra 1% for each month (12% per year) you waited to sign up. These penalties can be significant, especially since they are lifetime penalties. So, the lesson here is to enroll in Medicare when you first qualify, unless you have creditable coverage, such as coverage from an employer, former employer, or a union.

I was not taking any prescription drugs when I first became eligible for Medicare, so I signed up for the cheapest Prescription Drug Coverage I could find (it is currently under $8 per month), just to avoid paying the late enrollment penalty if I eventually need drug coverage later on in life. (And, fortunately, I'm still not taking any prescription drugs.)

Finally (whew), although you generally need to sign up for Medicare when you first become eligible, there is an Open Enrollment Period each year – in 2021 it is between October 15 and December 7 – during which you can join, switch, or drop a Medicare Health Plan or a Medicare Advantage Plan. Additionally, between January 1 and March 31 each year, if you are enrolled in a Medigap plan, you can switch to a different Medigap plan or back to Original Medicare and join a Medicare Prescription Drug plan. It is important that you use the Open Enrollment Period each year to review your coverages because the coverages and prices change for Medicare Part D (Prescription Drug Plan), and Medicare Advantage Plans. You may also want to consider changing your Medigap from one plan to another to adjust coverage, or from one provider to another that charges a lower premium (recall that the coverage under the various Medigap plans is the same from provider to provider but the premiums are different). Go to www.medicare.gov and sign in (or create an account if you don't already have one) to view the various plans and prices available to you. The site is very user friendly and allows you to put up several alternative plans on your computer screen and compare them. My husband and I just completed that process and saw that our prescription drug plan (we were both on the same plan) was increasing the monthly premium, and decreasing its drug coverage. We were able to switch to a different provider and reduce our combined annual drug cost by approximately $1,600 for next year (including both the monthly premium as well as the expected drug costs for the year for the prescriptions we entered onto the site).

I also saw that the cost for my Medigap Plan F was still the lowest of all the Plan Fs in my area.

## Long-Term Care Insurance

Chapter 5 addressed continuing care retirement communities (CCRCs). However, maybe your hope is to stay in your home and obtain assistance from family and friends, which is how the majority of people in the U.S. receive assistance. A detailed summary of the costs on a state-by-state basis for homemaker and health-aide services, community and assisted living services, and care at a nursing home facility, based on a 2020 survey by Genworth, can be found at https://pro.genworth.com/riiproweb/productinfo/pdf/282102.pdf. To summarize the highlights of the survey: In the United States, the median cost for homemaker services was $23.50 per hour and $24 per hour for a home health aide, with a range of $17 per hour in Louisiana to over $31 per hour for each of those services in the state of Washington. The median cost for living in an assisted living facility was $4,300 per month and in a nursing home facility $7,756 per month for a semiprivate room, and $8,821 per month for a private room. Again, these prices vary a lot depending on the location – Delaware was the priciest state at $6,690 per month, and Missouri the lowest at $3,000 for an assisted living facility. The median monthly cost for a semiprivate room ranged from an eye popping $37,413 in Alaska and (oddly) slightly less at $36,378 for a private room (making it pretty clear you would not pick Alaska as the place to go), to a low in Texas at $5,019 for a semiprivate room and in Missouri at $5,749 for a private room.

According to the Department of Health and Human Services Administration on Aging (AOA), long-term care assistance will be needed by about 70% of people 65 years old or older, with the average woman needing it for 3.7 years and the average man for 2.2 years. This includes care at home (either by family members, friends, or paid assistance) as well as care in an assisted living community or a skilled nursing facility. On average, 37% of people will need care in a facility but only for about a year (I guess that's the good news/bad news?). As a general rule, Medicare will not cover long-term care, except for limited periods following a hospital inpatient stay of at least three days (for more detailed information on this go to https://www.medicare.gov/Pubs/pdf/10153-Medicare-Skilled-Nursing-Facility-Care.pdf).

Although family and friends generally provide the majority of care people receive in the United States, it is clear from the costs just outlined that it could be expensive if you need to pay for it.

Medicaid does provide some basic long-term care needs, but you pretty much have to be at a poverty level, in terms of income and assets, in order to qualify, and the state will have a claim on any remaining assets remaining after your death, or after the death of your spouse if he or she survives you.

So, should you consider long-term care insurance? It is not for everyone, and it may well be that if you need it, you may not be able to afford it, and if you can afford it, you may not need it. According to the American Association for Long-Term Care Insurance, 7.5 million Americans had some form of long-term care insurance as of

January 1, 2020 and 55% of policyholders purchased the policy between age 55 and 65, 27% before age 55 and 18% after age 65.

Long-term care insurance covers care within day care or assisted living facilities, including skilled nursing services and hospice. Some policies will cover in-home care, including housekeeping and cooking, whereas other policies exclude them. In order to qualify for in-home benefits under these policies you must be unable to perform at least two of the following daily living activities, without assistance:

- Bathing
- Eating
- Dressing
- Transferring
- Toileting
- Continence

You might also trigger the policy benefits if you have severe cognitive impairment (dementia, Alzheimer's, etc.). Policies may cover preexisting conditions, but they will likely exclude them for a specific time period after the effective date of your policy.

The cost of a long-term care insurance policy will depend on your gender, age, and health when you purchase the policy, plus the maximum daily benefit amount and the period (days, months, or years) that the services will be covered as well as the maximum total benefit. Some policies have inflation protection and others do not. Importantly, the policies will usually have a so-called "elimination period," the period during which you are responsible for the full cost of your care, before the policy benefits start. The length of the elimination period will be an important factor in determining the cost of the policy, because the longer it is the cheaper the premiums will be. An elimination period of 90 days is common, but shorter elimination periods are available.

Insurance companies have been shying away from offering these policies, due to a lack of profitability, and those still offering them generally do not have fixed premiums like life insurance; the premiums could rise year after year, and could even become cost prohibitive, forcing you to have to cancel the policy. Some companies are now offering hybrid policies, which link permanent life insurance with long-term care insurance, and you can get a fixed premium for these policies.

When shopping for long-term care coverage, you should at least ask for a history of rate increases by the insurance companies you are considering. As far as companies you might consider, Investopedia listed the following companies as the best in 2021 for long-term care insurance:

- Best Overall: New York Life
- Best for Discounts: Mutual of Omaha
- Best for No Waiting Period: Lincoln Financial Group
- Best for Flexible Options: Pacific Life
- Best for Easy Benefits Payout: Brighthouse Financial

An easy-to-use calculator to get a handle on the cost of long-term care insurance can be found at https://www.ltcfeds.com/tools/premium-calculator. For example, it shows that a policy paying $200 per day for five years ($365,000 maximum) for a 55-year-old person would cost $297.19 per month. This policy has an automatic compound inflation option, which means the daily benefit amount and lifetime maximum increases 3% per year with no increase in the premium. The same policy purchased at age 65 would be $559.50 per month.

As you can see, the older you are when you purchase a long-term care policy the more it will cost.

So, should you consider long-term care insurance? The answer is yes, you should *consider* it, and at least determine what it would cover, how much it would cost, whether you can afford it, and what alternatives (self-pay, help from others, etc.) you have. If nothing else, it may give you peace of mind that there will be some money to take care of your health as you age. However, it is basically a gamble that the cost of your care covered by long-term care insurance will exceed the cost of the policy over the years. If you have significant assets and can afford the care without an insurance policy, it may not be a good investment, because you can afford the cost risk without significant hardship on either you or your family. Otherwise, unless Medicaid is your plan, it may come down to trying to predict your needs based on your current health and whether you can afford the premiums.

## Saving for Retirement

Before looking at managing your investments for retirement, you need to determine how much money you will need to retire to have the lifestyle you desire. There are a number of calculators that can help you in this process. If you do a Google search for "free retirement calculators," you'll get more than 37,000 possibilities. I tested the AARP retirement calculator at www.aarp.org/retirementcalculator using the following scenario: Eric and Jane, both 50 years old, plan to retire at 67, which is their full retirement age for Social Security, and expect to live at about the same financial level in retirement as they do currently. Eric has a salary of $80,000, savings of $150,000 and expects monthly Social Security benefits of $1,800. Jane's salary is $50,000, she has savings of $90,000 and expects monthly Social Security benefits of $1,000. The assumptions in the model (which can be changed) were a 6% return on savings before retirement and 3.6% return thereafter; annual salary increases for their remaining 17 working years of 2.5%, and with Eric living 20 years in retirement and Jane 23 years. In order to fund their retirement, the calculator determined that they would need to save about 14.5% of their combined salaries each year. Of course, these are all just assumptions, but it gives a good starting point. In reality they could earn more (or less) than 6% per year on their investments (before retirement) and could retire before or after age 67 (see discussion later in this chapter about Social Security and the impact of deferring the beginning date of payments). Alternatively, they could adjust their retirement lifestyle plans by, for example, downsizing their residence, possibly moving to a lower-cost location, maybe working part time, and so forth. Or, perhaps they could save more, or earn a bigger return on their investments and adjust their retirement lifestyle to something more exotic or, better yet, enjoy a bigger margin of comfort between their retirement income and expenses. However, remember the EBRI surveys in Chapter 2 which find, year after year, that many people end up leaving the workforce earlier than they planned, because they became ill, had to care for someone who was ill, were downsized or fired, and so forth. So plan for the best but prepare for the unexpected.

### You Might Want to Use a Financial Advisor

Some find the world of finance fascinating, and a challenge they are ready to tackle. However, for many, the thought of handling our own investments and/or retirement planning is daunting, overwhelming, or maybe just boring, and a job for which we need/want the services of a professional advisor. According to a 2020 study by Northwestern Mutual, only 29% of adults in the United States work with a financial advisor, although 71% admit that their financial planning needs improvement. The closer you get to retirement the more often you will likely be deluged by mailings and emails from stockbrokers, accountants, financial planners, Social Security planners, insurance salespeople, annuity purveyors, and on and on. Often there are group luncheon or dinner presentations. I have found that attending some of these are an informative and fun way to learn more about what help is out there (and it often is accompanied by a nice meal!), but in the final analysis it is the credentials and expertise of the advisor that are most important. Sticking with those who have received the appropriate training and passed the requisite tests to receive relevant professional certifications is the best course of action.

There are two kinds of financial advisors, and they have different professional standards for their advice. Financial advisors who are fiduciaries are required to act in your best interest and have a duty of care and a duty of loyalty to you. They should be recommending the lowest-cost solutions to meet your needs. Financial advisors who are not fiduciaries are generally held to a suitability standard of care that requires only that the recommended investments are suitable to your needs and circumstances, and may allow the advisor to recommend an investment more costly than a similar investment and that produces a higher commission to the advisor. When you are interviewing a prospective financial advisor, you should ask if he or she is a fiduciary and, if not, why not?

Financial advisors can be compensated by charging you a fee for their services or receive commissions on the products (insurance, annuities, etc.) you purchase through them, or by a combination of both. Some are working for a brokerage firm selling stocks and bonds, but could also be selling insurance, annuities, or similar financial products.

Financial advisors often have lots of initials after their name. It is important to know what these initials mean and which may be more important to you.

- A Certified Financial Planner (CFP) is probably the most recognized credential in financial planning. CFPs must have a bachelor's degree and complete additional coursework through a CFP Registered Program. The coursework includes, but is not limited to, financial planning, investment planning, insurance planning, estate planning, and tax planning. They must pass a six-hour board exam, have 4,000 to 6,000 hours of professional experience, and meet continuing education requirements.
- A Certified Public Accountant (CPA) has a four-year college degree and at least 150 hours of coursework. They are recognized for their expertise in accounting, auditing, and taxes. They must pass a Uniform CPA Exam, which covers four areas: business environment and concepts, financial accounting and reporting, auditing, and regulation. Although

the exam is standard throughout the United States the various states set other requirements, such as work experience and continuing education. A CPA is permitted to represent taxpayers before the IRS.

- A Personal Financial Specialist (PFS) is an additional specialty for a CPA and is awarded by the American Institute of Certified Public Accountants. This designation requires extensive work experience and passing an exam on personal financial planning, including the areas of tax, estates, retirement, investments, insurance, employee benefits, elder planning and several other areas.
- A Chartered Financial Analyst (CFA) must have a four-year college degree and four or more years of professional work experience, of which at least 50% must be directly involved in the investment decision-making process or producing a product that impacts that process. They also must pass a three-part exam over a four-year period, each part taking up to 300 hours of preparation.
- An Enrolled Agent (EA) is also permitted to represent taxpayers before the IRS. They must either have experience as former IRS employees or pass a three-part exam on business and individual tax returns. They also must complete continuing education requirements.

There are lots of other designations, such as a Life and Annuity Certified Professional (LACP), a Certified Annuity Specialist (CAS), and a Chartered Life Underwriter (CLU).

A financial advisor can perform a variety of services, including preparing a personal financial plan to help you reach your retirement goals, recommendations on how much you need to save to reach your retirement goal, the asset allocation you should use for your investment portfolio, the withdrawal pattern you should use when spending your savings, the ins and outs of maximizing Social Security benefits, and so forth. Although it is hard to quantify in dollars and cents the value of using an investment advisor, Vanguard has given it a shot in a detailed 28-page analysis, intended for the use of its investment advisors, which you can find at https://advisors.vanguard.com/iwe/pdf/ISGQVAA.pdf. In short, Vanguard concludes that their "advisors can potentially add about 3% in net returns per year by using the Vanguard Advisor's 'Alpha' framework." Not sure if this is believable or not, but 3% per year over a lengthy period of years is huge.

There are also so-called robo-advisors, which are computer based and use algorithms and software to help you choose and manage your investments, including regular rebalancing of your portfolio. You input information, based on a questionnaire, about your current financial situation and future goals (much like the information you would provide to any financial planner), and the robo-advisor uses this to automatically invest your assets and to offer advice. The recommended investments will generally be mutual funds and/or exchange-traded funds (ETFs) using passive indexing strategies (discussed later in this chapter), and not individual stocks and bonds. There is very little, if any, human interaction, but the cost is much lower than it would be using the services of a traditional financial planner.

Financial advisors charge either a flat fee per year, an hourly fee based on the services they provide, or an annual fee expressed as a percentage of your assets they have under management (AUM), and which ranges from about 0.2% to about 1.5% of your invested portfolio. Robo-advisors charge at the lower end of that range, and traditional advisors at the higher end. For either traditional or robo, the higher the amount of assets invested the lower the percentage. If the advisor is charging on an hourly basis, the rates should range between $200 and $400 per hour. If the planner is engaged to prepare a financial plan for a flat fee, the fee should range from about $1,000 to $3,000.

Asking your friends and acquaintances is a good way to locate financial professionals in your area. Your attorney or accountant would also be good potential sources for a recommendation and referral. Another way would be to contact the National Association of Personal Financial Advisors by phone at 847-483-5400 or by using their web-based advisor locator service at https://www.napfa.org/find-an-advisor. If you are looking for a certified financial planner (CFP), contact the Certified Financial Planner Board of Standards at www.cfp.net and click on "Find a CFP Professional." If a Certified Public Accountant who is also a Personal Financial Specialist is what you are looking for, contact the American Institute of Certified Public Accountants (AICPA) at https://www.aicpa.org/forthepublic/financial-planning-resources.html and click on "Find a CPA/PFS." Once you locate a few possible candidates, make an appointment to meet with them to see if there is a good fit, both in their expertise, personality, and fee structure. As I noted at the beginning of this chapter, a CFP or a CPA with the Personal Financial Specialist designation would be a good first choice, and if you could locate an advisor with both professional designations it, would be a homerun.

## Funding Your Retirement

Once you have a handle on your expected expenses in retirement it is time to consider how you will pay for them. Although most workers in the United States will receive a Social Security benefit when they retire, this will likely not be adequate to completely fund the retirement you desire. You will need to supplement with funds from other sources, such as from an employer pension, an Individual Retirement Account (IRA), a Section 401(k) or 403(b) account, investments, a reverse mortgage, or even by working part time. Let's look at these different ways to fund your retirement.

## Social Security

Social Security is the major source of retirement income for most of us, and on average it amounts to approximately 40% of retirees' pre-retirement income. In 2021, the maximum Social Security benefit at the full retirement age of 66 was $3,148 a month, but hardly anyone actually received that much for a number of reasons, including retiring and starting benefits before full retirement age, not earning the maximum amounts subject to Social Security tax for the 35 years includable in the determination of their benefit, or both. The maximum benefit at age 62 was just $2,324 per month and the average benefit was $1,543 per month.

In order to qualify for Social Security, the general rule (there are other rules in the case of disability or blindness) is that you must be age 62 or older, a U.S. citizen or legal resident, have earned at least 40 Social Security credits, which you earn when you work, and pay Social Security taxes either on your wages or on your self-employment income. Credits are based on the amount of your taxed earnings and you can earn up to a maximum of four credits in a calendar year – thus it takes at least 10 years of employment to qualify. The amount of earnings needed for a credit in 2021 was $1,470 per year, or $5,880 per year to earn the maximum of four credits for the year. The earnings amount needed can change and has been increasing over time.

An oversimplification of how your Social Security benefit will be calculated is that it is based on an average of your indexed monthly earnings (indexing is explained below) subject to Social Security tax over the 35 years in which you had the highest earnings – and yes, if you have not worked for the full 35 years, you will have some zeros in the calculation. This may not be as bad as it seems, as the ultimate calculation of your monthly benefit gives greater weight to lower average earnings than to higher average earnings, as explained later.

The indexing of your annual earnings over the years of your working career brings your prior years' earnings up to current values to reflect the general rise in the standard of living that occurred during your working lifetime. For example, $32,400 of earnings in 1982 would be indexed to $108,456 for a worker born in 1956 and retiring in 2022. Once the annual earnings have been indexed for each year, the average of the indexed earnings for the highest-earning 35 years is used to determine your benefit at your full retirement age (which is currently between 66 and 67, depending on the year you were born). The calculation of the benefit is based on separating your average monthly earnings into three groups, which are adjusted each year for changes in the National Wage Index. For workers reaching age 62 in 2021 the first group is $996, for which you will get a monthly benefit of 90%, the second group is the next $5,006, for which you will get a benefit of 32%, and the final group is the rest of your total average monthly earnings, for which you will get 15%.

The total is your monthly benefit at full retirement age. As an example, showing how the calculation gives greater weight to lower earnings than to higher earnings, assume Ralph P. has indexed monthly earnings of $60,000 ($5,000 per month). His monthly benefit at full retirement age would be $2,178. If his indexed monthly earnings had been $90,000 ($7,500 per month), his monthly Social Security benefit would have only increased by $545. The increase in his indexed earnings was 50% but the increase in his benefit was only 25%.

The good news about trying to figure out what your Social Security benefit will be is that you can go to https://www.ssa.gov/myaccount/statement.html, set up an account, and then have access to a statement that shows your expected Social Security benefit at age 62 and for each age thereafter to age 70. The calculation of the benefit is based on your lifetime earnings subject to Social Security taxes, and with future taxable earnings projected based on your current earnings. You should also use this as an opportunity to check your lifetime earnings, which are listed on a year-by-year basis. The statement also includes information on how to report an error in your earnings record.

If you have not set up a "My Social Security" account, the Social Security Administration will mail the statement to you three months before your birthday each year, starting with the year you turn age 60, up to the year you file for Social Security benefits.

Be aware that some people will have their calculated benefit reduced or eliminated, under the Windfall Elimination Provision (WEP) or the Government Pension Offset (GPO) rule. WEP can apply if you worked for an employer that did not withhold Social Security taxes from your salary, such as a foreign employer or a government agency, and you are getting a pension from that work. The rule is applied by reducing the 90% of your first $996 averaged monthly earnings to as low as 40% in calculating your Social Security benefit, which would reduce your monthly benefit by as much as $498. There is a special rule that could soften or eliminate this benefit reduction based on how many years, if any, that you had income which was subject to Social Security taxes.

GPO applies when you are entitled to Social Security spousal or widow benefits and are also receiving a federal, state or local government pension based on your own work for which you did not pay Social Security taxes. It can reduce your monthly Social Security benefit by two thirds of your monthly government pension. Thus, for example, if you are getting a $1,200 per month government pension, up to two-thirds of that, or $800, will be deducted from your Social Security benefit. If you are eligible for a Social Security benefit of $1,000 per month, it will be reduced to $200. As you would expect, there are a number of exceptions to the application of GPO, including when the government pension you receive is not based on your own earnings, or when you paid Social Security taxes on your earnings during the last 60 months of government service.

If your full retirement age is 66 (you were born between 1943 and 1954), and you start collecting at age 62, your benefit will be reduced by 25%. If your full retirement age is 67 (born in 1960 or later), your benefit will be reduced by 30%. On the other hand, if you defer the starting date of Social Security until you are 70, your benefit will be increased by 24%. The increase, or decrease, in your benefit is calculated on a month-by-month basis. Thus, retiring at age 67½ will give you a bigger benefit than retiring at age 67. As an example of how this works, assume John D. will reach his full retirement age of 67 in 2027 at which time he would have a Social Security benefit of $25,000 per year. If he decides to retire at age 62, his benefit will be reduced to $17,500 and if he waits until age 70, his benefit will be increased to $31,000.

The decision to start receiving Social Security should be based on (1) whether you intend to keep working (in which case you should probably consider waiting to start Social Security); (2) your life expectancy, based on your health and family history of health (the longer you expect to live determines how many years you expect to collect the larger benefit earned by waiting, which you can compare to the number of Social Security payments you did not receive because you waited); and (3) whether you need the money more now or if you can wait until the future for the benefit to start. Obviously waiting has a huge impact on the benefit; in the preceding example, John D.'s benefit increases by over 77% by waiting until age 70 as compared to starting early at age 62.

Despite the benefit of deferring the start of Social Security, age 62 has historically been the most popular age for retirees to file for Social Security. However, an analysis in late 2021 by *The Washington Post* reported that, even though the number of new retirees nearly doubled during the pandemic, the number of workers that applied for Social Security benefits fell 5% during the year ending in September compared to the year before. A number of reasons were given for this significant drop, including the generous federal stimulus payments, a soaring stock market and home prices, as well as the closing of Social Security field offices, which forced seniors to apply online.

If you start collecting Social Security benefits before your full retirement age and continue to work, your benefits may be reduced. For 2022, the amount of the reduction is $1 for each $2 you earn over $19,560. For example, if you retire at age 62 in 2022, have a calculated Social Security benefit of $12,000 per year and continue to work for a salary of $24,000, a total of $2,220 ($185 per month) will be withheld from your monthly Social Security checks ($1 for each $2 of the $4,440 in salary you receive over the limit of $19,560). In the year you retire, a special rule applies to only count your compensation after you retire in applying this earnings test. Also, in the year you reach full retirement age, the amount of compensation you can receive with no reduction in your Social

Security benefit is increased to $51,960 and only compensation up to the month prior to the month you reach full retirement age is counted. So, in summary, if you work prior to reaching your full retirement age while receiving Social Security payments, and earn more than the aforementioned amounts, your monthly benefit will be reduced or even eliminated. However, all is not lost. Once you reach full retirement age your monthly benefit will increase to take into account the amounts that were withheld.

A spouse, who is at least age 62, of an individual who has filed for Social Security benefits can file to claim a spousal benefit once the marriage has lasted for at least a year. If his or her full retirement age is 66, the benefit at age 62 will be 30% of the spouse's benefit, whereas at age 66 it would be 50%. Spousal benefits do not increase by waiting past full retirement age to start collecting, and the maximum benefit at full retirement age is 50% of the spouse's benefit at his or her full retirement age.

A method some use to increase a couple's total Social Security benefits in a situation where both qualify for Social Security based on their own earnings record is to have the spouse, whom I will call John, and who has a lower benefit, file to start Social Security at age 62 or later and the other spouse, whom I will call Beth, and who has the higher Social Security benefit, defer filing to age 70. This ends up with a much larger benefit for Beth when she files at age 70 and still provides a Social Security benefit to the couple for the intervening eight years.

If you are a widow or widower and were married for at least nine months (with some exceptions), you can receive full Social Security benefits at your full retirement age based on your spouse's earnings record, or reduced benefits as early as age 60, if your deceased spouse worked long enough to qualify for Social Security, even if you remarried, as long as it was after you reached age 60.

If you are divorced and were married for at least 10 years, you can claim Social Security benefits based on your ex-husband's or ex-wife's earnings record up to as much as 50% of your ex-spouse's benefit at full retirement age, as long as you have not remarried.

If your ex-spouse is deceased, you can receive benefits up to as much as 100% of your deceased spouse's benefit as long as you were married for at least 10 years, and can remarry once you are age 60 or older and keep your divorced survivor benefit. In fact, multiple former spouses can collect Social Security benefits based on the same ex-spouse's earnings record, as long as they otherwise qualify. And surprisingly, the receipt of Social Security benefits by one or more qualifying ex-spouses does not impact the benefit of the ex-husband or ex-wife on whose earnings record the ex-spouse is filing. As you can see, Social Security can be the gift that keeps on giving!

Based on a U.S. Supreme Court's decision in 2015 that same-sex couples could marry, the Social Security Administration recognizes these marriages for purposes of eligibility for spousal benefits. This recognition is now provided for same-sex marriages in the United States and, based on facts and circumstances, in various foreign countries. This still left open an issue for surviving same-sex spouses who were not able to marry in most states prior to the Supreme Court's decision and were being denied survivor Social Security benefits. This now seems to be a resolved issue, based on the Biden administration deciding on November 1, 2021, not to appeal several court cases filed against the Social Security Administration that held that same-sex couples who were unable to meet the marriage requirements for survivor's benefits because of marriage laws that were discriminatory should be entitled to those benefits.

## Pensions and Defined Contribution Retirement Accounts

### Pensions

A 2021 survey by the National Institute on Retirement Security found that 77% of Americans feel that all employees should be entitled to a pension, where the employee gets a fixed monthly benefit for life, and in fact in times past many workers did retire with a pension. Under a pension plan the benefit, which may or may not adjust in future years for cost-of-living increases, is generally based on a formula that looks to the number of years the retiree worked for the employer and the average compensation over the last three or maybe five years of employment. The retiree does not have to worry about how to invest the retirement funds, as the employer is responsible for all of that. While there is some risk that the employer would go out of business and the plan would have insufficient assets to continue the payments, many pensions are covered by the Pension Benefit Guaranty Corporation (PBGC). This is a guarantee of up to a maximum annual amount that is determined under a formula, and which could be less than the pension benefit the employee was entitled to under the employer's plan. According to a 2021 report by the Congressional Research Service 81% of full-time state and local public workers participated in a defined benefit pension plan in 2020, but only about 14% of private sector employers did so. The employers in the private sector that do provide pensions are generally companies where there is a strong union and many of the companies are trying to get rid of the pension obligation, generally intending to replace it with a defined contribution retirement plan.

If you have a pension plan, you may have the option to take a lump-sum distribution from the plan when you retire, instead of getting the lifetime fixed monthly benefit. If you do have this option, you should look at it carefully to see which choice is better for you. You could, for example, take the funds and roll them over tax-free into an Individual Retirement Account (IRA) and purchase an annuity with some or all of the distribution to pay fixed payments to you for life. Although the current very low interest rates have the effect of increasing the cost of an annuity, they also have the effect of maximizing the lump-sum benefit you would receive, thus giving you more funds to use for the purchase. Alternatively, you could invest the funds on your own in the IRA. A lump-sum distribution may be especially attractive if your pension is larger than the PBGC guarantee and your employer is in a high-risk business because you would be removing the risk of losing some of your retirement benefit should your employer go bankrupt. See the discussion above on the PBGC guarantee, which may or may not be applicable to your pension, but you would be taking on the investment risk inherent in maximizing your retirement funds.

### Using Insurance as an Alternative to Electing a Joint and Survivor Benefit from a Pension Plan

If you are fortunate enough to have a pension plan at your place of employment, you will have to decide either to have the full pension paid out to you over your lifetime, or to have the same pension benefit – or alternatively a reduced pension benefit (e.g., 75% or 50% of your benefit) – paid to your spouse after your death, for the remainder of his or her lifetime. This is not an easy decision because your pension payments will be reduced if you select payment over both your lifetime and that of your spouse, and the cost could be as much as a 10–20% reduction depending on your age and the age of your spouse. The decision will have to be made around the time of your retirement and, once made, can usually not be changed. Thus, if a lifetime benefit is elected for you and your spouse, but your spouse dies first, your pension would have been reduced in anticipation of a benefit that never materialized. Hopefully, though, you're more saddened by the death of your spouse than the lower benefit!

One potential solution to this pension choice, for which the numbers work sometimes, but not always, is to elect the full pension for yourself, and nothing for your spouse, and purchase a life insurance policy on your life large enough to replace the loss of the pension benefit your spouse would have had if you elected to have the pension paid out over both lifetimes. If your spouse dies first, you could cancel the life insurance policy and stop paying the premiums (after mourning his or her demise, of course). Alternatively, if you die first, the proceeds of the policy would generate a lifetime income for your spouse. Keep in mind that the life insurance death benefits payable to your spouse would not be subject to either federal income or estate tax.

As an example of this strategy, consider Ralph T., and his spouse, Joyce, who is 10 years younger than Ralph. Ralph's employer has a pension plan that will pay him $36,000 per year ($3,000 per month) for the rest of his life when he retires at age 65. He has several choices for providing a continuing benefit for Joyce if he predeceases her and is considering the one that will pay her $27,000 ($2,250 per month) for the rest of her life. Under this election, Ralph's pension benefit will be reduced to $28,440 ($2,370 per month). In the event that Joyce predeceases Ralph, even if very early in his retirement, his pension benefit will continue at the reduced rate of $28,440. To protect Joyce, and assuming he is healthy, Ralph could use the extra $7,560 pension benefit ($36,000 less $28,440) to purchase a life-insurance policy that would pay enough to Joyce for her to purchase an annuity that would pay her $2,250 a month. Whether this idea works or not would depend on the pricing of life insurance policies at the time of his election decision.

## Defined Contribution Accounts

The most common defined contribution accounts are Individual Retirement Accounts (IRAs), which are opened up and funded by individual taxpayers at a financial institution, and Section 401(k) plans and Section 403(b) plans, both of which are set up by employers for the benefit of their employees.

Section 403(b) plans are used for employees of public schools and tax-exempt organizations, whereas Section 401(k) plans are used for employees of other entities. The funds going into these accounts usually come from employee contributions and are matched in part by employer contributions. This relieves the employer of the obligation to provide adequate future funds to pay a pension obligation, and puts the burden on the employee to contribute adequate amounts to his/her retirement account and to decide how those funds should be invested in order to help finance their retirement years. The amounts contributed to these accounts are not included in the Form W-2 of the employee as taxable wages, and are, therefore, what are described as pretax contributions. In 2022, the maximum amounts you can contribute to either of these accounts is $20,500 unless you are age 50 or older, in which case the limit is $27,000.

An Individual Retirement Account (IRA) is an account you can set up at a financial institution (e.g., banks, investment companies, and insurance companies) to help you save for retirement. With a Traditional IRA you will often be able to deduct your contributions for income tax purposes (see discussion later). In 2022, the maximum amount you could contribute to an IRA is the lesser of your earnings from employment or $6,000, unless you are age 50 or older, in which case the maximum is $7,000. Taxability of all earnings in the IRA is deferred until the funds are withdrawn, potentially many years later. You can invest the funds in the account in many types of investments, including individual stocks, mutual funds, exchange-traded funds, bonds, and certificates of deposit.

When you retire and take distributions from your Traditional IRA, Section 401(k) or Section 403(b) account, the amounts received are generally fully taxable. However, because of limits on how much of the amounts you contributed to the IRA can be deducted on your income tax return, distributions from IRAs for which there were nondeductible contributions will be partially nontaxable.

The general rule for distributions from a Traditional IRA, Section 401(k) or Section 403(b) account is that they should not start before either reaching age 59½ or retiring (there are some exceptions that allow earlier distributions), at which time the withdrawals would be taxable. There are also rules that require you to begin distributions at age 72 (certain exceptions apply) of amounts that are no less than those calculated based on IRS tables of life expectancy. Early withdrawals are subject to a 10% penalty, in addition to being included in taxable income. The penalty for failing to make sufficient distributions each year starting at age 72 is

50% of the required amount that was not distributed. This required distribution rule is covered more fully in Chapter 8.

Eventually these traditional retirement plans were enhanced by the introduction of a Roth feature, under which you could contribute after-tax dollars into the account and qualified distributions would be tax free after reaching age 59½ or after you have retired. Contributions to a Roth Section 401(k) or 403(b) plan would be included in your Form W-2 as taxable wages, whereas your contributions to a Roth IRA would be nondeductible. Many employers currently offer a Roth option to their Section 401(k) or Section 403(b) plans. In addition, individuals can set up their own Roth IRA, as an alternative to a Traditional IRA.

The decision to use a Roth account instead of a traditional one is not just based on your tax rate while working versus your expected tax rate in retirement, but also on the number of years the funds will be compounding in the account before withdrawal. And don't just assume your tax rate will be lower when you retire. Your tax rate in retirement may be lower than when you were working, but there is also the possibility that tax rates, in general, will be higher in the future. In fact, the significant tax rate reductions in the Tax Cuts and Jobs Act expire at the end of 2025, not to mention the possibility of tax rates being increased in the future to rates far higher than we have now, or even had before the Tax Cuts and Jobs Act was enacted. In any event the number of years that earnings in the funds will be compounding tax free in a Roth account should create a benefit that more than offsets the possibility of lower tax rates in the future. Another issue that could be important to some is that there is currently no requirement to distribute funds from your Roth IRA account, whereas there is a required minimum distribution amount for Traditional IRAs (as well as from Roth Section 401(k) and Section 403(b) accounts – even though qualified distributions from these accounts are not taxable), starting in the year you turn 72 years old. Of course, this would only be of importance if your retirement planning indicates that you would not need to distribute amounts to fund your retirement that are at least as great as your required minimum distribution amounts. Once you reach age 59½ there are no limits on the maximum amounts you can withdraw from these retirement accounts. Chapter 8 includes a discussion of the required minimum distribution amounts (RMD) and how to avoid the required distribution rules for a Roth Section 401(k) or 403(b) account. These are, perhaps, great issues to discuss with your financial advisor.

There are limits to how much you can contribute to your IRA, Section 401(k) or Section 403(b) account each year. First, and importantly, you cannot contribute more than the amount of your earned income, meaning income from providing services, such as salary, wages, and consulting fees. In addition, there are upper limits on the total amount you can contribute each year. Traditional IRAs (for which contributions are generally deductible on your tax return, and distributions are generally taxable) have a maximum amount you can contribute in 2022 of $6,000 plus $1,000 if you were age 50 or older for a total of $7,000. For Roth IRAs (for which contributions are not deductible on your tax return, and qualified distributions are not taxable), the general contribution limit is the same as for Traditional IRAs, but there is an additional limitation if your modified adjusted gross income exceeds $129,000 if single and $204,000 if married, with no contributions allowed if your income exceeds $144,000 if single and $214,000 if married.

Contributions to a Traditional IRA are deductible if neither you nor your spouse was covered by a retirement plan, such as a Section 401(k) plan or a pension plan at work. Otherwise, your deduction can be limited or eliminated. In 2022, the limitations apply if your modified adjusted gross income (essentially your total income with certain adjustments) exceeds $68,000 if single and $109,000 if married. Once your income reaches $78,000 if single or $129,000 if married, none of the contribution is deductible. If your deductions to a Traditional IRA would be limited by this rule, you probably should be using a Roth IRA instead, in order to make all future qualified retirement distributions tax free.

239

The contribution limit in 2022 for Section 401(k) plans and Section 403(b) plans, both Traditional and Roth, is $20,500 plus an additional $6,500 catch-up contribution if you are age 50 or older, for a total of $27,000. Since your employer could also contribute to your Section 401(k) or Section 403(b) plan, there is an additional limit for the total contribution (both yours and your employer's) of $61,000, not including the extra $6,500 if you are age 50 or older. All of these limits are indexed for inflation so they are increased every few years.

Important: Amounts held in defined contribution retirement accounts, whether they are IRAs, Section 401(k)s or Section 403(b)s, can be a major source of your retirement income, along with a pension, if you are one of the lucky few to have a pension. You should make your best effort to maximize the amounts you contribute to an IRA each year, but also to a Section 401(k) or Section 403(b) plan at your place of employment. Importantly, since many employers offer a matching contribution in the case of these two plans, such as matching them dollar for dollar or maybe 50 cents for each dollar, you should be very sure to contribute at least the amount needed to get the largest possible matching contribution.

### *"Lost" Retirement Accounts*

We live in a very mobile society and many of us have changed jobs a number of times and moved from state to state. You may have lost retirement funds in the process. It is possible that you have one or more retirement accounts that belong to you, but are still being held by, or for, a former employer who doesn't know where you are. Over the years the rules for vesting within retirement programs have changed, and you may have a vested benefit that is yours for the asking. Or perhaps you participated in a Section 401(k) or Section 403(b) plan at a former employer and left the funds behind when you switched jobs. One place you can search for lost retirement plan funds is at the National Registry of Unclaimed Retirement Benefits at https://unclaimedretirementbenefits.com/.

Although the database of this registry is certainly not 100% complete, it is a good starting place for your search for lost retirement funds, and the search is free. A better course of action would be to call your former employers and ask if you have either a vested pension benefit or left behind funds in a Section 401(k) or Section 403(b) account from your years on the job. Most larger employers have an employee benefits group, or at least a human resources department, and that is where you should direct your call. Lois K., who recently lost her husband who had worked at a major corporation, discovered a vested pension benefit he had earned by calling their Human Resources department and asking them to check.

## Working in Retirement

I know, working in retirement sounds like an oxymoron, but it can be an important source of funds in retirement, especially in the early years as you adjust to new spending and living patterns. Go back to Chapter 3 for a discussion of hot careers, part-time jobs with (or without) health benefits, and working from home (now more popular and possible than ever).

## Investments

For many retirees, Social Security plus a pension (for the lucky few that have one) and/or distributions from their Section 401(k) or Section 402(b) retirement plans will not be enough to fund the lifestyle desired in retirement. They will need to rely on other funds saved in preparation for retirement and a major issue will be where to invest these funds so that they not only produce an appropriate amount of earnings, but will also last for the rest of their lives. For most, depending on age and circumstances, a combination of stocks, bonds, and savings accounts works best, but for some, annuities and reverse mortgages will work out great in their retirement planning.

Banks are paying interest rates so low on savings that the accounts are little more than a place to keep funds safe, while their values are eroded by inflation. It is hard to justify keeping much money in a savings account paying interest of 0.5% (if you are lucky) when inflation is running close to 2%. So, assuming you have a reasonable amount of risk tolerance, you will likely need to have some of your assets invested in stocks and bonds. If you have a Section 401(k) or 403(b) account with your employer, your choices of investments will be limited to those offered by the plan. Unless these choices meet your needs, you should consider taking a lump-sum distribution from these accounts when you retire and rolling them (tax free) into an IRA at a major investment firm offering a wide range of investments. Examples would be Vanguard (https:// investor.vanguard.com/home), Fidelity (https://www.fidelity.com/), Wells Fargo (https://www.wellsfargo.com), and Schwab (https://www .schwab.com).

Forbes ranked Fidelity Investments as one of the best, partially due to its low costs, and Vanguard as the runner-up, again due to its low costs. You can set up new accounts online at most major investment firms and fund them either by mailing a check or by making transfers of funds electronically.

If you are doing a tax-free rollover of your pension or of the balance in your Traditional (i.e., non-Roth) defined benefit account to an IRA, you must deposit the funds distributed to you within 60 days into the IRA in order to accomplish a fully tax-free rollover. One problem that will arise is the requirement to have 20% federal income tax withheld from the distribution, leaving you with insufficient funds to do a 100% tax-free rollover. For example, if the balance in your account is $100,000, there will be $20,000 federal income tax withheld, leaving you with only $80,000 available to rollover, and $20,000 in taxable income, unless you can come up with the $20,000 withheld from other sources and include that in your rollover. The way to avoid this issue is by requesting the payer to directly roll over the distribution into your IRA, rather than sending you a check.

## Investment of Short-Term Cash

You should not put all your investments in stocks and bonds, if for no other reason than to have a ready source of cash to meet current expenses and unexpected emergencies. Interest rates are currently so low that you don't want to have any more of your short-term cash in a bank savings account than is absolutely necessary. For the cash that you do want or need to put in a savings account, consider an Internet-based bank, rather than the bank down the street, but keep your checking account locally for your convenience in cashing checks, using an ATM, and so forth. You will be able to put most of your short-term cash in a savings or money market account at an Internet-based bank and transfer that cash electronically to your local bank's checking account when needed. In addition, with most Internet-based banks you will be able to deposit checks using your cell phone (by taking a picture of the deposit check on the bank's app, or by making deposits at your local bank and moving the funds electronically to the Internet-friendly bank).

Examples of banks that offer higher interest rates than local banks and are Internet accessible are Marcus by Goldman Sachs (https://www.marcus.com/us/en), Citibank (https://www.citi.com/), and Ally Bank (https://www.ally.com/) – but there are many more and you can find them by Googling "highest interest rates on savings accounts." Be sure any bank you pick is insured by the Federal Deposit Insurance Corporation (FDIC). Look for the FDIC sign on the website, call the bank, or better yet, use the FDIC's BankFind tool (https://banks.data.fdic.gov/bankfind-suite/bankfind).

## Investing in Stocks and Bonds

A well-diversified investment portfolio should include both stocks and bonds, if you want to at least keep up with inflation and hopefully do even better than just "keep up." Within your stock or bond holdings you would not want to have a significant concentration in just one company or industry; for example, you would not want 10% of your total stocks invested in just Tesla or Apple stock, nor would you want 50% invested in financial institutions or automobile manufacturers. (Don't put all your eggs . . . well, you know the saying.)

Although bonds are considered less risky than stocks, they are not without risk. Besides the risk of repayment there is the risk of rising interest rates. Rising interest rates are great for bonds, if you are buying bonds with the higher interest rate. The problem is that a rise in interest rates will cause the value of existing bonds that you own to go down. For example, if you own a bond that is paying an annual interest rate of 4% and the going interest rate on bonds rises to 5%, the value of your bond will decrease. This is not necessarily a problem if your intention is to hold the bond until its maturity (when the face value of the bond will be repaid to you). However, it is a problem if you have to sell the bond at a loss, and it also means you are getting a lower than current market interest rate. Of course, the flipside is that the value of your bond will go up if market interest rates go down.

There is an inverse relationship between the price of stocks and bonds, meaning that when stock prices are rising, people are selling bonds and buying stocks; thus, the value of bonds goes down as the value of stocks goes up. On the other hand, when the value of stocks goes down, the value of bonds generally goes up because investors are selling stocks and buying bonds. For this reason, most financial advisors recommend your portfolio include both stocks and bonds to reduce the volatility of the overall portfolio.

The safest portfolio would be one that is invested 100% in bonds, while the riskiest portfolio would be 100% invested in stocks. One theory over the years has been to have a 60/40 portfolio, with the 60 representing the percentage invested in stocks and 40 the percentage invested in bonds. However, although this may be a good mix for some, a younger person should have a higher percentage in stocks and an older person a lower percentage, because the younger you are, the more time you have to recover from a bad stock market, and over the long-term stocks do better than bonds.

There other theories about the allocation of your portfolio between stocks and bonds. One long-held theory says that the percentage in stocks should equal 100 less your age. For example, if you are 55 years old, your portfolio would be 45% stocks and 55% bonds. There are many detractors of this theory who feel that the mix of stocks should be higher, maybe 10% to 20% higher than the calculation under the old theory, because of the availability of mutual funds, especially index funds (see discussion later) that offer the opportunity to have significant diversification of your stock investments, plus the longer lifespans today compared to the past. These advisors recommend that the percentage in stocks should equal 110, or maybe even 120, less your age. For example, using 120 less your age would result in a portfolio that is invested 70% in stocks at age 50 and 60% at age 60, with the balance invested in bonds.

Soon we will discuss mutual funds, but I want to mention here that one category of mutual funds is target-date funds, because these funds are designed to match the mix of investments within the fund based on the investor's expected retirement date. Thus, they relieve you of the need to change the mix of your investment portfolio between stocks and bonds as you age. For example, a 40-year-old person planning to retire at age 65 would pick a target-date fund in 2022 aimed for retirement around 2047. As that retirement date approaches, the fund will take care of moving its investments from largely stocks, to a heavier concentration of bonds and this shift will continue into the retirement years.

An interesting booklet by Vanguard titled "Vanguard's Principles for Investing Success" at https://about.vanguard.com/what-sets-vanguard-apart/principles-for-investing-success/ISGPRINC_062020_Online.pdf includes a chart of stock and bond returns from 1926 through 2019, based on varying mixes of stocks and bonds. It shows that a portfolio 100% invested in stocks would have returned an average of 10.3% per year while a portfolio invested 100% in bonds would have returned 5.3% per year. Quite a difference, but another big difference is that the range of the best and worst one-year returns for a portfolio invested 100% in stocks was a high of 54.2% and a low of –43.1%, whereas the similar range for bonds was a high of 32.6% and a low of –8.1%. Would you have bailed out of stocks during a year where the returns were running at a negative 43.1%?

Once you have decided on a mix of your investments between stocks and bonds, you need to turn your attention to *which* stocks and bonds should be included in your portfolio. Many of us enjoy this process, but it is important to realize that to do it well requires a lot of analysis. You need to not just identify companies that have good prospects, but also determine if the price of their stock justifies your investment. A good company whose stock is overpriced is not a good investment. Unless you plan to devote significant time and effort to this process, you might be better off considering investing in mutual funds and/or exchange-traded funds.

## *Mutual Funds and Exchange-Traded Funds*

One way to invest in a variety of stocks and bonds without having to select each one individually is to invest in mutual funds or exchange-traded funds (ETFs). Mutual funds are pools of money invested in stocks, bonds, money market instruments and/or other assets, and provide investors with professionally managed portfolios and diversification. Investors in the funds realize a proportional piece of the profits and losses of the fund, based on their percentage ownership in the fund. Many mutual funds are so-called load funds, for which an investor pays a commission that goes to the broker who sells the fund and which can sometimes be significant, whereas others are no-load funds, for which no commissions are paid. ETFs are similar to mutual funds in what they invest in, but are traded on the stock exchanges the same as company stocks, and the only commission you would pay is the relatively small commission charged by your brokerage for any stock purchase. A purchase or sale of a mutual fund share is always at the closing price of the fund for the day in which the purchase or sale takes place (after all the individual investments within the fund are priced out). On the other hand, an ETF trades on the stock market in the same manner as stock in individual companies, thus providing you with a definite purchase or sales price at the time of the transaction, instead of a price at the end of the day. Some mutual funds have ETFs that essentially mirror the investments in the mutual fund.

Mutual funds and ETFs can be separated into broad categories including money market funds, stock funds, bond funds, and balanced funds (stocks and bonds) and then into actively managed funds, where financial professionals research companies in order to select the individual stocks to put into the fund, and passively managed index funds, where the investments in the fund mirror the companies in an index. There are many different types of index funds, but the better-known ones are those tracking major stock indices, such as the Dow, the S&P 500, the Nasdaq, and the Russell index, as well as index funds tracking various bond indices, such as the U.S. Universal Index and the Bloomberg Barclays U.S. Aggregate Index.

There are now numerous index funds, tracking a variety of indices. For example, there are index funds tracking the total U.S. stock market, growth stocks, value stocks, dividend stocks, bank stocks, and so on. There are also numerous bond index funds to choose from.

Information about individual funds is readily available on the Internet, including at Morningstar mutual fund ratings (www.morningstar.com), which uses one to five stars to rate most funds, which is one way to compare funds with similar investment profiles, as well as on the websites of brokerages that are selling these funds. For Morningstar, go to their website and enter the mutual fund ticker symbol (for example, VFIAX for the Vanguard S&P 500 index fund) in the search bar. It will take you to a brief summary of the fund and a star rating (1 to 5 stars).

Although ratings such as those on Morningstar are a useful source for evaluating potential fund investments, the effect of the expenses paid by the fund (termed the expense ratio) has been shown in studies to be very important. The average expense ratio of actively managed mutual funds is between 0.5% and 1% per year, although some can be much higher, and in some cases as high as 2%, whereas the average expense ratio for passively managed index funds is about 0.2%. The impact of an extra 1% or more in expenses each and every year over an extended investment horizon is huge. For example, an investment of $100,000 for 25 years in a fund generating a 6% annual growth in its portfolio and with a 0% expense ratio would be worth $430,000, whereas the same investment in a fund with a 2% expense ratio would only be worth $260,000. Quite a difference. You can readily find the expense ratios of funds on the Internet, including at sites like Morningstar, which was discussed earlier, or by googling the fund's mutual fund ticker symbol to get to a summary of the fund.

Studies have shown that managed funds (as contrasted to index funds) as a group do not beat the market. And when you think about it, why should they when they have to generate gains in excess of the market gain just to cover their expenses? In 1975, John Bogle, the founder of Vanguard, created the first index fund, which was a fund designed to track the S&P 500 index. The idea behind this fund was essentially that a fund that invests passively in the companies that are within a selected index will not have all the expenses inherent in a managed fund, because they can be largely managed by a computer program, without the need for a large staff to evaluate and select specific investments to include in the fund. Thus, the annual return of an index fund will usually be just slightly lower than the increase or decrease in the index it tracks, due to the expenses of the fund itself. And a well-managed index fund should have very low expenses. For example, the Vanguard S&P 500 index fund (VFIAX) has an expense ratio of just 0.04% and the Fidelity S&P 500 index fund (FXAIX) is even lower at 0.015%. Thus, the annual expenses borne by a $100,000 investment would be between $15 at Fidelity and $40 at Vanguard while the expense born by a $100,000 investment in a fund with a 2%

expense ratio would be $2,000 per year. And, you are not only losing profit on your investment each year in the fund with the high expense ratio but also all the future compounded earnings you lost due to the higher expenses.

Warren Buffett, often referred to as the Oracle of Omaha, is regarded as one of the most astute investors of all times. Although he has become famous for his ability as an active investor to pick specific stocks for the investments of the company for which he is the Chairman and CEO, Berkshire Hathaway, his advice for others is to do as he says, not as he does, because "active investing as a whole is certain to lead to worse-than-average results" because you are not going to devote all your waking hours doing investment research. He also advises against investing in mutual funds that are actively managed by financial professionals, largely because they cannot consistently beat the market averages over time, partly because, as noted earlier, they have to beat the market average by enough to cover their own fees, which can amount to a substantial amount over time. In fact, over a 15-year period ending in 2019 only about a third of actively managed funds beat their benchmark index in any given year, according to Morningstar. What are the odds that you would find a fund that beats its benchmark index every year?

So, what does the Oracle of Omaha recommend we do? He says to invest in a low-cost index fund that tracks the S&P 500 index (an index of 500 large companies listed on the U.S. stock exchanges). He felt so strongly that an investment in a S&P 500 index fund would outperform hedge funds (a popular investment medium used by high-net-worth investors, which uses a wide range of investment strategies) that he offered to wager $1 million that an investment in a low-cost S&P 500 index fund would outperform an investment in hedge funds over a 10-year period. Only one person took him on, a former co-manager of a specialized asset management and advisory firm. Not surprisingly, the Oracle's investment in the S&P 500 index would have earned $854,000 over the 10 years compared to only $220,000 by the hedge funds selected by his opponent. (Warren Buffett's winnings were contributed to Girls Inc.)

Many advisors also recommend that the stock portion of your portfolio should be invested in a mixture of U.S. stocks and as much as 25% in international stocks. As you will probably guess, there are also international stock index funds for this purpose. Keep in mind, however, that when investing in international stocks, whether in an index fund or by picking individual stocks, your overall gains or losses will be derived from both the performance of the foreign company's stock price change, as well as from the fluctuations in the value of the U.S. dollar against the currencies in which the foreign stocks are denominated. For example, if the stock in a U.K. company you invested in rose by 10%, but the U.S. dollar rose by 5% against the U.K. pound, you would only have gained 4.5% after converting your investment in U.K. pounds back into U.S. dollars. The converse would hold true also so that your gain would be in excess of 11.55% if the U.K. pound rose 5% against the U.S. dollar.

Even investing in a fund tracking an index does not assure you of achieving the average market return of the fund. A study in 2020 by the research firm Dalbar concluded that, even though the S&P index had an annualized return of 10% per year in the 25 years that ended in 2019, the average investor only earned 7.8% per year. Why? – because the average investor had poor market timing, often buying when the market was soaring and selling when the market tanked.

### Annuities

As noted earlier, the days of employers paying a pension to their retirees are drawing to a close. Getting a monthly check in retirement was a wonderful benefit, but one that is hard to come by these days. An alternative for those who long for the good old days is to use some of your savings (or maybe the proceeds of a lump-sum distribution from your employer's pension plan) to purchase an annuity that will pay you a monthly benefit for the rest of your life. If an annuity is attractive to you, consider waiting until interest rates rise from their current historically low levels. Buying fixed annuities when interest rates are low, as they are currently, means either smaller monthly payments to you or a higher purchase price for the annuity.

In simple terms, an annuity is an insurance product, under which you make a payment to an insurance company in exchange for its promise to make periodic payments to you, generally for the rest of your life. Annuities can be very complicated, with a multitude of features that can be included or excluded from your contract. Examples are immediate annuities, which start paying you right away, and annuities that start payments to you at a later date. Annuity payments can be fixed amounts (with or without cost-of-living adjustments) or can be variable, such as based on the performance of the stock market, or a combination of both.

Since you make a large payment up front for an annuity that pays you over an extended future period, it has the effect of locking up your funds. So, be sure to keep enough of your portfolio outside of the annuity so you can be prepared for any need that requires immediate access to cash.

Once you purchase an annuity, if you change your mind later on, you are likely going to have to pay surrender charges, which may decrease over time. Because of their complexity, you should consider getting assistance from a financial advisor to help you select the right annuity.

Finally, the promise to make payments to you is only as good as the ability of the issuer of the annuity to honor its commitment. Thus, you need to be concerned with the solvency of the insurance company. You can find financial strength ratings from services like AM Best (www.ambest.com). Some experts recommend buying annuities from several insurers to minimize the risk.

## Reverse Mortgages

A reverse mortgage is another way to generate an upfront payment, periodic payments, a line of credit, or a combination of these options. The money you get is generally not taxable, and will not impact your Social Security or Medicare benefits. What you are actually doing is borrowing some or all of the equity in your home while retaining ownership and continuing to occupy it as your residence. You will be required to continue to maintain your home, pay all utilities, repairs, and taxes, but will not have a mortgage payment. Generally, you do not have to repay the money received as long as you continue to live in the home. The interest on the funds paid to you will be added to the principal balance of the loan, which will reduce your equity. When you die, vacate, or sell your home, the loan is repaid. In order to get a reverse mortgage, you must be at least 62 years old and, of course, own a principal residence that has enough equity to justify the reverse mortgage.

Reverse mortgages are complex and involve lots of fees, so you need to be comfortable with how the costs compare to how much you receive in loan advances and how much equity will remain at the end of the reverse mortgage period.

There are three types of reverse mortgages – single-purpose reverse mortgages, proprietary reverse mortgages, and home equity conversion mortgages (HECMs). Single-purpose reverse mortgages are the cheapest option, but are not offered everywhere. They are offered by state and local governments, and some nonprofit agencies, and must be used for a specific purpose (e.g., home repairs or improvements). Proprietary reverse mortgages are private loans, and may provide you with a larger advance than the other alternatives. Home Equity Conversion Mortgages are federally insured and backed by the U.S. Department of Housing and Urban Development, and can be used for any purpose. This is the most popular of the three types of reverse mortgages and is only available through an FHA-approved lender. According to the Federal Trade Commission, "Most reverse mortgages have something called a 'non-recourse' clause. This means that you, or your estate, can't owe more than the value of your home when the loan becomes due and the home is sold."

The amount you can borrow depends on a number of factors, including your age, the value of your home, the amount of your current mortgage, and current interest rates. The older you are, and the more equity you have in the home, the more you will be able to borrow.

Before you apply for an HECM, you will be required to meet with a counselor from an independent government-approved housing counseling agency, who is required to explain the costs involved and the financial implications of the loan. In addition, the alternatives to an HECM will also be covered, and the counselor will be able to help you compare the different types of reverse mortgages and their costs and payment options. You will be charged a fee, generally about $125, by the counseling agency. You might also want to consider the services of a financial advisor before you commit to a reverse mortgage.

For more information on reverse mortgages go to the Federal Trade Commission site at https://www.consumer.ftc.gov/articles/0192-reverse-mortgages and also check out the reverse mortgage pamphlet prepared by the Consumer Finance Protection Bureau at https://files.consumerfinance.gov/f/documents/cfpb_reverse_mortgage_rights_responsibilities.pdf.

Whew! Lots of thoughts, approaches, and possibilities for making your money last as long as you do. Let's not be like my almost-retired friend Jonathan, who says: "I'm retiring on July 1, and living off my savings. I have no idea what I'll be living off on July 2." But we know that whatever money we have, "The Taxman Cometh." That's the next chapter, and the only consoling thought is that (author unknown): "A fine is a tax for doing something wrong. A tax is a fine for doing something right."

## Compare Your Housing Costs

|  | Your Home per Year | New Home per Year |
|---|---|---|
| Mortgage/Rent Payments | $_____ | $_____ |
| Homeowner Dues | $_____ | $_____ |
| Property Taxes | $_____ | $_____ |
| Utilities | $_____ | $_____ |
| Sewer/Water | $_____ | $_____ |
| Gas-Electric | $_____ | $_____ |
| Phone | $_____ | $_____ |
| Cable TV/Internet | $_____ | $_____ |
| Trash Service | $_____ | $_____ |
| Insurance | $_____ | $_____ |
| Home | $_____ | $_____ |
| Car(s) | $_____ | $_____ |
| Memberships: (Golf, swim, etc.) | $_____ | $_____ |
| **TOTAL:** | $_____ | $_____ |

## How Much $$$ Do You Need for Retirement?

### MONTHLY EXPENSES

|  | Prior to Retirement | Postretirement |
|---|---|---|
| Ongoing: |  |  |
| Mortgage/Rent | $_____ | $_____ |
| Car payments | $_____ | $_____ |
| Credit card bills | $_____ | $_____ |
| Other loan repayments | $_____ | $_____ |
| Taxes (income, property, etc.) | $_____ | $_____ |
| Home insurance | $_____ | $_____ |
| Medical/Dental insurance | $_____ | $_____ |
| Auto insurance | $_____ | $_____ |
| Other insurance (life, etc.) | $_____ | $_____ |
| Utilities | $_____ | $_____ |

## Dollars and Sense

|  | Prior to Retirement | Postretirement |
|---|---|---|
| Cable | $_____ | $_____ |
| Telephone | $_____ | $_____ |
| Groceries | $_____ | $_____ |
| Clothing/Laundry | $_____ | $_____ |
| Entertainment | $_____ | $_____ |
| Gas for autos | $_____ | $_____ |
| Subscriptions | $_____ | $_____ |
| Memberships | $_____ | $_____ |
| Saving for retirement | $_____ | $_____ |
| TOTAL | $_____ | $_____ |
| Multiply by 12 for annual expenses | $_____ | $_____ |
| Irregular Expenses (calculate annual total): | | |
| Gifts | $_____ | $_____ |
| Education | $_____ | $_____ |
| Household maintenance | $_____ | $_____ |
| Auto maintenance | $_____ | $_____ |
| Medical/Dental expenses | $_____ | $_____ |
| Travel/Vacation | $_____ | $_____ |
| Donations | $_____ | $_____ |
| Other | $_____ | $_____ |
| TOTAL | $_____ | $_____ |
| TOTAL ANNUAL EXPENSES | $_____ | $_____ |

(Keep in mind that sometimes there are large, onetime expenditures such as replacing a roof, renovating a kitchen, replacing a deck, buying a car, etc.)

## Will You Have Enough to Fund Your Retirement?

Now, take a look at possible sources of income when you are retired.

| | |
|---|---|
| Salary/wages/tips | $_____ |
| Social Security* | $_____ |
| Pensions** | $_____ |

(*continued*)

255

| | |
|---|---|
| IRA/401(k) distributions | $_____ |
| Investment income | $_____ |
| Net rental income | $_____ |
| Partnership income | $_____ |
| Alimony | $_____ |
| Other | $_____ |
| TOTAL INCOME | $_____ |
| Multiply by 12 for annual income | $_____ |

Subtract your total annual retirement expenses from your total annual retirement income. If there is nothing left over, or the answer is negative, you must increase your income or cut your expenses. How will you go about bridging this gap?

---

*If you have not set up a "My Social Security" account, where you can review a statement of your projected benefit, the Social Security Administration will mail the statement to you three months before your birthday each year, starting at age 62, up to the year you file for Social Security benefits.

**Contact employer(s) for a description of the plan and the estimated benefits.

# More Resources

## *Books*

Barry, Patricia. *Medicare for Dummies*. For Dummies, 2020.

Birken, Emily Guy. *The 5 Years Before You Retire, Updated Edition: Retirement Planning When You Need It the Most*. Adams Media, 2021.

Kotlikoff, Laurence. *Money Magic: An Economist's Secrets to More Money, Less Risk, and a Better Life*. Little, Brown Spark, 2022.

Krantz, Matt. *Retirement Planning for Dummies*. For Dummies, 2020.

Orman, Suze. *The Ultimate Retirement Guide for 50+: Winning Strategies to Make Your Money Last a Lifetime*. Hay House, 2020.

Peterson, Jonathan. *Social Security for Dummies*. For Dummies, 2020.

Petrow, Steven. *Stupid Things I Won't Do When I Get Old*. Citadel, 2021

Quicken Willmaker & Trust 2022: Book & Software Kit, 2022nd edition.

Slott, Ed. *The New Retirement Savings Time Bomb; How to Take Financial Control, Avoid Unnecessary Taxes and Combat the Latest Threats to Your Retirement Savings*. Penguin Books, 2021.

Thaler, Richard. *Nudge: The Final Edition*. Penguin Books, 2021.

Vernon, Steve. *Don't Go Broke in Retirement: A Simple Plan to Build Lifetime Retirement Income.* Rest of Life Communications, 2020.

## *Websites*

Let's crush your money goals: www.nerdwallet.com

How Work Affects Your Benefits: https://www.ssa.gov/pubs/EN-05-10069.pdf

https://www.medicare.gov/Pubs/pdf/12026-Understanding-Medicare-Advantage-Plans.pdf

## *Podcasts*

Kiplinger: https://www.kiplinger.com/article/retirement/t047-c032-s014-top-5-retirement-podcasts-everyone-should-try.html

Jean Chatzky: https://hermoney.com/t/podcasts/

Dave Ramsey: https://www.ramseysolutions.com/shows/the-ramsey-show

## *Quizzes*

https://trsurveys.survey.fm/what-is-your-social-security-iq-2020

https://trsurveys.survey.fm/what-is-your-medicare-iq

# CHAPTER 8

# The Taxman Cometh

■ ■ ■

"The only difference between a taxman and a taxidermist is that the taxidermist leaves the skin" (Mark Twain). According to the Tax Foundation (www.taxfoundation.org), the tax system in the United States generated $5.2 trillion in 2019, and 41.5% of that was paid by individuals. This tax total put the United States in the number-one position for collecting the most tax revenue of the 38 countries that are members of the Organisation for Economic Co-operation and Development (OECD). Yes, that sounds like we are being taxed to death, but surprisingly our total taxes only equaled 24% of our gross national product, compared to a weighted average of 34% for the other OECD member countries. So we collected the most, but we also have the highest population of all the OECD countries. Maybe our tax burden is not so bad after all.

Although retirees face most of the same tax issues as everybody else, certain issues are more likely to arise when planning our retirement years. These issues include the tax treatment of selling your home, the state tax considerations involved in relocating, the rules for determining the taxability of Social Security payments (yes, we could be taxed on our Social Security benefits after paying

Social Security taxes throughout our working careers), retirement distributions, and, finally, estate and inheritance taxes.

## Sell Your Home and Avoid Income Tax on the Gain

The good news is that many retirees who choose to move, either because they are downsizing or maybe moving to another state, will realize a gain on the sale of their home, especially after the huge increase in home prices that occurred during the (bad news) coronavirus pandemic. Although the tax law generally taxes the gain on selling any asset, there are special rules relating to the sale of your principal residence that will help you avoid tax on a gain when selling your home. In the past, up to 1997, you could defer the gain on the sale of your residence as long as you reinvested the net proceeds (selling price less costs of the sale, but not less your mortgage) into a replacement principal residence. The gain that was not taxed was required to be used to reduce your tax cost of the replacement residence. The gain deferral could continue with house sale after house sale, as long as the net proceeds were reinvested in a new principal residence. This worked great for most home sales but not so much for retirees who were downsizing. After all, the main point of downsizing is to reduce costs and that usually means the net proceeds of the sale would not be reinvested into a replacement residence, thus causing some or all of the gains that were built up over the years on the sales of your principal residences to come to roost.

Fortunately, in 1997 Congress changed this rule and replaced it with a far kinder and gentler tax break, especially for retirees who wanted to downsize. Under the new rule, which is currently still in place, some or all of the gain on a sale of a principal residence is no longer taxable, as long as the taxpayers owned and lived in the residence as their principal residence for at least two years during the five-year period ending on the date of the sale. The maximum amount of gain that can be excluded from taxable income is $250,000 for a single person (or a married person filing separately), and $500,000 for a married couple filing a joint income tax return. Importantly, this gain is not deferred as under the old rules, and does not reduce the tax cost in the replacement residence, and has no impact on calculating gain on the future sale of the replacement residence. In fact, there is no requirement to even purchase a replacement principal residence, and, believe it or not, this rule can be used to eliminate up to $500,000 in gain every two years. In my community there are builders who build a new principal residence and live in it for two years and then sell it and move into another principal residence that they built, and then after two years do it again. Sounds like this should not be allowed, but maybe it is proof that tax rules can work better for some taxpayers than for others.

The term *principal residence* was used several times in the preceding discussion, and it is important to know what that term means for taxpayers who own two or more residences, because only one of them can be their *principal* residence. Generally speaking, the principal residence is located in the same state in which the taxpayers are domiciled, and is the home in which they live most of the time. A principal residence can be a single-family home, townhouse, duplex, cooperative apartment, condominium, or mobile home, but cannot be just a lot. In fact, a principal residence, in some cases, can even be a houseboat or yacht. Your principal residence will usually correspond to the address on your voter registration card, driver's license, and on your federal and state income tax returns. It is usually located near religious organizations of which you are a member, and where you work and bank.

For example, Christine and Garrett own a residence in which they reside in Cincinnati, Ohio. They also own and occupy a second residence that they occupy for three months each winter in Orlando, Florida, plus a few additional weeks several times a year – they are snowbirds. Their Cincinnati residence is their principal residence, and any gain on its sale would come under the aforementioned rule, assuming they had met the use as a principal residence for at least two of the five years preceding the sale. A gain on the sale of their Orlando residence would be fully taxable.

It is important to ensure that the required two years of use as a principal residence in the five-year period ending on the date of sale is met. Imagine the pain if the sellers could not get a sale to settlement in time to qualify. Assume, for example, that Christine and Garrett had purchased their Cincinnati residence in 1990, and used it as their principal residence until January 1, 2019, at which time they moved into their Orlando residence and rented their Cincinnati home, until they sold it with settlement scheduled for December 31, 2021. Due to the coronavirus pandemic the settlement was delayed until January 2, 2022, and they lost the entire break. Why? Because not settling until January 2, 2022, meant that they had not occupied the residence as their principal residence for a full two years of the five years preceding the date of the sale.

As is often the case in taxation, there are several exceptions to meeting the required two years of use as a principal residence test, which are intended to soften the requirement under certain circumstances. If the taxpayers needed to sell their residence prior to meeting the two-year ownership and use test, the sale will still qualify if the primary reason for selling was due to (1) a change in employment, (2) health reasons, or (3) unforeseen circumstances. In each of these cases the maximum amount of the exclusion ($500,000 or $250,000) is reduced by a formula that compares the number of qualifying days (or months) of ownership and use prior to the date of the sale to 730 days (or 24 months).

For example, if Christine and Garrett needed to sell their Cincinnati residence after only owning and living in it for one year, because of a change of jobs requiring they move to Cleveland, the exception to the two-year use as a principal residence requirement would apply, but the amount of maximum exclusion would be reduced from $500,000 to $250,000 (half of the maximum as they only met half of the two-year requirement). This is still a pretty good deal, as most homes don't appreciate more than $250,000 in one year.

The health exception applies if the sale is due to either your illness or injury or that of a close relative (such as a spouse, parent, grandparent, child, sibling, or mother-in-law). The third exception, unforeseen circumstances, covers a number of contingencies that could force a sale of a principal residence. Examples could be divorce or legal separations, multiple births resulting from the same pregnancy (probably not an issue for most retirees), unemployment, and death, including the death of a close relative.

Finally, the rule allowing the elimination of up to $500,000 of a gain on the sale of a principal residence can only apply once in every two-year period, although there are some exceptions to this rule also. This once-in-every-two-year requirement would not stop you from selling your principal residence that met the two years of ownership and use test and eliminating up to a $500,000 gain and then moving into your already-owned vacation home, occupying it as your principal residence for at least two years, and then selling that home and eliminating up to a $500,000 gain again.

To read more about the taxation of the gain from the sale of your home, go to www.irs.gov and enter Publication 523 into the search bar.

## Other Home-Selling Issues

- Any points you may have paid on a prior refinancing of your home that have not already been deducted are deductible in the year of sale when the mortgage is paid off.
- Any prorated property taxes shown on the settlement sheet for the sale as borne by you are deductible in the year of the sale.
- Any gain on a sale of a previous principal residence prior to 1998 that was deferred due to the purchase of a replacement residence, as discussed earlier, must be used to reduce the cost of the first residence sold on or after 1997, which could be the residence you are now selling.

## Don't Forget the Impact of State Taxes When Deciding Where You Want to Live

Taxes may not be the most important issue to consider in deciding where you want to spend your retirement years, but they are certainly a consideration. Federal taxes will be the same no matter where you live, even if you move to a foreign country. The United States taxes the worldwide income of its citizens and legal residents, no matter where they choose to live, and if you move to a foreign country, you may also be subject to its income tax, although the United States does provide for a tax credit for some or all of the foreign income tax you pay. However, the amount of state taxes will be largely based on where you reside and where you work, should you choose to work in retirement.

Let's face it. Each state needs to raise revenue in order to meet its obligations. Some get revenue from unique sources such as oil reserves (Alaska) or gaming revenue (Nevada), but most states get their revenue from the local taxpayers. The tax rates and the various exemptions, such as for retirement income, vary by state and by type of tax. So don't just assume you should move to a state without a broad-based income tax, like Florida or Texas, as you might find that their real-estate tax, sales tax, or something else swings a different state into the number-one tax position for you. An example would be a state that does have an income tax but not on the type of income you will be living on, which makes it better for you from an overall tax standpoint.

Each of our 50 states, and the District of Columbia, has its own tax system that determines your state and local income taxes, sales taxes, property taxes, estate and inheritance taxes, and more. Currently Alaska, Florida, Nevada, South Dakota, Texas, Washington, and Wyoming do not have a broad-based income tax and two states, New Hampshire and Tennessee, only tax interest and dividends.

State taxable income is generally determined by starting with federal income and then making a series of additions and subtractions to arrive at the state's taxable income. Common subtractions from federal income are U.S. government interest, such as from Treasury Bonds and Social Security income. Some states allow deductions as shown on your federal tax return (mortgage interest, charitable contributions, etc., but not including a deduction for state income taxes paid). There is often a standard deduction allowed, usually as an alternative to itemizing deductions (similar to the choice on your federal tax return) and a deduction for personal exemptions. A few states tax your gross income with essentially no deductions. As noted earlier, a common subtraction from federal income in arriving at state taxable income is Social Security income, but 13 states could tax some of your Social Security income. (See the "State Tax Rates – 2021" at the end of this chapter.)

After determining your state taxable income, most states apply some type of a graduated tax rate to calculate the total tax, although Colorado, Illinois, Indiana, Kentucky, Massachusetts, Michigan, New Hampshire, North Carolina, Pennsylvania, and Utah use a flat tax rate. The chart at the end of this chapter shows the high and low end of tax rates for each state and the District of Columbia. (see "State Tax Rates – 2021" at the end of this chapter).

Four states (Delaware, Montana, New Hampshire, and Oregon) do not have a state, county, or local sales tax, and one state, Alaska, does not have a state sales tax but allows its counties to charge a county sales tax. According to the Tax Foundation, combining state and local sales taxes by state for those states with a sales tax shows a weighted average ranging from a high of 9.55% in Tennessee and Louisiana and a low of 1.76% in Alaska.

Cities are allowed to impose an income tax on individuals in 17 states. Although that does not mean all the cities within those states do impose an income tax, it does mean that you should inquire about the existence of a city income tax in any location you are considering for relocation.

All 50 states and the District of Columbia impose a property tax and, according to the Tax Foundation, the mean effective tax rate on owner-occupied housing for calendar year 2019 was 1.03 % of property value, with a high of 2.13% in New Jersey and a low of .31%

in Hawaii. Although the property tax rate is important, other issues, including the availability of homestead and senior citizen exemptions, can also be a significant factor in your total tax package, but they vary so much from location to location that it is almost impossible to provide a meaningful table to help you. It is equally important to understand how properties are valued and assessed. For example, one jurisdiction may typically value real estate much lower than its fair market value, while another may be right on the money. Therefore, just comparing the tax rates of two alternative states you are considering will not necessarily lead you to a good conclusion as to which imposes the higher property tax and which the lower because it ignores the valuation issue. Call the county assessor's office and find out what the current tax rate is per thousand dollars of value, and at what percent of fair market value you can expect a residence to be assessed for property-tax purposes. If that is too cumbersome for you, ask the real-estate agents you speak with how property taxes are determined in areas of interest to you, and talk to people who have recently relocated to or purchased homes in the area.

Obviously, when deciding where to live from a tax perspective, the entire tax package in the area you are contemplating must be considered. There are nuances in the tax rules in the various states. For example, as noted earlier, Tennessee and New Hampshire have an income tax, but it is only imposed on interest and dividends. Thus, depending on your facts, their income tax may end up costing you a lot or maybe nothing. Pennsylvania has an income tax but pensions are not taxable and, with a few exceptions, IRA and Section 401(k) distributions also escape taxation there. If you move to Pennsylvania and your major sources of income are pension, IRAs or Section 401(k) distributions and Social Security, your income tax could be zero. Another nuanced example would be Florida, where the property tax as a percentage of value of the homes is in the middle of the pack compared to the other 49 states. However, it has a special provision that limits the annual increase in the assessed value of "homesteaded" homes to the lesser of 3% or the inflation rate. That can be very important to your future property tax increases in Florida, if your Florida residence is your primary residence, particularly when there are significant increases in real property values related to the movement of people, such as what happened due to the coronavirus pandemic.

## Tax Freedom Day

One way to try and get a handle on the tax burden in the various states is by looking at "Tax Freedom Day" (https://taxfoundation .org/publications/tax-freedom-day/), which is determined from time to time by the Tax Foundation. Tax Freedom Day, which arrived on April 16 in 2019 for the entire United States, is the day on which the average American's federal, state, and local tax bill is fully covered by his or her year-to-date earnings. In other words, this is the day (on average) that an individual has made enough to pay Uncle Sam, plus state and local government taxes, and is now beginning to make the money that he or she will be able to spend on other things. As taxes get higher, this day comes later in the year, while a decrease in taxes causes Tax Freedom Day to come earlier. So, the earlier Tax Freedom Day occurs, the sooner your tax obligation has been met!

The latest determination of Tax Freedom Day, which was for 2019, put Alaska in the top position, with the big day arriving on April 5, reflecting its overall low tax costs. Not surprisingly, New York and the District of Columbia tied for worst, with their Tax Freedom Day not arriving until May 3. Since I already noted that the U.S. federal tax burden is essentially the same no matter where you live, the high and low ranking of Alaska and New York also put them in the top and bottom places for their state and local tax burdens as a percentage of income with Alaska at 5.8% and New York at 14.1%.

## What If You Purchase a Second Home?

Are you thinking about purchasing a second home in a different state for your retirement years? If so, a question that will come up is how a state determines who is subject to its income tax. In general, states tax all the income of those who are residents of the state, and also those who are domiciled in the state, even if not currently residing there. Usually, but not always, a person living in a state is also domiciled there. A domiciliary is someone who has a permanent home in a state even if they are not physically present there for most of the year, whereas a resident (sometimes referred to as a statutory resident) is someone who is not a domiciliary, but who has a place of abode in a state where he or she resides for more than a minimum amount of time during the year, with 184 days often being the point where this test is met. For example, George P., who is domiciled in Virginia, where he normally lives, took a two-year temporary job in New York City, rented an apartment there and was physically present in New York for 184 or more days during each year. He ended up being subject to income tax on all of his income in Virginia, as a domiciliary, and also in New York state and New York City by reason of meeting (or maybe I should say failing) the physical presence test there. George received a tax credit in Virginia for the income tax he paid to New York state. Unfortunately, however, the Virginia tax credit was less than the tax George paid to New York State, whose tax rate is much higher, plus he had to pay New York City tax.

The distinction between domiciliary and resident can become particularly important when you have two places of abode, such as the sunbirds who live in Florida for much of the year and head "home" to the north to escape the hot, humid Florida summers. Often their place of abode outside of Florida is in a location where they had been both residents and domiciled for a number of years. For example, Dennis and Cathy B. lived in Virginia for many years. After retiring they purchased a home in Naples, Florida, and claimed it as their principal residence in order to escape income tax in Virginia, and also to qualify for the Florida limit on annual property tax valuation increases on homesteaded properties, which was mentioned earlier in this chapter. In 2021 they lived in Florida from January 1 through April 30, when they returned to Virginia.

On November 1 they were back in Naples and stayed there for the rest of the year. Unfortunately, even though they were domiciled in Florida and thought of themselves as income tax free, Virginia taxed them on all of their income because they were physically present in their Virginia home for 184 days. Surely, they wished they had kept better track of their days and stayed one day longer in Florida.

The reverse could also happen. Consider the situation of a couple domiciled in Virginia who lived there for fewer than 184 days during the year. Virginia would continue to tax them due to their status as domiciliaries. Thus, while it is easy to count days to avoid taxation in a state due to physical presence, it is important to understand what makes you a domiciliary, especially if you have more than one home. As you might expect, it is a common tactic of taxpayers to claim domicile in a state that does not have an income tax, such as Texas or Nevada, while continuing to maintain a residence in one of the many states that does have an income tax. This raises the question of how you determine (and prove) your state of domicile. Over the years, the courts have used a number of factors in resolving this issue. The more important criteria have been the state of your voting registration, driver's license, ownership of real estate, and automobile registration. Other, less important tests have included the location of your banks, country club memberships, church memberships, and the address used on your federal income tax returns.

So, if you are going to own homes in several states, it would be wise to seek professional advice in order to gain a complete understanding of each state's rules on where you will be subject to taxation. If your new domicile is more tax- friendly than your old one, move quickly to satisfy the criteria listed earlier, in order to clearly establish the date of the change. And keep very good records of which home you lived in during each day of the year. Forewarned is forearmed – these rules can be used to your advantage, but to do so you need to understand them (or find someone who does!).

## Will You Be Taxed on Your Social Security Income?

According to the Social Security Administration, an average of 65 million Americans per month will receive a Social Security benefit in 2021, totaling over one trillion dollars in benefits paid during the year. Since you paid Social Security taxes throughout your working life to earn this benefit, you might be surprised to learn that our legislators saw fit to tax this source of income, starting in 1984, after 49 years of it not being taxed. And to make matters a bit worse, there is a sometimes-complicated formula for determining whether and how much of your Social Security income will be taxed.

In general, the amount of Social Security that is included in your federal gross income is determined by making a comparison between a "base amount" and the total of one-half of your Social Security benefits plus 100% of the rest of your income, including your nontaxable income. For simplicity, let's call this second amount your "benchmark income." If your benchmark income is equal to or less than your base amount, none of your Social Security benefits are going to be includable. However, if your benchmark income exceeds your base amount, up to 85% of your benefits will be includable. So, what are the base amounts that your benchmark income must not exceed in order to avoid taxation?

- $25,000 if you are single, a head of household, or a qualifying widow(er)
- $25,000 if you are married, filing separately and lived apart from your spouse for the entire calendar year
- $32,000 if you are married and filing jointly
- $0 if you are married, filing separately, and lived with your spouse at any time during the year

Once your benchmark amount exceeds the base amount, up to 50% of your Social Security benefit will be included in your federal income. However, if your benchmark income exceeds

$44,000 on a joint return or $34,000 on a single return, up to 85% of your benefit will be includable. As I am sure you realize, having a benchmark amount of $44,000 ($32,000 if single) is not a very high litmus test, and many will find that up to 85% of their Social Security benefit is includable in their federal income. For example, Scott and Christine L. received $9,000 in Social Security in 2021 benefits and also had a taxable pension of $20,000 and nontaxable interest income from their state of Ohio bonds of $4,000. Their benchmark income is $28,500 (half of the $9,000 Social Security benefit + all of the Ohio bond interest of $4,000 + all of the $20,000 pension). Since this is less than their base amount of $32,000 none of the Social Security benefit is in their federal income.

Because nontaxable income, like the Ohio bond interest, is included in the determination of your benchmark income, situations could arise where this could cause up to 85% of your Social Security benefit being taxable, thus effectively converting your nontaxable Ohio bond interest income into being up to 85% taxable. Retirees who are close to having a benchmark income in excess of the base amount should think carefully about whether investing in municipal bonds is worthwhile.

Using a base amount of $0 for married persons who choose to file separate income tax returns prevents retirees from escaping includability of the Social Security benefits of the spouse with the lower earnings by using married-filing separately status.

There is a special method for calculating the taxability of your Social Security benefits if they include a lump-sum payment relating to prior years. Under this method, you recalculate the taxable part of your benefits in each prior year to which the lump-sum payment relates, including the applicable portion of the lump sum, and then subtract the total from the amount you reported as taxable Social Security income in the prior year(s). The result is how much of the lump sum is includable in your federal income.

271

## *Taking Distributions from Your Retirement Accounts*

There are specific tax rules dealing with how soon you can start, and how late you must start, to take distributions from your IRA, 401(k), or 403(b) plan accounts. The rules dictating when you must start taking distributions do not apply to Roth IRA accounts but do apply to Roth Section 401(k) and 403(b) accounts even though, as noted in Chapter 7, qualified distributions from Roth accounts are not taxable. The rules are in place to prevent withdrawing the retirement funds too soon rather than having them available to cover your expenses in retirement, or, alternatively, leaving them to accumulate in the tax-deferred accounts and eventually bequesting them to your beneficiaries as an inheritance. The general rule is that you can't take distributions before you reach 59½ years old, and must start distributions in the year you turn age 72. An exception to the age 72 requirement is that you can defer the date to start distributions from an employer-sponsored plan ((401(k) and 403(b) plans) if you are still working for that employer, as long as you are not a 5% or more owner of the business.

The exceptions to the general rule against taking distributions before age 59½ are for early retirement, disability, and distributions made after the death of the plan participant, and in some cases, distributions of your contributions to a Roth account.

Although there are no rules limiting the amount of distributions you take each year from your retirement accounts after turning age 59½, there are rules that prescribe required minimum distribution (RMD) amounts that you must distribute, starting with the year in which you turn age 72. The effect of these rules is to have you distribute your retirement funds over your expected lifetime, instead of saving them for your beneficiaries after your death. Your RMD is calculated each year by dividing the total value of your retirement account(s) as of December 31 of the previous year by a "distribution period," which is prescribed in a set of tables published by the IRS, and which is based on your remaining life expectancy. The new Uniform Life Table, which is the one most, but not all, retirees are required to use for 2022 and later years, shows a "distribution period" for each age through age 120. You divide the December 31 balance in your account by the distribution period and the answer is your RMD. For example, Patricia R. was 73 years old in 2022 and had a balance in her IRA on December 31, 2021, of $400,000. The Uniform Life Table shows that a 73-year-old person has a distribution period of 26.5 (yes, I realize that would indicate she will live to age 99.5), so her RMD for 2022 is $15,094. The table also shows that 26.5 is equivalent to 3.78%, which would indicate that her account balance will likely be higher at the end of the year, assuming she realizes an average return during the year in excess of 3.78% on her investments in the account. As you get older, the distribution period gets smaller and smaller, and is 6.4 (15.63%) at age 100 and 2 (50%) at age 120.

IRS Publication 590-B includes a summary of the rules on distributions as well as worksheets and the Life Expectancy tables, which you can download by going to www.IRS.gov and putting 590-B in the search bar. One word of caution, however, is that as of late 2021 the updated Publication 590-B for 2021 showing the new Life Expectancy Tables that are first effective for 2022 has not been issued. You should ensure that Publication 590-B for 2022 indicates that the tables are the new ones.

Those of us who don't want the aggravation of having to calculate our RMDs will be happy to know that IRA custodians are required to either send you a notice showing your RMD on or before January 31 each year, or offer to calculate it for you.

The RMD must be distributed on or before December 31 each year, except that the RMD calculated for the year in which you turn 72 can be distributed either during that year or up to April 1 of the following year. However, if you wait to distribute your first RMD until the next year, you will have two RMDs to distribute that second year, which could end up increasing your tax bite by raising the overall tax rate on the extra RMD.

The penalty for not distributing at least as much as the calculated RMD is 50%, so it is important that you distribute at least the minimum amount. In the earlier example, Patricia R. had an RMD of $15,094 for 2022. If she only distributed $10,000, her penalty would be $2,547 (50% of the shortfall of $5,094).

The RMD rules do not apply to a Roth IRA, but they do apply to a Roth 401(k) and a Roth 403(b) account, but this can be avoided by a tax-free rollover of the balance in these accounts to a Roth IRA.

Since your assets within these retirement accounts are generating earnings (such as interest, dividends, and appreciation) on a tax-deferred (and for Roth accounts on a tax-free) basis, it is frequently best to hold off as long as possible before you start taking distributions, and when you reach age 72 taking no more than your RMD in order to keep investing the maximum amounts in your retirement accounts. Of course, this assumes you have other sources of funds on which you can live, such as a pension, previously taxed earnings, or lower-taxed dividends and capital gains income. You must also take into account our system of progressive tax rates, under which your earnings start off at a zero or very low tax rate and then, as your earnings increase, the tax rates on the increased amounts get higher. Thus, for example, you would generally not want to defer taking a qualified distribution from a retirement account in a year in which you are in a 15% tax rate and then take a larger one a few years later if it would be taxed at 25% in that later year. Of course, it is possible that you could come out ahead if the future year of taxation is far enough in the future, if the benefit of continued compound earnings on the untaxed assets within your retirement account would offset the 10% tax rate difference.

So, a quick and easy answer would be to defer distributions as long as possible (of course, you must take your RMD each year – but that does not start until you reach age 72), but only if your tax rate is not expected to go up. If you do expect it to increase, then you need to do your homework to determine whether to take distributions sooner than required, rather than later.

## A Word About Estate and Inheritance Taxes

Due to significant increases in the federal estate tax exemption in 2011 and 2018, very few of us will have estates that end up paying this federal tax. In addition, as shown in the chart "State Tax Rates – 2021" at the end of this chapter, only 12 states plus the District of Columbus impose an estate tax and only six have an inheritance tax, with Maryland having both. So, for many of us, estate and inheritance taxes are not an issue of concern (unless, of course, changes in the tax law significantly reduce or eliminate these large exemptions or more states add estate and/or inheritance taxes to their arsenals).

Federal estate tax is imposed on the taxable estate of a decedent, which is determined by adding up pretty much everything owned at the time of death minus deductible liabilities and expenses, and importantly, an unlimited deduction for property left to a spouse and an exemption amount. The federal exemption deduction was raised to $11.18 million in 2018, and it is increased further each year for inflation, and amounted to $11.7 million in 2021. Any portion of the decedent's exemption amount not needed on the estate tax return can be transferred to the surviving spouse, potentially giving the second person to die an exemption of $23.4 million in 2021. Thus, the combination of the unlimited deduction for property left to a spouse and the large exemption amount renders the federal estate tax only applicable to the very wealthy.

In 2026, the exemption amount will be reset at $5.49 million, adjusted for inflation, with an expectation that this will be approximately $6 million. Not as good as $11.7 million, but still keeps this tax a concern for only the wealthy. If you are unlucky (some would say lucky) enough to have an estate large enough to pay the tax, the rates are graduated from 18% to 39% on the first $1.0 million and then at 40% on the remaining balance.

There is more of a possibility of paying estate and/or inheritance taxes if you live in or move to one of the states or the District of Columbia imposing one or the other of these taxes (Maryland imposes both). Each state has its own rules on estate and inheritance taxes, but in computing the taxable estate each of the states provide exemptions, ranging from $1 million in Massachusetts and Oregon to $7.1 million in Connecticut (which is scheduled to increase to the federal exemption amount in 2023). The estate tax rates imposed are at various rates starting at a low of 0.8% in Maryland to a high of 20% in Hawaii.

Some states impose a tax on the transfer of property after death – often with exceptions for specified transfers, such as transfers to spouses and lineal heirs, and sometimes with different rates for specified classes of beneficiaries. For example, Nebraska does not tax transfers to spouses, and imposes tax at 1% on transfers to immediate relatives, 13% for transfers to remote relatives and 18% for all others. The estate pays the inheritance tax, not the beneficiary.

Due to the diversity of the estate and inheritance taxes in the 17 states imposing one or both of these, plus the District of Columbia, it is impossible to generalize about their potential impact on you, but you should consider seeking professional advice on their potential cost if you live in or plan to move into one of them.

Do you feel "intaxicated" after all that tax discussion? The next chapter will hopefully make you feel better, since it includes money-saving tips and ideas that will stretch those retirement dollars.

## State Tax Rates – 2021

| State | Personal Income Tax Rate (%) Note 1 | State and Local Sales Tax Range (%) Note 2 | State Does NOT Tax Social Security Benefits | State Has an Estate Tax | State Has an Inheritance Tax |
|---|---|---|---|---|---|
| Alabama | 2.0–5.0 | 4.0–9.22 | X | | |
| Alaska | None | 0–1.76 | X | | |
| Arizona | 2.59–8.0 | 5.6–8.4 | X | | |
| Arkansas | 2.0–5.9 | 6.5–9.48 | X | | |
| California | 1.0–13.3 | 7.25–8.82 | X | | |
| Colorado | 4.55 | 2.9–7.72 | | | |
| Connecticut | 3.0–6.99 | 6.35 | | X | |
| Delaware | 2.2–6.6 | None | X | | |
| District of Columbia | 4.0–8.95 | 6.0 | X | X | |
| Florida | None | 6.0–7.01 | X | | |
| Georgia | 1.0–5.75 | 4.0–7.33 | X | | |
| Hawaii | 1.4–11.0 | 4.0–4.44 | X | X | |
| Idaho | 1.125–6.925 | 6.0–6.02 | X | | |
| Illinois | 4.95 | 6.25–8.83 | X | X | |
| Indiana | 3.23 | 7.0 | X | | |
| Iowa | 0.33–8.53 | 6.0–6.94 | X | | X |
| Kansas | 3.1–5.7 | 6.5–8.7 | | | |
| Kentucky | 5.0 | 6.0 | X | | X |
| Louisiana | 2.0–6.0 | 4.45–9.55 | X | | |
| Maine | 5.8–7.15 | 5.5 | X | X | |
| Maryland | 2.0–5.75 | 6.0 | X | X | X |
| Massachusetts | 5.0 | 6.25 | X | X | |
| Michigan | 4.25 | 6.0 | X | | |
| Minnesota | 5.35–9.85 | 6.875–7.47 | | X | |
| Mississippi | 3.0–5.0 | 7.0–7.07 | X | | |
| Missouri | 1.5–5.4 | 4.225–8.25 | | | |
| Montana | 1.0–6.9 | None | | | |
| Nebraska | 2.46–6.84 | 5.5–6.94 | | | X |

(*continued*)

| State | Personal Income Tax Rate (%) Note 1 | State and Local Sales Tax Range (%) Note 2 | State Does NOT Tax Social Security Benefits | State Has an Estate Tax | State Has an Inheritance Tax |
|---|---|---|---|---|---|
| Nevada | None | 6.85–8.23 | X | | |
| New Hampshire | 5.0 | None | X | | |
| New Jersey | 1.4–10.750 | 6.625–6.6 | X | | X |
| New Mexico | 1.7–5.9 | 5.125–7.84 | | | |
| New York | 4.0–8.82 | 4.0–8.52 | X | X | |
| North Carolina | 5.25 | 4.75–6.98 | X | | |
| North Dakota | 1.1–≠2.9 | 5.0–6.96 | X | | |
| Ohio | 2.850–4.797 | 5.75–7.22 | | | |
| Oklahoma | 0.5–5.0 | 4.5–8.95 | X | | |
| Oregon | 4.75–9.9 | None | X | X | |
| Pennsylvania | 3.07 | 6.0–6.34 | X | | X |
| Rhode Island | 3.75–5.99 | 7.0 | | X | |
| South Carolina | 3.0–7.0 | 6.0–7.47 | X | | |
| South Dakota | None | 4.5–6.4 | X | | |
| Tennessee | None | 7.0–9.55 | X | | |
| Texas | None | 6.25–8.19 | X | | |
| Utah | 4.95 | 6.1–7.19 | X | | |
| Vermont | 3.35–8.75 | 6.0-6.24 | | X | |
| Virginia | 2.0–5.75 | 5.3–5.75 | | | |
| Washington | None | 6.5–9.29 | X | X | |
| West Virginia | 3.0–6.5 | 6.0–6.51 | X | | |
| Wisconsin | 3.54–7.65 | 5.0–5.43 | | | |
| Wyoming | None | 4.0–5.39 | X | | |

Note 1. Eleven states allow for a local (City or County) tax, which are not included in these rates. They are Alabama, Delaware, Indiana, Iowa, Kentucky, Maryland, Michigan, Missouri, New York, Ohio, and Pennsylvania.

Note 2. Some states allow for the imposition of an additional sales tax at the local level, resulting in a range of possible total sales taxes in those states. The upper range in this chart reflects the population weighted average of these local sales taxes.

*Source:* Tax Foundation.

# More Resources

## *Books*

Deloitte. *2020 Tax Planning for US Individuals Living Abroad.* www2.deloitte
.com/content/dam/Deloitte/us/Documents/Tax/us-tax-planning-
for-us-individuals-living-abroad-2020.pdf.

Matthews, Joseph. *Social Security, Medicare & Government Pensions: Get the
Most Out of Your Retirement and Medical Benefits* (27th ed.). NOLO, 2022.

Pfau, Wade. *Retirement Planning Guidebook: Navigating the Important Decisions
for Retirement Success.* Retirement Researcher Media, 2021.

## *Helpful IRS Publications (Find these at www.irs.gov)*

Publication 17, Your Federal Income Tax

Publication 523, Selling Your Home

Publication 550, Investment Income and Expense

Publication 554, Tax Guide for Seniors

Publication 590-B, Distributions from Individual Retirement
Arrangements (IRAs)

Publication 915, Social Security and Equivalent Railroad Retirement Benefits

Publication 939, General Rule for Pensions and Annuities

# CHAPTER 9

# Money Saving Tricks and Tips

■ ■ ■

What sounds better? Eating 80% lean ground beef or eating 20% fat ground beef? When purchasing meat, most of us would purchase the package labeled 80% lean ground beef, although both choices are equivalent (and indeed, experiments that did exactly this in stores showed this prediction to be true). We think we are rational creatures, but "behavioral economists" demonstrate in study after study that many of us are easily "tricked" by psychological concepts. Let's take a look at several of these and see how we can conquer being "predictably irrational" in decisions regarding money . . . and other things.

- **Anchoring.** You go into a store looking to buy a pair of new jeans. You see the "original" price in big letters (which sets the "anchor" price in your mind) and then you see the sales price, and figure you are getting a good deal. What if there hadn't been that anchor? Would you feel the same about the deal? Probably not. Or, you plan to go on a cruise. You're thrilled to see the cruise is on "sale." The "normal" price sets the anchor, and you feel you've scored a deal, without really knowing if it's a good deal or not. The MSRP on a car is another "anchoring" purchase. Most of us know that the price that is on the windshield is not really the beginning point of the negotiation, although the intent is to create an "anchor" in our minds. Knowing what the dealer paid for the car or what others have paid for the same make/brand/year is a far better reference point. Thinking about buying a house? The listing price creates an anchor, but is it realistic? Anchoring occurs when we use an initial piece of information to make subsequent judgments. It's a very powerful way to sell us stuff. Imagine you're at a nice restaurant and there's a $95 bottle of wine on the menu (the anchor). Suddenly, the $32 bottle of wine seems like a good price. Here's an iconic advertising example that drives the point home: "How do you sell a $2,000 watch? Put it next to a $10,000 watch." Anchor!

Anchors can result in purchases that can negatively affect our finances, because we're tricked into these false comparisons. Solution: Counteract anchors by doing your homework beforehand and know the real value of what you want to purchase, and negotiate from that point. You might save a bundle.

- **Analysis Paralysis** (also called hyperchoice). Having many choices seems to be a good thing, right? Wrong. It's called the "hyperchoice paradox" – too many choices are counterproductive, causing decisions to become less likely, and experiencing a drop in choice satisfaction when you *do* choose. For example, think about relocation. In Chapter 5, I mentioned that being able to move *anywhere* after retiring can be overwhelming, so for many it's easier to decide not to decide, and just stay put. Staying where you live now *may* be the best decision, but for many it's the one requiring the least effort. Or, consider Medicare Advantage plans. In 2021, there were 3,550 plans available nationwide, although when I limit it to those available in my ZIP code, there are only 34 . . . still overwhelming!

How to fight "analysis paralysis"? Narrow your choices by prioritizing your goals, doing research, and seeking input from those whose opinion you respect, recognize there is rarely ever one "perfect" answer, trust your instincts, and set a time limit to come up with a choice. The best choice *may* be the status quo, but don't go down that path because of analysis paralysis. For example, staying in your home because it's easier to do nothing can become a huge issue when one of you can no longer negotiate the steps to the bedroom. Relocating can suddenly become a crisis – both emotional and financial. One final example (confession) . . . I live in a community with a Homeowners Association (HOA), and needed to get approval for changing the color of my house. After going through the Sherwin-Williams paint deck of more than 2,000 colors and agonizing for a week or more, I decided to re-paint it . . . the same color. I was overwhelmed by too many choices and stuck with the status quo. On the other hand, when choosing a place to move after my husband retired, we made a list of several things we *had* to have in a new location – recall from Chapter 5 we called these our "nonnegotiables" – on the East Coast of the United States, good medical care, on the ocean, a new (easier to meet people) community with a Homeowners Association (I like communities with rules – many people do not), a vibrant tennis program, good transportation, nice climate, and low taxes (I can work remotely, so that aspect was not an issue). Once I narrowed my list, I found a place within a few months – and we're still happily here, 15 years later).

- **Status Quo Bias.** Yes, it's often easier to do nothing, but it's not always the right choice. For example, many companies have instituted opt-out versus opt-in retirement savings plans, because companies understand it's easier *not* to sign up for the company savings plan, even though it's usually a smart thing to do. Many businesses take advantage of status-quo bias. It explains why we might keep unread magazine subscriptions, cable plans, gym memberships – for some, it's easier to have something auto-renew than to actually cancel it, even though it costs us a lot of money. To fight status quo bias, start small. Try eating something you've never had before at a restaurant, rather than the same exact order every time you go; read a book that's not in your normal genre; cut ties with toxic people; approach someone you don't know well and start up a conversation; go someplace different for your next vacation. Fighting status quo bias can enrich your life. . .and your wallet. But, recognize that for most, change is not easy.

- **Future Discounting.** On January 1, I will . . . Tomorrow, I will . . . As soon as (fill in the blank), I will . . . this is future-discounting thinking. It's our tendency to idealize our future self's behavior, although our present self is weak. It's why we finish off that chocolate ice cream tonight, vowing we won't eat any junk food tomorrow; it's how we promise we'll walk two miles in the morning, while we're watching TV in the evening. It why we say we'll start saving for retirement with the next paycheck, but blow it on some new gadget instead. What to do? Set up an automatic savings plan if you're still working. And, envision your future self. In studies that aged people digitally about 20 years, those who actually saw their "future selves" started saving more for the future than those who did not. At the least, find pics of yourself as a kid – and now, and envision yourself even farther along.

- **Loss Aversion**. Here's the thing . . . we generally feel twice as bad about a loss as we feel good about a similar gain. Most of us would feel worse about losing a $20 bill than we'd feel good about finding a $20 bill. It's why we spend money on extended warranties, which most experts agree are not worth it. It's why people have a tough time taking less for the sale of their home if they feel it's worth more (although a house is really only worth what people are willing to pay for it), and why it's so painful to downsize – it's viewed as a loss, even though it's the right decision. It's why people have trouble cutting their losses on bad investments and selling that dog stock; or, they pull out their investments as soon as the market takes a dip, because the "loss" feels so painful; and it's why research shows that in the Olympics, the Bronze winner is happier than the Silver winner: the Bronze winner is happy he/she is at least standing on the podium . . . the Silver winner is feeling the loss of just missing the Gold. Knowing you're suffering from loss aversion is itself very helpful. Work to separate your emotions from your actions. Or, ask yourself how long you have to work to buy that car, purse, pair of shoes you covet . . . it will help you avoid loss aversion.

- **Framing.** The example we started with (the 20% fat vs. 80% lean ground beef) is an example of framing. The way we frame things can make a huge difference. For example, there was a study involving a financial planner who asked her clients if they could cut 30% of their living expenses. The answer was generally an emphatic "no." However, when the question was reframed, and comparable clients were asked if they could live on 70% of their current income if necessary, the answer from the majority was "yes." Framing things differently can help us save money. For example, reframing a purchase, such as "How many hours do I/did I have to work to buy those shoes/car/piece of jewelry?" can make a difference. Or, say you're considering starting a business in retirement; which is more likely to make you take the leap: You'll have a 50% chance of success . . . or . . . you'll have a 50% chance of failure? One does sound more encouraging than the other, even though they are both exactly the same, right? My favorite example of framing is when a little decal of a fly was placed close to the drain in the men's urinals in a Dutch airport. By "reframing" the target for the men's urine, they drastically reduced "spillage" (about 50%), and lowered cleaning costs. This framing idea has been copied in many other locations with great success.

- **Confirmation Bias.** Confirmation bias is the tendency for people to seek or interpret information that confirms their beliefs. These days, with the political divide, people tend to watch the news that reinforces their own views, such as Fox News or CNN. Or, people listen to religious leaders who espouse the beliefs they already hold. We see and hear what we want to see and hear, and ignore information that doesn't conform to our own views. And, we often are friends with people who share the same ideas/beliefs. But, this bias can cause problems in retirement planning, because we often do not make the best choices when we are only consulting like-minded people. So, be sure to look at all aspects of an investment, and find people who have divergent opinions, and try to keep an open mind. Seek out sources that challenge what we think. Marie M. has lost thousands of dollars by buying individual funds recommended by a subscription service. They confirm her own investment views, but she finally realized they may not have *her* best interest at heart.
- **Overconfidence Bias.** We tend to have an overinflated view of ourselves. Our confidence in our knowledge and judgment is often lower, when measured objectively, than we think. Although overconfidence bias may be good for our ego, and can propel us to do things we wouldn't ordinarily do (such as accepting a challenging position, or starting a new business or making new friends), it can be a bad thing when it comes to saving for retirement. For example, people with overconfidence bias may do research about investing and saving for retirement, but research information in such a way that they only look for examples that confirm their biases, not challenge them.

Knowing, understanding, and recognizing some of the unconscious ways we think and act and how to counteract these behaviors will help us make our retirement planning more successful. We'll make better financial (and nonfinancial) decisions, become savvier consumers, and as Dan Ariely, the James B. Duke Professor of Psychology and Behavioral Economics at Duke University, says, become less "predictably irrational."

## From Irrational to Rational

Now, let's pivot from the "irrational" workings of how our brain can trick us into making some less-than-ideal money decisions, and look at some specific, concrete tips that can increase the money in our wallets:

- **Use Credit Cards That Pay You.** It goes without saying that you should try to avoid carrying a balance on your credit cards because the interest rates charged can be outrageous. According to WalletHub, the average rate in October 2021 for new accounts was 18.24%, and 14.54% for existing accounts. If you must carry a balance, look for a credit card with the lowest interest rate possible. If you are not carrying a balance, you should look for a credit card that pays you the most in cash-back benefits. A number of credit cards offer cash back on purchases at rates up to 5%, but with limits on the category of purchases (e.g., groceries, gas, restaurants, etc.) that qualify for these high rates, and also limits how much in purchases qualify for the high cash-back percentage. These limitations can surely put a damper on the total amount of cash back you will earn. However, there are currently a few cards that pay cash back rates of 2% on all purchases, with no category limitations, and no annual fees. Examples of these are the Wells Fargo Active Cash Card (Google "Wells Fargo Active Cash Card"), which is currently also offering a $200 cash bonus for new cardholders who spend $1,000 in the first three months, and the Citi Double Cash Credit Card (https://www.citi.com/credit-cards/citi-double-cash-credit-card), which pays a 1% cash back bonus when you charge a purchase and an additional 1% bonus when you pay for the purchase, for a total of 2%.

- **Audit Your Credit Card Bill.** While we are on the topic of credit cards, another suggestion is that you periodically review your monthly statement very carefully, looking for charges for services that you don't want or need. Over the years you may have signed up for services that automatically charge your credit card, but which you no longer even use, or perhaps free trials that required a credit card number and after a month the free part disappeared. Examples would be magazine subscriptions and credit monitoring services that provide little benefit. When you add up these monthly charges and multiply by 12, they can add up to a nice piece of change. Call and cancel them.
- **Say Good-Bye to Foreign Transaction Fees.** Although many if not most credit cards charge up to a 3% fee for all charges made in foreign countries, some do not. Get rid of those fees by using a card that does not impose that extra charge. As an added bonus, some cards not only waive this fee, but also have no annual fee and pay you up to 1.5% in cash back for all your charges. On a two-week trip to Europe, you could easily spend $5,000 or more on hotels, restaurants, trains, entertainment, and airfare and save $150 by not paying foreign transaction fees while you earn $75 more in cash back. Examples of cards that waive the foreign transaction fee, have no annual fee, and pay a cash back reward are the Bank of America Travel Rewards Card (https://www.bankofamerica.com/credit-cards/products/travel-rewards-credit-card/) and the Capital One Quicksilver Cash Rewards Credit Card (https://www.capitalone.com/credit-cards/quicksilver/).
- **Property Tax on Your Home.** The two major variables that determine how much you will pay in property tax on your home are the tax rate imposed by the state/county/city and the valuation of your home by the property tax assessor. You can exercise your right as a citizen to protest the rate, but that needs a lot of support from the residents of your taxing jurisdiction, and is rarely successful. So that leaves fighting

the valuation on your home as your best course of action. The first step is to review your assessment, including the information on which it was based (which is available from the assessor), such as the square footage of your home, the number of bathrooms, whether your basement is finished or not, and importantly, how it compares to the selling prices of comparable homes in your neighborhood. If you feel there is a reasonable basis to protest the valuation, you should discuss it with your tax assessor. While a more formal appeal may be necessary, I have successfully appealed the property tax valuation on all four of the homes I have owned and only once had to make a formal appeal. The other three times a lower assessment was worked out with the assessor, either by telephone or by meeting and discussing my concerns, armed with the data I put together to demonstrate an overassessment existed. The magic of a successful appeal is that it is a gift that keeps giving in future years.

- **Refinance Your Home.** We have enjoyed historically low interest rates on home mortgages over the past few years. Interest rates are likely to rise in the future and it is quite possible that the current rates are lower than what you are paying on your home mortgage. Refinancing to a lower rate will not only reduce your interest costs, potentially by thousands of dollars, but if you also change to a shorter mortgage period, you will not only enjoy an even lower interest rate but you will pay off your mortgage sooner. Wouldn't it be great to go into retirement without a home mortgage, or with only a few years left to pay it off?

- **Cut the Cost of Television.** Do you really watch very many of the channels you are paying your cable (or satellite) company to provide? Premium content means premium costs. It may be time for you to look at the cost of the TV package you are paying for and then compare it to a lower cost package to see if you would lose any channels that are important to you. Even better, are you willing to consider "cutting the cord" and streaming all your programming over the Internet? If you have a smart TV (a smart TV can connect to your home Internet and offers a range of applications for programming), it is easy to sign up for a series of applications that very well may give you all the TV entertainment you need. Some of the available applications are free and others come with what is usually a small monthly cost, especially when compared to your cable or satellite programming packages. Even if you don't have a smart TV, inexpensive devices like Roku and Fire TV Stick plug into the back of your TV and offer pretty much the same functions and applications of a smart TV. If this does not sound appealing to you, how about putting an antenna on your roof, or maybe even in your attic, and getting all the local channels for free – or maybe do both, an antenna for local channels and streaming for all else.

If changing to streaming your TV programming does not sound appealing to you, how about just calling your cable or satellite company and letting them know their cost is too high and you are planning on cutting the cord if they can't reduce the monthly fee. This often works, and is quick and easy to do.

- **Cost of Drugs.** Prescription drug costs are constantly going up. Ask your doctor if there is a generic drug that works just as well and costs considerably less. Also, check websites like GoodRx (www.goodrx.com) for coupons that provide savings on your drugs. On the GoodRx website you can input the drug you need and it will provide the cost at a number of local pharmacies, for which you can print out a discount coupon. Another possibility is the Optum Perks discount card (https://perks.optum.com/). GoodRx and Optum Perks don't always produce a lower drug cost, but sometimes they have a lower cost that is very significant. The only downside, which may or may not be an issue for you, is that drugs purchased with these discount cards do not count against any drug cost deductible you may have on a drug plan (such as a Medicare Part D plan). If you are not going to meet your deductible anyway, that won't matter.

- **Gym Membership.** Many of us have signed up for a gym membership in the past, maybe as part of a New Year's resolution or just because we decided it was time to get in better shape. However, lots of us ended up not really using the gym very much, or maybe not at all. Yet, the monthly charge keeps showing up on our credit card bill. Is it time to cut your costs and cancel the membership? Consider exercising at home using your TV; workout programming is available on smart TVs, some of which is free if, for example, you are already streaming programming on applications that include this, such as Apple TV and Netflix. It is a lot more convenient and can save you the cost of the gym membership.

- **Self-Storage Units.** Are you like many of us who rented a self-storage unit a long time ago to store household stuff that you were no longer using? It can be psychologically tough to get rid of items that may have served you well over the years, but you really should take a look at how much you are paying to store them. If it is likely that you are never going to use the items again, maybe you can make a nice contribution to charity (Goodwill, Habitat for Humanity, AMVETS, Salvation Army), stop the monthly rental, and pick up a tax deduction. And guess what . . . your kids aren't going to want that stuff, either.

- **Search for Missing Money.** All states have escheatable property laws under which unclaimed property must be turned over to the state. According to the National Association of Unclaimed Property Administrators, approximately 10% of people in the United States have unclaimed property that is being held by U.S. state governments and treasuries. In 2020 Smart Asset estimated the total at $49.5 billion.

    Examples of unclaimed properties include uncashed paychecks, dormant checking and savings accounts, stocks, utility deposits and contents of safe deposit boxes. You can do a free search for any unclaimed property of yours that is being held by the various state sites by going through the National Association of Unclaimed Property Administrators at https://unclaimed.org/.

Another possible source of lost money is unredeemed U.S. Treasury bonds and other government securities. The current estimate is that there are 80 million matured, unredeemed bonds, with a total value in excess of $29 billion. You can quickly and easily search to determine if there are any of these bonds in your name by going to an online search tool run by the Treasury Department at www.treasuryhunt.gov and entering your name, social security number, and state of residence. The search will also include missing payments on series H or HH savings bonds.

- **Visit Our National Parks on the Cheap.** Our national parks are a national treasure and wonderful places to visit. A great vacation is a road trip to visit several of them at a time. However, there is an entrance fee at the 108 national parks, ranging as high as $35 per vehicle. The good news is that those aged 62 or older can purchase an annual senior pass for $20, or a lifetime senior pass for $80 that gets you into all of them (plus more than 2,000 federal recreation areas). These passes can be purchased at any federal recreation site, including the national parks, that charges an entrance fee. Proof of age and residency is required. Those accompanying the pass holder in a noncommercial vehicle are admitted into the parks for free; and three additional people are admitted with a passholder at per-person fee sites. An incredible deal.

- **Sell Your Car Online Instead of Trading It at the Dealership.** Buying a car at a dealership can be frustrating enough without the added hassle of negotiating a fair trade-in value for your current car. One way to make this process easier, and maybe even eliminate it, is to price your current vehicle online at sites like Carvana (https://www.carvana.com/

sell-my-car) or CarMax (https://www.carmax.com/sell-my-car). They will offer you a "guaranteed" offer price based on the information you provide, good for seven days, which gives you the ability to determine if the dealer will give you a comparable or even better offer (you can provide the dealer the Internet offer you already have as a bargaining tool). If the dealer won't, you can go ahead and sell your vehicle to Carvana or CarMax, or one of the other sites that make these offers. They may even pick up your vehicle at your residence. One thing to keep in mind is that the purchase of an automobile is generally subject to a state sales tax, and some states tax the net (of the trade-in value) purchase price, in which case you would need to factor this in when deciding if the dealer trade-in value is comparable to or better than the internet offer you have.

- **Get a Smart Thermostat.** A significant portion of your monthly electricity and/or gas bill is the cost of heating and cooling your home. If you still have an old-style thermostat that does not allow you to preprogram the desired temperatures by time of day and day of week, consider getting one. There is no need to have room-comfortable temperatures when nobody is home, and maybe you prefer cooler temperatures at night while sleeping, but you don't bother turning the temperature down every evening. You can save a lot by using a smart thermostat to automatically adjust temperatures to maximize savings without giving up any comfort.

- **Medical Procedures.** Going out of network for medical services can get very expensive. Even if you know your doctor is in your medical network you should confirm that all involved in your case are also in network before having an elective procedure. This includes the surgery center or hospital, and the anesthesiologist, and the labs that will be used. Peter M. had a colonoscopy last year and confirmed that the doctor and surgery center were in network for his insurance plan. He was shocked a month later when he was billed for almost

$3,000 by the anesthesiologist and pathology lab; it turned out that neither was in network for him. He was able to negotiate the bills down, but still ended up paying over $1,000.

- **The High Cost of Death.** As Benjamin Franklin said in 1789, ". . . in this world nothing can be said to be certain, except death and taxes." Although he did not comment on the costs of both, we know that taxes are expensive and, if we don't already know, we will find out that funeral arrangements can be very pricey as well. According to the National Funeral Directors Association, the average cost of a funeral (excluding burial plots, transportation, flowers, etc.), is a bit over $7,000, plus about $1,400 more if the graveyard requires a vault. A mausoleum may or may not be as expensive as a burial plot. The average cost for a cremation is about $1,000 less than these average costs, and going with a direct cremation, where the body is cremated soon after death, and there is no embalming, viewing, or visitation, can lower the cost to around $1,000.

  In 1984 the Federal Trade Commission set forth rules that prohibit funeral homes from exerting leverage to get customers to buy services and products they don't really need or want. The rules mandate a number of things, including requiring the funeral home to show a list of the price of caskets as well as all the other products and services available, provide pricing details over the phone, and allowing you to provide your own casket or urn.

  Although dealing with the death of a loved one is a very difficult time, if you want to significantly reduce funeral costs, you should consider (1) visiting several acceptable funeral homes in your area to compare their services and prices, and (2) pricing and purchasing a casket online. Caskets can be one of the most expensive funeral costs, averaging over $2,000 and ranging up to $10,000 and more. You can price caskets and purchase them online at such outlets as Walmart, Amazon, and Costco, with prices starting just under $1,000 and delivery in as little as three days. Overnight Caskets (www.overnightcaskets.com) has a wide selection of caskets in the $1,300 to $1,400 range and guarantees overnight delivery to the funeral home of your choice. My friend Ann L. purchased a casket from Costco (not available for shipping in Alaska or Hawaii) for her spouse, who died after a long bout with cancer, and was very satisfied with the cost, efficiency, and quality.

- **Use a Library Card.** Libraries are a wonderful place to get access to thousands of books, movies, magazines, and newspapers. Why buy a book to read if you can read it for free? Many also provide free use of a computer, networked to the Internet.

- **A Health Savings Account Can Provide Long-Term Tax Benefits.** Many employers pair a high deductible health insurance plan with a Health Savings Account (HSA) for their employees. The HSA may be funded by employer contributions, employee pretax contributions, or maybe a combination of both. The funds are generally put into a low-interest-paying bank account from which the employee can draw funds to pay out-of- pocket medical expenses. The maximum amounts that can be contributed into an HSA in 2022 are $3,650 for an individual and $7,300 for a family plan. If you have a high deductible medical insurance plan ($1,400 or more for an individual and $2,800 or more for a family) and contributions to your plan at work are less than the maximum allowed, or if there is no plan at work, you can set up an HSA on your own to bring the annual contribution up to the maximum. If you set this up through a financial provider that provides options for investing the account in mutual funds and leave them there year after year, the balance in the account can build to a nice nest egg. For example, if you contribute $5,000 into an HSA each year for 10 years and invest it in a mutual fund averaging an 8% annual return, you would have over $78,000 in the HSA at the end of the 10 years.

Withdrawals from an HSA are tax free only if used to pay eligible medical expenses, but there is no requirement that the withdrawal be made in the same year as the expense was incurred. So, be sure to keep a file of all your medical and dental bills that are reimbursable by an HSA so you can support the tax-free withdrawals that you might choose to make years after the expense was incurred. The HSA can also be used to reimburse you for premiums for Medicare Parts B and D and for Medical Advantage plans, but not for your premiums for Medicare supplemental policies. Reimbursing yourself years later on a tax-free basis makes the HSA even better than a Roth IRA – you receive a tax deduction for your contributions, accumulate earnings over a number of years, and then make withdrawals tax free.

- **Overpaying Income Tax on Stock Dividends.** The federal income tax rate on qualified dividends (which includes most dividends paid by U.S. corporations on stock which you have held for one year or longer) is lower than the tax rate on all other income. If your brokerage account is set up to allow margin purchases of securities, it likely also allows the brokerage house to borrow your securities and use them for covering short stock sales of their customers (known as hypothecation), regardless of whether you have ever made a short stock sale yourself. This can result in you receiving "payments in lieu of dividends" from the brokerage house, instead of dividends from the stock that was borrowed. While you are being fairly compensated for the loss of the dividend on the stock that was borrowed, the payment in lieu of your dividend does not qualify for the preferential tax treatment and will likely cost you more tax dollars. Check this out with your broker and, if you are not buying stocks on margin, delete the margin option on the account. This is not an issue for stocks you hold in a tax-deferred account, such as an IRA or Section 403(b) account.

296

- **Become a Shareholder with Perks.** The reason for investing in stocks is to make money, from dividends and from appreciation in the value of the stock. However, there are some companies that give benefits to its shareholders. If a company's stock looks like a good investment, and there are additional benefits, it would be a win-win.

  A number of the major cruise companies are giving onboard credits to their shareholders. Examples are Carnival Corporation, which owns Carnival, Holland America, and Princess; Norwegian, which owns Norwegian, Oceania, and Regent Seven Seas; and Royal Caribbean, which owns Royal Caribbean and Celebrity. They each give shareholders owning at least 100 shares of stock an onboard room credit of $50 to $250 per stateroom per cruise, depending on the length of the cruise. Bon voyage!

  Examples of other companies giving shareholder benefits are InterContinental Hotels, Irish Continental Group, and Lenovo Group, each of which provides purchase discounts to its shareholders.

- **Finally, Just Ask.** It is a very competitive world out there, and vendors never want to lose a good customer. You probably get lots of solicitations in the mail for things like cable and satellite TV, newspapers, gym memberships and on and on. When you see a significant difference between what is being offered to new customers compared to what you are paying (even if you are using a competitor), why not give the customer service representative a call to ask for a comparable discount? You will be surprised at how often this will result in lowering your monthly charge.

"A penny saved is a penny earned." Although this adage is attributed to Benjamin Franklin, he never actually said it. What he really wrote in the 1737 *Poor Richard's Almanack* was "A penny saved is two pence clear." But, you get the idea. Reducing your day-to-day expenses, both before and after retirement, should be an important part of your planning.

The best thing about money is that it provides options, opportunities, and freedom. Money can help us achieve our goals and purpose. That's what the next – and last – chapter is about; determining who we really are, and what we want to accomplish and share with others as we enter what is often called the "third age" of our lives.

## More Resources

### Books

Ariely, Dan. *Predictably Irrational, Revised and Expanded: The Hidden Forces That Shape Our Decisions.* Harper, 2009.

Thaler, Richard. *Nudge: Improving Decisions About Health, Wealth, and Happiness.* Penguin Books, 2009.

### Websites

www.AARP.org (Put "99 New Great Ways to Save Money" into the search bar)

Nerd Wallet: https://www.nerdwallet.com/article/finance/how-to-save-money

U.S. News: 15 Creative Ways to Save Money: https://money.usnews.com/money/personal-finance/saving-and-budgeting/articles/creative-ways-to-save-money

# CHAPTER 10

## The Final Chapter

■ ■ ■

"Find out who you are, and do it on purpose." Dolly Parton nailed it with this quote. If you do a search for the word "purpose" on Google, you get 2,820,000,000 (that is almost 3 *billion*) results. That tells us that purpose is something important. How do we find/know our purpose in life? Many of you reading this may have figured it out; for others, it may be something you think is worthwhile, but haven't yet crystallized; some may think it's just the newest retirement buzzword, and you're just doing the best you can to plan/get through this last third of your life.

This book addresses the "ingredients" for a successful retirement; what to do with your 168 hours a week; the innumerable possibilities of where to live; how to choose a place, and how your location can shape how you live; strategies to stay or become healthy in mind, body, and spirit; the vital importance of connections; and how to make your money last. This chapter will explore how to hopefully leave this earth with no regrets, and ways to leave a financial and/or nonfinancial legacy.

Okay, I'll be honest . . . some of this chapter is a little more "touchy-feely" than the others, but it could be the most important chapter in the book.

# Regrets

Chapter 1 addressed the secrets for a successful retirement, and shared some of the common *financial* regrets from those who have already retired, including not starting to save early enough and/or not saving enough; having too much debt (cars, credit cards, educational loans for kids/grandkids); having a house that is more than you need/more expensive than you can easily afford, and so forth.

But, how about nonfinancial regrets at the end of life? The following list is compiled from three sources: *The Top Five Regrets of the Dying* by Bronnie Ware (Ware cared for people in their homes during the last weeks of their lives); Quora, an online site that invites the community to answer questions (the question was: "What are the lessons people most often learn too late in life?"), and the "Top 10 Regrets in Life by Those about to Die" by Joel Brown, the CEO and founder of Addicted2Success, who interviewed elderly residents in nursing homes and palliative care.

These three sources, perhaps not unsurprisingly, had similar themes and a lot of overlap. Here they are, condensed, combined, reworded, and summarized:

1. I wish I had realized that happiness is a choice – my choice.
2. I wish I realized that time passes much more quickly than we realize.
3. I should have done more of what I wanted to do, rather than what others expected me to do.
4. I should have said "I love you" more often.
5. I wish I had spent more time with family and friends. People are far more important than work or things.
6. I should have resolved my conflicts with others.
7. I wish I had been more compassionate, and helped others who were less fortunate.
8. I wish I had the courage to express my feelings, rather than hold in bitterness and resentment.

9. I realized jealousy and envy are wasted emotions. There will always be others who are more attractive, richer, more popular, more athletic, smarter, etc. I wish I had accepted this.
10. If you don't take care of your body while you're younger, it won't take care of you when you're older.

Powerful stuff. And, note that it's not money that takes center stage when it comes to the end of our life. So, take some time and imagine you are in *your* final days. What would be your regrets and wishes? And, think about Cher's lyrics, "If I could turn back time." We know that's not possible, so act on banishing those regrets and fulfilling those wishes *now*.

## Tom Sawyer, Steve Jobs, and Eulogies

Did you read *The Adventures of Tom Sawyer* by Mark Twain (Samuel Clemens)? One of the memorable plot lines was Tom attending his own funeral, hidden from the congregation. The townspeople, erroneously assuming Tom (and his friends Huckleberry Finn and Joe Harper) were dead, held a service for the boys. Their neighbors praised and mourned them, and wished they had been nicer to the three of them. The townspeople regretted they had been so tough on them. It brings up an interesting question – what will people say about you at *your* funeral?

There's a thought-provoking book called *The Road to Character* by David Brooks, in which he discusses the difference between "resume virtues" and "eulogy virtues." Our resume virtues include accomplishments like graduating from Harvard or Yale, rising to a high position in a corporation, becoming a best-selling author or famous celebrity, or inventing a new technology. They are symbols of external success. Eulogy virtues are the ones people talk about at funerals. These are things like kindness, compassion, honesty, and integrity. There is certainly nothing wrong with resume virtues, but we should strive to give equal weight to developing our eulogy virtues.

Most of us would agree Steve Jobs of Apple fame is an example of someone who had incredible resume virtues. Yet, let's take a look at his graduation speech at Stanford in 2005, when he was famous and wealthy, but had recently been diagnosed with a pancreatic neuroendocrine tumor. At the time of this speech, Job's doctors thought his cancer was curable. That scare (unfortunately, it was not curable, and Jobs died in 2011), changed the way he thought about life. A few of his quotes: "No one wants to die. Even people who want to go to heaven don't want to die to get there. And yet death is the destination we all share. No one has ever escaped it. And that is as it should be, because Death is very likely the single best invention of Life. It is Life's change agent." "Your time is limited, so don't waste it living someone else's life. Don't let the noise of others' opinions drown out your own inner voice. And most important, have the courage to follow your heart and intuition." Heavy stuff. Bottom line: Our values should drive our actions.

## Values and Purpose

Steve Jobs's Stanford talk was about the importance of living your values and figuring out your purpose. Purpose is why we do what we do and our values help us determine our purpose. Generally, of course, our day-to-day actions should reflect our purpose and values. The great thing about values is that they are voluntary; we get to choose them. They are the things we consider important in life. Purpose and values are popular discussion points in retirement these days, and it's no wonder – as we get older and thoughtfully look forward – and back – upon our life, hopefully our values and purpose align with our behaviors and actions. We don't want to be on our deathbeds and thinking about our regrets – what we *wished* we had done with our time on this earth.

For example, if we say health is one of our values, but we don't eat or exercise accordingly, it's time to reevaluate if it's really a value . . . or a wish. Or, if we say family is very important, but we only connect or get together on obligatory holidays or special occasions, or out of a sense of guilt, there is a disconnect between our values and our actions. If we claim we want to help make the world a better place, but always turn down even simple volunteer requests, or we say we value honesty, but routinely cheat on our taxes . . . you get the idea. Values are what we do when no one is looking, and no one finds out about them . . . and we're fine with that. For example, if someone leaves a very hefty tip for a waitperson who seems to be struggling . . . and tells no one. Or, we provide money to fund our grandchildren's higher education . . . but only tell their parents. Or bequeath a sizable sum to a charity . . . and keep that knowledge private.

If you're struggling to identify *your* values, sometimes seeing a list of values can help crystallize and pinpoint what's important to you. It reminds me of the famous quote by Justice Potter Stewart in 1964, when he was trying to explain what is obscene or "hard-core" pornography, and famously said, "I know it when I see it." So, perhaps some additional examples of values will resonate with you: caring, empathy, fairness, kindness, loyalty, making a difference, relationships, service, spirituality, thankfulness, and understanding. It can also be helpful to think of people you truly admire, and think about what it is about them that makes them so special. Chances are they have values that you value. Your hobbies, what you share on social media, what you like to read, and even the pictures you like to take can provide some clues to your values. The demands of day-to-day life often get in the way of determining our values, so we may need to carve out some time to think about and list them. (There's a link to a longer list of values at the end of the chapter.)

Once you have your list of values, and some/many of your values may be aspirational – we aren't always our best selves. Values can help us formulate our purpose and guide our decision-making and our behavior. Your purpose is individual and unique; it's often what gets you out of bed in the morning. But, if you struggle to come up with one, Richard Leider, author, coach, speaker, and pioneer of the global purpose movement, suggests a wonderful example: "Our life purpose is to GROW and to GIVE." Pretty much says it all!

A few examples of famous people and their purpose: Mother Teresa: to help "the unwanted, the unloved and the uncared for." Dali Lama: "It is the practice of compassion." Steve Jobs found his purpose when he was young: "I was lucky – I found what I loved to do early in life. Woz and I started Apple in my parents' garage when I was 20." If you haven't found it yet, keep looking within yourself. Remember how long it took Dorothy to click her heels and say, "There's no place like home."

Many find their purpose later in life. Colonel Sanders was so confident about the way he pressure-fried chicken as a younger man, he spent years (unsuccessfully) trying to get restaurants to try his recipe, and he didn't start KFC until he was 65. J.K. Rowling of Harry Potter fame was 28, divorced, a single mom, broke, and on welfare. But, as she said after she was famous – as the commencement speaker at Harvard University – of her earlier years: "I still had an old typewriter and a big idea." We may not be in their league, but we can certainly make the world a better place.

## Retirement Re-Do

Consider retirement as an opportunity to reinvent yourself. If you leave your primary career, and if you move to a new location, you can really start over as the person you've always wanted to be (or the person your dog thinks you are!). Companies have done it – why not you? Did you know, for example, that Avon began as a company that sold books door-to-door? That Wrigley originally sold soap and baking powder? Tiffany began as a stationer, selling pens, paper, and other writing materials. We can change and evolve if we want to do so. Start living your life as you want to be remembered after you're gone.

Research shows we *can* change. One example is the concept of "Do Good, Be Good." University of Virginia professor Timothy Wilson demonstrated that people who volunteer often change their beliefs about themselves. They start viewing themselves in a different light – that they are the kind of person who does good things for other people. Wilson's research demonstrates that we can tell ourselves new stories, and change our behavior and ourselves. Sort of a variation of "fake it 'til you make it."

## Put Your Money Where Your Values and Purpose Are

We've heard the saying "Love of money is the root of all evil." Let's look at a few possible positive ways your money can reflect your values and purpose – whether you are dead or alive.

- **Consider setting up a Section 529 plan to provide funds for your grandchildren's college education**

    Paying for college is a financial worry for most parents. Setting up a Section 529 plan is a wonderful way to help not only your adult children, by helping to remove this worry, but also your grandchildren, by helping to fund their college education. These plans are state-sponsored investment accounts that you can set up at a number of financial institutions, such as Vanguard, Schwab, Fidelity Investments, and most banks. It's best to start contributing to the Section 529 plan early and allow the funds to accumulate tax-free over a long period of time. You can make contributions to the plan periodically, and your adult children can also contribute to the plan.

    Although there is no federal tax deduction for amounts contributed to the Section 529 plan, withdrawals to pay an unlimited amount of a beneficiary's college expenses (tuition, fees, books, certain room and board expenses, and more), as well as K–12 tuition (limited to $10,000 per year) are tax-free – allowing the earnings in the plan to escape taxation forever. A number of states do provide a tax deduction for residents but generally require that the contributions are made to their own state's plan, so you should consider this in deciding which state to use in setting up the plan. More importantly, however, is that you should set up the plan with a financial institution that offers a variety of investment options, and which has low costs, as the annual fees and other costs will add up over the long stretch of time these funds will be invested. See the end of the chapter for more information about setting up one of these plans.

For example, Carla and Juan T. have three grandchildren and wanted to set up a 529 plan for them, and remove that financial responsibility and worry off the shoulders of their three adult children and their spouses. In December 2000, after looking at the alternatives for where to set up the plans and how to invest the funds, they selected Vanguard and contributed $20,000 into each grandchild's Section 529 account and invested it in an index fund which tracks the S&P 500. The ensuing years were unusually favorable for the U.S. stock market, and each account as of the end of 2020 had over $73,000 accumulated for each grandchild's education.

- **Leave money to a charity**

    If you'd like to leave money to a charity in your will, and you don't know one or more that are legit or reflect your values/purpose, be sure to vet them carefully. Two excellent websites, mentioned in Chapter 2, are Charity Navigator (www.charitynavigator.org) and Charity Watch (www.charitywatch.org). Your goal is probably to get the most money to the programs you want to support, rather than diverting a sizable chunk of your donation to fundraising efforts and administrative costs. These sites provide that important information. And, if you're searching for specific charity suggestions, Charity Navigator has what it calls its "Top 10 List," which can take the guesswork out of your decision-making by providing well-vetted possibilities.

- **Socially responsible investing**

    There is a growing interest among investors to invest in companies that have a positive social or environmental impact, but which also achieve positive financial returns. This has resulted in some financial professionals digging deeper into a company's operations, products, and personnel, so they can recommend investments that correspond to their clients' preferences and beliefs. In addition to investing in individual companies, there are also some mutual funds and exchange-traded funds (ETFs) that are focused on sustainable investing. Fidelity Investments, for example, currently offers 11 such funds, including funds focused on climate, water, and alternative and renewable energy as well as index funds tracking companies with high ratings on outcomes shaped by environmental, social, or governance (ESG) factors. For more information on these funds go to https://www.fidelity.com/mutual-funds/investing-ideas/sustainable-investing. *Forbes* has a list of what it feels were the best ESG funds in 2021 at https://www.forbes.com/advisor/investing/best-esg-funds/.

## Ethical Wills/Legacy Letters/Forever Letters

A will can spell out what you want others to *have*, but an ethical will, legacy letter, or forever letter spells out what you'd like others to *know*. They aren't legal documents, but they are a way to share life lessons, values, and (hopefully) wisdom to those who read them.

Ethical wills have an interesting 3,500-year-old Jewish origin, and are first mentioned in the Bible when Jacob, nearing death, gathered his 12 sons and blessed them, gave them moral advice, and passed on his values and thoughts about how they should live after his death. Ethical wills or legacy letters can include hopes for the future, lessons learned, meaningful family stories, and perhaps apologies for past hurts. They are basically love letters (they can be oral or video as well) to loved ones that remind them, after you're gone, how important they were to you, although you don't have to wait until you are gone to share your ethical will. If you find the concept interesting, but need some help formulating an ethical will or legacy letter, see the end of this chapter for a free template for an ethical will by Beth La Mie, as well as a few suggested books for composing your own ethical will, legacy letter, or "forever letter."

One of the nonfinancial legacies of the pandemic is that it propelled about a third of American adults to discuss end-of-life issues, and reflect upon what they wanted to pass on to those they love, including lessons learned, memories, transmission of experiences and values, and discussions about inheritance, according to a 2021 poll conducted by Edward Jones in partnership with Age Wave and The Harris Poll. For many, this was the first time these issues had been discussed.

### Wills, Advance Directives, Funeral Preplanning: The Nitty-Gritty

Like the title of the 2012 horror movie *Nobody Gets Out Alive*, we know that in the end, there is an end. We know it's important to make plans for that eventuality. A 2021 Gallup poll found that 46% of adults 50–64 don't have a will; nor do 24% of those 65 and older. It's not easy facing our mortality, or perhaps there are disagreements with your spouse about the disposition of your assets, or it's too hard, or you think you don't have enough money to worry about, or you're single and okay with the way your state decides who gets what upon your death. But, do a will anyway.

In addition to a will, being in control of your health decisions is important, and an advance health directive allows you to define what you'd like – or not like – and under what medical circumstances (sometimes called a "living will"), as well as who can speak for you (a healthcare agent) if you are unable to speak for yourself. Finally, you can make your death easier on your loved ones by doing some prefuneral planning for yourself. Difficult, perhaps, but it'll ease the burden on your family members when the time comes.

A power of attorney for finances is also important; someone who can take over if you are no longer able to handle your own money matters, with restrictions; they cannot modify your will or take your money, for example. Some experts recommend the same person be responsible for both your healthcare decisions and your financial affairs; others suggest two different people.

Don't forget your digital assets. Who should be able to access your online accounts when you're gone? Your spouse/children/a trusted friend? From Kindle books to email accounts to Amazon, to cryptocurrency, and everything else that exists online, it's important to consider. Make a list of all your online accounts, and what you'd like to happen to them after you're gone, and who is responsible for accessing them. And, of course, you'll need to create a list of passwords and log-in info that can be accessed when you're gone. Facebook, for example, will either permanently delete your account if someone tells them you have passed away, or your site can be "memorialized." But, you need to select a Facebook "legacy contact" to carry out your wishes. The directions to do this are on Facebook. Perhaps your digital executor will be the executor of your will, or perhaps it'll be someone you feel is more tech savvy.

One well-ranked software program where you can create your will, living trust, healthcare directive, financial power of attorney, and other essential documents yourself (my husband and I used it) is the Nolo Quicken Willmaker and Trust (https://store.nolo.com/products/quicken-willmaker-plus-wqp.html). There are a few jurisdictions where it is not valid, but the site includes this information.

And, of course, be sure to *share* the location of these documents with those who need to know your wishes. Something shoved into a drawer that no one knows about isn't helpful. Jack B., who did the financial planning, created a booklet for his wife, Anna, called "If I Die." He compiled all the information, including where to find everything, and included all the passwords and log-ins, and any other info that would be helpful to Anna if he preceded her. Anna then added her own info that would be helpful to Jack if she preceded him.

Someone needs to know where all the money/important papers are located! Sure, our survivors can piece a lot together from brokerage and bank statements that arrive in the mail, but for the last several years banks and brokerages have been tripping over themselves trying to get us to accept all this information by email. This makes it much harder for your financial picture to be assembled. Yes, a lot of information can be gleaned by reviewing past income tax returns, especially Schedule B, which is included in Form 1040, and which lists the sources of interest and dividend income being reported, but what about everything else that will be important?

Make it easy on your loved ones. You should assemble a file of important documents to be accessible to your spouse or loved ones (again, be sure they know where it is!) and this should include, at a minimum:

- Your will and any relevant trust documents
- Advance health directive
- Financial power of attorney
- Birth certificate
- Marriage license
- Social Security number
- Copy of your last few years' income tax returns
- Listing of all financial accounts, including account numbers and name of a contact person (account representative, financial advisor, etc.)
- Location of brokerage account and bank account recent statements
- Listing of cost basis of all investments in taxable brokerage accounts (unless this information shows on your brokerage statements)
- List of all auto, home, and life insurance policies
- Information on any pension plans and retirement accounts still held by current or prior employers
- Location of titles for home, autos, etc.
- Listing of all credit card accounts
- Login information for all financial accounts, credit card accounts, insurance policies, etc.
- Information on any preplanned or paid funeral arrangements
- Names and addresses of all beneficiaries
- Listing of all debts (mortgages, auto leases, etc.)
- Ethical wills/legacy letters/forever letters

These important documents should be put in place when we are still hale and hearty, and while we can calmly and thoughtfully think about end-of-life issues.

There are helpful links at the end of this chapter about these end-of-life topics, and a terrific checklist, "Planning for Someone Who Has Died," from My Farewelling (www.myfarewelling.com) is available at the end of this chapter. Access their site for additional thoughtful and helpful checklists and ideas.

So take risks. Like John Maxwell said, "Sometimes you win/sometimes you learn." Use retirement to make positive changes . . . what's the **best** that can happen? And, to repeat that clever title from the Michael J. Fox book, there's *No Time Like the Future*. Let's go!

## Farewelling Checklist: The Farewelling 5

********

## Planning for Someone Who Has Died

If you're planning a farewelling now for someone who has died, we understand this is a difficult time. We hope you'll use this checklist to streamline your planning and help you personalize. We've divided the tasks and elements into the five most important sections to make it more manageable, and if you find you want more info, you can visit the myfarewelling.com site for the clickable version of this list. We also have detailed provider listings on the site in case you need to find a funeral home.

### 1. Well Loved: What to Do First

If a loved one has died, these are likely the first things to deal with. Use these guidelines to keep you on track, and ask for help where you need it.

☐ Verify whether the person was an organ donor or wanted their body donated to science.

☐ Find out if funeral arrangements were made in advance (often funeral plans are found in a will or in a separate folder from a local funeral home).

☐ If there is no will, determine whether any final wishes were shared.

☐ If they've died at home and they were not under the care of a doctor or hospice, contact your local police.

☐ If they've died in hospice or hospital, research a funeral home.

☐ Contact your chosen funeral home and make initial decisions with your funeral director.

NOTES: _____

_____

_____

_____

## 2. Well Documented: Important Records

Depending on your situation, you'll need some combination of the documents below, so hopefully this list will be helpful as you plan. It can be good to gather documents you do have into one central file for safekeeping.

☐ Organ Donation Paperwork

☐ Farewelling File/Funeral Plans

☐ Identification Documents (Drivers License, Passport, Birth Certificate)

☐ Social Security Card

☐ Marriage Certificate and/or Divorce Record

☐ Last Will and Testament

☐ Statements for Bank, Retirement, Investment, Credit, and Loan Accounts

☐ Passwords and Pin Codes to all Accounts

☐ Deeds or Proof of Ownership for Home, Car, etc.

☐ Business-related Documents

☐ Insurance Policies

☐ 10 copies of the Death Certificate (request these from your funeral director (you may need them to access accounts, etc.)

NOTES: _____

_____

_____

_____

## 3. Well Planned: The Service and Celebration

This is a chance to honor your loved one in a personal, beautiful way, taking into account their wishes, their values, and even their style. Remember that ceremony and ritual may help us to heal. Often there are at least two parts to a funeral: the service and a celebration or gathering following (or in place of) the service.

☐ Share wishes/plan timing/personalize the service with your chosen funeral director.

☐ Notify Veterans Administration to receive funeral benefits if applicable.

☐ Confirm the funeral service format (religious, nontraditional, eco-friendly).

☐ Contact officiant/celebrant/religious leader.

☐ Select personal readings for the service.

☐ Choose and coordinate anyone who will speak at the service.

☐ Write eulogy or speech.

☐ Select any desired flowers for the service.

☐ Choose music for the service and/or related celebrations.

☐ Create a program or prayer card for the service.

☐ If desired/permitted, select food and drinks for service.

☐ Choose and pack your loved one's clothing and any accessories for the service (include any items that will be buried with them).

☐ If you'll have a celebration (pre- or postservice or in place of a formal service) to honor your loved one, choose a venue.

☐ Select food and drinks.

☐ Add personal details to the celebration.

☐ Share details (times/venues, etc.) for all events with family, friends, and loved ones.

☐ Appoint someone to bring items to the service and celebration.

☐ Arrange any special transportation (limos, etc.).

NOTES: _____

_____

_____

_____

## 4. Well Organized: All the Practicalities

We've listed the following tasks in order of priority. The first may be more pressing, whereas the others can likely wait a bit till you have the time. Do check for any documents you may need under the well-documented section of this checklist, because those might be required when closing out accounts, and so forth. Note that not every one of these items will necessarily apply in your planning.

☐ Collect any personal items from the hospital/hospice.

☐ Put a hold on active credit cards as soon as you can.

☐ Make sure their home is secure.

☐ Are there pets? If so, arrange for their care.

☐ File any claims for prepaid funeral expenses or life insurance.

☐ You'll likely want to notify important contacts:

    ☐ Personal and/or business attorney

    ☐ Workplace colleagues

    ☐ Landlord

    ☐ Member organizations (military, volunteer, civic, religious, etc.)

    ☐ Car companies to cancel lease

    ☐ Department of Motor Vehicles

    ☐ Social Security administration

    ☐ Insurance providers

    ☐ Other ongoing service providers (telephone, cable, cell phone, automatic prescriptions, etc.)

    ☐ Voter registration office

    ☐ U.S. post office

☐ Organize any details regarding their home.

☐ Close bank, investment, and retirement accounts.

☐ Settle debts and credit accounts.

☐ Cancel subscriptions to newspapers, magazines, streaming services, home deliveries.

☐ File a final tax return.

☐ Complete the processing of the will and distribution of any assets.

☐ After the will has been processed (this can take time), donate, store, sell or give away any applicable items.

NOTES: _____

_____

_____

_____

## 5. Well Remembered: Legacy Matters

This section is less about practicalities and logistics and more about staying connected to the memory of your loved one.

☐ Write and submit an obituary.

☐ Select/design memorial headstone or etching.

☐ Organize any donations in the person's name.

☐ Resolve social media and digital accounts.

☐ Write thank-you notes.

☐ Share your memories via photos and stories.

☐ Create traditions to honor and celebrate your loved one.

_____

_____

_____

_____

_____

_____

\*\*\*\*\*\*\*\*

*Farewelling*

*Celebrating a beautiful life, beautifully*
www.myfarewelling.com

# More Resources

## *Books*

Baines, Barry. *Ethical Wills: Putting Your Values on Paper*, 2nd ed. DaCapo Lifelong Books, 2006.

Jameson, Marni. *What to Do with Everything You Own to Leave the Legacy You Want*. The Experiment, 2021.

Leider, Richard. *Who Do You Want to Be When You Grow Old?: The Path of Purposeful Aging*. Berrett-Koehler Publishers, 2021.

Riemer, Rabbi Jack. *Ethical Wills & How to Prepare Them: A Guide to Sharing Your Values from Generation to Generation*, 2nd ed. Jewish Lights Publishing, in the date of publication, 2015.

Strecher, Victor. *Life on Purpose: How Living for What Matters Most Changes Everything*. Harper One, 2016.

Wilson, Timothy. *Redirect: Changing the Stories We Live By*. Little, Brown Spark, 2015.

Zaiman, Elana. *The Forever Letter: Writing What We Believe for Those We Love*. Llewellyn Publications, 2017.

## *Websites*

List of 60 of the most common values: https://www.actmindfully .com.au/wp-content/uploads/2019/07/Values_Checklist_-_Russ_Harris.pdf

"Unlock the Power of Purpose": https://richardleider.com/

529 Plan info: https://www.savingforcollege.com/intro-to-529s/ what-is-a-529-plan

Ethical Will Template: https://www.knox.org/wp-content/ uploads/2017/05/ethical_wills_template_2011.pdf

Farewelling (good advance planning checklists for yourself or someone else): https://www.myfarewelling.com/pages/the-farewelling-checklist-advance-planning

Free Advance Directive Forms by State (from AARP): https:// www.aarp.org/caregiving/financial-legal/free-printable-advance-directives/

# References

Abramowitz, J. "New Insights on Self-Employment of Older Adults in the United States." *Innovations in Aging* 4, supplement 1 (December 2020): 460.

Age Wave and Edward Jones. "The Four Pillars of the New Retirement: What a Difference a Year Makes." March 2021.

Allen, Jacob M. et al. "Exercise Alters Gut Microbiota Composition and Function in Lean and Obese Humans." *Medical Science Sports Exercise Journal* 50, no. 4 (April 2018): 747–757.

"America's Health Rankings: 2021 Senior Report." United Health Foundation, 2021.

Binette, Joanne and Kerri Vasold. *2018 Home and Community Preferences: A National Survey of Adults Age 18-Plus.* Washington, DC: AARP Research, August 2018; revised July 2019.

Blume, Christine, Marlene H. Schmidt, and Christian Cajochen. "Effects of the Covid-19 Lockdown on Human Sleep and Rest-Activity Rhythms." *Current Biology* 30, no. 14 (July 2020): R795–R797.

Brady, Samantha et al. "Reducing Isolation and Loneliness Through Membership in a Fitness Program for Older Adults." *Journal of Applied Gerontology* 39, no. 3 (2020): 301–310.

Campisi, Natalie. "Baby Boomers Retired at a Record Pace in 2020. Here's Where They're Looking to Move." *Forbes,* February 23, 2021.

Cherkas, Lynn. "Sedentary Lifestyles Associated with Accelerated Aging Process." *JAMA*, 2008.

Chopik, William J. "Are Friends Better for Us Than Family?" *Science Daily,* June 6, 2017.

# References

Chopik, William. "Associations Among Relational Values, Support, Health, and Well-Being Across the Adult Lifespan." *Personal Relationships* 24, no. 2 (2017): 408–422.

Collinson, Catherine. "What Is Retirement? Three Generations Prepare for Older Age." 19th Annual Transamerica Retirement Survey of Workers, April 2019.

Cruwys, Tegan, Catherine Haslan, Niklas K. Steffens, S. Alexander Haslam, Polly Fong, and Ben C. Lam. "Friendships That Money *Can* Buy: Financial Security Protects Health in Retirement by Enabling Social Connectedness." *BMC Geriatrics* 19, no. 319 (2019).

Degges-White, Suzanne (in review). "Strong Friendships Predict Happiness in Adulthood: What's the Magic Number of Friends That We Need?" *2021 Retirement Risk Readiness Study*. Allianz Life.

Duffin, Erin. "Total Monthly Payment Forecast of Military Retirees in the United States from 2021 to 2031, per Participant." Statista, March 2, 2021.

Elliott, Brianna, RD. "The Nine Best Foods and Drinks to Have Before Bed." *Healthline*, August 2020.

Employee Benefits Research Institute and Greenwald Research. "2021 Retirement Confidence Survey – United States, 2020." April 2021.

Farida B. Ahmad, Jodi A. Cisewski, Arialdo Miniño, and Robert N. Anderson. "Provisional Mortality Data." *Morbidity and Mortality Weekly Report* 70, no. 14 (April 9, 2021): 519–522.

Fidelity Investments. "Couples and Money Study." 2018. https://www.fidelity.com/bin-public/060_www_fidelity_com/documents/pr/couples-fact-sheet.pdf.

Finkelstein, Amy, Matthew Gentzkow, and Heidi Williams. "Sources of Geographic Variation in Health Care: Evidence from Patient Migration." *Quarterly Journal of Economics* 131, no. 4 (November 2016): 1681–1726.

Fox, Michelle. "Dreaming of Retiring Abroad? Here's What You Need to Know." *CNBC*, September 14, 2020.

Frey, William H. "Census 2020: First Results Show Near Historically Low Population Growth and a First-Ever Congressional Seat Loss for California." Brookings, April 26, 2021.

Fryar, Cheryl D., Margaret D. Carroll, and Joseph Afful. "Prevalence of Overweight, Obesity, and Severe Obesity Among Adults Aged 20 and Over: United States, 1960–1962 Through 2017–2018" National Center for Health Statistics, 2020.

# References

Gaesser, Glenn and Siddhartha S. Angadi. "Obesity Treatment: Weight Loss versus Increasing Fitness and Physical Activity for Reducing Health Risks." *iScience* 24, no. 10 (October 22, 2021).

Generations United. "Family Matters: Multigenerational Living Is on the Rise and Here to Stay," 2021. https://www.gu.org/resources/multigenerational-families/.

Giles, Lynn, Gary Glonek, Mary Luszcz, and Gary Andrews. "Effect of Social Networks on 10-Year Survival in Very Old Australians." *Journal of Epidemiology and Community Health* 59 no. 7 (2005): 574–579.

Glass, Thomas, Carlos Mendes de Leon, Richard A. Marattoli, and Lisa F. Berkman. "Population-Based Study of Social and Productive Activities as Predictors of Survival Among Elderly Americans." *British Medical Journal* 319, no. 8 (1999): 478–483.

Harlow, Harry F., Robert O. Dodsworth, and Margaret K. Harlow. "Total Social Isolation in Monkeys." *Proceedings of the National Academy of Sciences of the United States of America* 54, no. 1 (1965): 90–97.

Harvard Health Publishing. "The Health Benefits of Strong Relationships," 2010. https://www.health.harvard.edu/staying-healthy/the-health-benefits-of-strong-relationships.

Hearts & Wallets. "Retirement Resurgence: Americans Who 'Aspire to Retire' by 55," March 16, 2021. https://www.heartsandwallets.com/docs/press/press_release_2021-03-16_Retirement_Resurgence_Americans_Who_Aspire_to_Retire_by_55_Goal_More_Income_Sources.pdf.

Heijtz, Rochellys Dias, Ayoze Gonzalez-Santana, and Jon D. Laman. "Young Microbiota Rejuvenates the Aging Brain." *Nature Aging* 1 (2021): 625–627.

ideal-Living. "2020–2021 Executive Report." Ideal-Living/RPI Media, LLC, 2020.

Intriago, Joy. "Religion and Spirituality in Older People." Seniors Matter, 2021. https://www.seniorsmatter.com/religion-spirituality-older-people/2492159.

Jachimowicz, Jon M., Ruo Mo, Adam Eric Greenberg, Bertus Jeronimus, and Ashley V. Whillans. "Income More Reliably Predicts Frequent Than Intense Happiness." *Social Psychological & Personality Science,* December 7, 2020.

Kaiser Family Foundation/The Economist. "Survey on Loneliness and Social Isolation in the United States, the United Kingdom, and

Japan," conducted April–June 2018. https://www.kff.org/other/report/loneliness-and-social-isolation-in-the-united-states-the-united-kingdom-and-japan-an-international-survey/.

Kellogg School of Management at Northwestern University. "How Old Are Successful Tech Entrepreneurs?" Kellogg Insight, May 15, 2018. https://insight.kellogg.northwestern.edu/article/younger-older-tech-entrepreneurs.

Kiecolt-Glaser, Janice K. et al. "Omega-3 Fatty Acids, Oxidative Stress, and Leukocyte Telomere Length: A Randomized Controlled Trial." *Brain, Behavior, and Immunity* 28 (2013): 16–24.

Koenig, Harold G., Harvey Jay Cohen, Linda K. George, Judith C. Hays, David B. Larson, and Dan G. Blazer. "Attendance at Religious Services, interleukin-6, and other biological parameters of immune function in older adults." *International Journal of Psychiatry in Medicine* 27, no. 3 (1997): 233–250.

Lawton, Ricky N., Iulian Gramatki, Will Watt, and Daniel Fujiwara. "Does Volunteering Make Us happier, or Are Happier People More Likely to Volunteer?" *Journal of Happiness Studies* 22 (2021): 599–624.

Lindholm, Maléne H. et al. "An Integrative Analysis Reveals Coordinated Reprogramming of the Epigenome and the Transcriptome in Human Skeletal Muscle after Training." *Epigenetics* 9, no. 12 (2014): 1557–1559.

Maniglia, Bobbi. "2020's Migration Trends: Where Is Everyone Moving?" North American Moving Services, February 2, 2021.

Marist Poll/NPR. "Amazon Is a Colossus in a Nation of Shoppers." 2018 https://www.npr.org/about-npr/617470695/npr-marist-poll-amazon-is-a-colossus-in-a-nation-of-shoppers.

Mather Institute. "The Age Well Study Report: Year 1 Findings." January 2019. https://www.matherinstitute.com/senior-living-professionals/free-industry-information/age-well-study-report-2019/.

Melov, Salimony, Mark A. Tarnopolsky, Kenneth Beckman, Krysta Felkey, and Alan Hubbard. "Resistance Exercise Reverses Aging in Human Skeletal Muscle." *PLoS ONE* 2, no. 5 (2007): e465.

McKinney, James, Daniel J. Lithwick, Barbara N. Morrison, Hamed Nazzari, Saul H. Isserow, Brett Heilbron, and Andrew D. Krahn et al. "The Health Benefits of Physical Activity and Cardiorespiratory Fitness." *British Columbia Medical Journal* 58, no. 3 (2016).

# References

Merrill Lynch and Age Wave. "Healthy and Retirement: Planning for the Great Unknown," 2014. https://agewave.com/wp-content/uploads/2016/07/2014-ML-AW-Health-and-Retirement_Planning-for-the-Great-Unknown.pdf.

Mirsha, Arul, Himanshu Mishra, and Tamara M. Masters. "The Influence of Bite Size on Quantity of Food Consumed: A Field Study." *Journal of Consumer Research* 38, no. 5 (2011): 791–795.

MKM Partners Quantitative Survey Group. "Baby Boomers and Generation X Agree: Bigger Is Better and City Life Is Overrated," Business Wire, April 17, 2019.

Moore, Jim. "Could active adult housing be a solution to the middle-market affordability challenge?" *McKnight's Senior Living* 19, no. 4 (August 2021).

Moen, Phyllis, Jungmeen E. Kim, and Heather Hoffmeister. "Couples Work/Retirement Transitions, Gender, and Marital Quality." *Social Psychology Quarterly* 64, no. 1 (2001): 55–71.

Moss, Wes. "Finding Your Core Pursuits for 2021." *The Atlanta Journal Constitution, January* 1, 2021.

Movement Advancement Project (MAP) and Sage. "Understanding Issues Facing LBGT Older Adults," 2017. https://www.lgbtmap.org/understanding-issues-facing-lgbt-older-adults.

National Association of Realtors. "2020 Profile of Home Buyers and Sellers," 2020. https://www.nar.realtor/sites/default/files/documents/2020-profile-of-home-buyers-and-sellers-11-11-2020.pdf.

National Center for Health Statistics. "Life Expectancy in the U.S. Declined a Year and Half in 2020." Centers for Disease Control and Prevention, July 2021.

National Center for Health Statistics. "Anthropometric Reference Data for Children and Adults: United States, 2011–2014." Centers for Disease Control and Prevention, 2014.

National Institute on Aging. "Health and Retirement Study," ongoing. https://hrsparticipants.isr.umich.edu/sitedocs/databook/HRS-Telling-the-Story-of-Aging-in-America.pdf.

Newcomb, Sarah. "How Social Comparisons Affect Your Client's Well-Being." Morningstar, February 27, 2018.

PBS News Hour. "Why More Seniors Are Going Back to College – to Retire." May 14, 2014. https://www.pbs.org/newshour/show/seniors-retiring-college-campuses.

# References

Pew Research Center. "A Profile of Single Americans." 2020. https://www.pewresearch.org/social-trends/2020/08/20/a-profile-of-single-americans/.

Pew Research Center. "Religious Landscape Study," 2021. https://www.pewforum.org/religious-landscape-study/.

Puterman, Eli, Jue Lin, Elizabeth Blackburn, Aoife O'Donovan, Nancy Adler, and Elissa Epel. "The Power of Exercise: Buffering the Effect of Chronic Stress on Telomere Length." PLoS ONE 5, no. 5 (2010): e10837.

Rapacon, Stacy. "Top 25 Part-Time Jobs for Retirees." AARP, 2020.

Redfin. "42% of Americans Are Hesitant to Move to a Place Where They'd Be in the Political Minority, Up From 32% in June," October 27, 2020. https://press.redfin.com/news-releases/news-release-details/42-americans-are-hesitant-move-place-where-theyd-be-political.

Robinson, Matthew M. et al. "Enhanced Protein Translation Underlies Improved Metabolic and Physical Adaptations to Different Exercise Training Modes in Young and Old Humans." *Cell Metabolism* 25, no. 3 (2017): 581–592.

Senior Living.org. "The Best & Worst States for Older Americans," March 2021. https://www.seniorliving.org/best-states-older-adults/.

Self Financial, Inc. "Life of Tax: What Americans Will Pay in Tax over a Lifetime," 2021. https://www.self.inc/info/life-of-tax/.

Sharif, Marissa, Cassie Molginer, and Hal E. Hershfield. "Having Too Little or Too Much Time Is Linked to Lower Subjective Well-Being." *Journal of Personality and Social Psychology* 121, no. 4 (2021): 933–947.

Smart Asset. "Where Retirees are Moving—2021 Edition," February, 2021. https://smartasset.com/financial-advisor/where-retirees-are-moving-2021.

Solemimani, Mohammad, Simin Zarabadi-Pour, Seyedeh Ameneh Motalebi, and Kelly-Ann Allen. "Predictors of Quality of Life in Patients with Heart Disease." *Journal of Religious Health* 59, no. 4 (2020): 2135–2148.

Soriento, Daniela, Eugenio Di Vaia, and Guido Iaccarino. "Physical Exercise: A Novel Tool to Protect Mitochondrial Health." *Frontiers in Physiology* 12 (April 27, 2021): 660068.

Steiner, Clyde and Shari Steiner. *Steiner's Complete How-To-Move Handbook.* San Francisco: IIP Consumer, 1999.

# References

The National Association of Realtors. "Existing Housing Home-Sales Housing Snapshot," June 2021.

TopRetirements.com. "10 Best of the Best Places to Retire in 2021," January 2021.

United Nations Population Division. "Life Expectancy of the World Population," 2020.

Villablanca, J. R. and D. A. Hovda. "Developmental Neuroplasticity in a Model of Cerebral Hemispherectomy and Stroke." *Neuroscience* 95, no. 3 (2000): 625–637.

Wang, Ninjian et al. "Long-Term Night Shift Work Is Associated with the Risk of Atrial Fibrillation and Coronary Heart disease." *European Heart Journal* 42, no. 40 (2021): 4180–4188.

Wansink, Brian, Koert van Ittersum, and James E. Painter. "Ice Cream Illusions: Bowls, Spoons, and Self-Served Portion Sizes," *American Journal of Preventive Medicine* 31, no. 3 (2006): 240–243.

Watson, Kathleen B. et al. "Physical Inactivity Among Adults Aged 50 Years and Older." Morbidity and Mortality Weekly Report 65, no. 36 (2016): 954–958..

Weir, Kirsten. "The Extra Weight of Covid-19." American Psychological Association, July 2021.

Wettstein, Gal and Alice Zulkarnain. "How Much Long-Term Care Do Adult Children Provide?" Boston: Center for Retirement Research at Boston College, June 2017.

Wiese, Bettina S. "Successful Pursuit of Personal Goals and Subjective Well-Being." In *Personal Project Pursuit: Goals, Action and Human Flourishing*, edited by Brian R. Little, Katariina Salmela-Aro, and Susan D. Phillips. Hillsdale, NJ: Lawrence Erlbaum Associates, 2007.

Wu, Chenkai and Michelle Odden. "Association of Retirement Age with Mortality: A Population-Based Longitudinal Study Among Older Adults in the USA." *Journal of Epidemiology and Community Health* 70, no. 9 (2016): 917–923.

Yanping, Li et al. "Healthy Lifestyle and Life Expectancy Free of Cancer, Cardiovascular Disease, and Type 2 Diabetes." *BMJ* 368 (2020): 116669.

# About the Author

Jan Cullinane is a recognized expert on holistic retirement. Her books include two previous editions of the best-selling *The New Retirement: The Ultimate Guide to the Rest of Your Life* (Rodale), the award-winning *The Single Woman's Guide to Retirement* (Wiley), and *Retire Happy* (Hallmark gift series). She is the "Healthy Living" columnist for *ideal-LIVING* magazine, and a contributor to *Everybody Has a Book Inside of Them* (Career Press, 2019) and *The Weekend Book Proposal* (Writer's Digest Books, 2014).

Jan has given numerous presentations about retirement; clients include AARP, the Smithsonian, In-N-Out Burger, Wells Fargo Advisors, Ford Motor Company, Deloitte, Ameriprise Financial, and the federal government. She is frequently interviewed for print and online media, and has appeared on national and local TV and radio shows.

Her educational credentials include a BS and an MEd from the University of Maryland, and she is ABD from Rutgers, The State University of New Jersey. She lives in Palm Coast, Florida with her husband, Roger, has three married children, five (adorable – of course!) grandchildren, and sincerely believes these years are the best years . . . if you're prepared. And, she can speak backwards fluently!

Follow her on Twitter @jancullinane and visit at www.jancullinane.com.

# Index

**A**

AARP, 50, 56, 57, 75, 140,
192–193, 222
Abramowitz, Joelle, 58
Accra, Ghana, 123
ACT (test), 36
Active-adult communities, 131–133
Active retirees, locations
for, 112–113
Addicted2Success, 300
Administration on Aging, 219
Advance directives, 308–311
Aegon Center for Longevity and
Retirement, 82
African American Travelers, 49
Age-Friendly Institute, 57
Age Wave, 19, 21, 45, 186, 204,
212–213, 308
"The Age Well Study," 134
Aging in place, 99–105
AICPA (American Institute
of Certified Public
Accountants), 225
Aiken, S. Car., 146
Airbnb, 62
Alabama, 77, 92, 93, 114, 141
Alaska, 264, 265, 267

Albert Lea, Minn., 192–193
Alcoholics Anonymous, 49
Alexandria, Va., 142
Algarve region, Portugal, 126
Allen & Rocks, Inc., 128
Allianz Life, 18
Ally Bank, 243
Alzheimer's disease, 186
Alzheimer's Foundation of
America, 188
AMA Waterways, 49
Amazon, 60, 67
Ambergris Caye, Belize, 115, 125
AM Best, 251
American Association for Long-
Term Care Insurance, 219–220
American College of
Cardiology, 201–202
American Heart
Association, 201–202
American Institute of Certified
Public Accountants
(AICPA), 225
American Psychological
Association, 189
American Red Cross, 38
AmeriCorp, 38

Americorps Senior Companion
    Program, 41
Analysis paralysis, 282–283
Anchoring (cognitive bias), 281–282
Annapolis, Md., 142
Annuities, 250–251
Anytime Fitness (gym), 180
Apple, Inc., 302, 304
AreaVibes, 89
Arizona, 10, 76, 77, 114, 121, 128,
    130, 141, 144–145, 147
Arizona State University,
    36, 200–201
Arkadelphia, Ark., 113
Arkansas, 113
Aron, Arthur, 9
Artists, communities for, 143–144
Asheville, N. Car., 111, 114,
    130, 144–145
Astronomy lovers,
    communities for, 144
Atlanta, Ga., 121, 123
Augusta, Ga., 123
Austin, Tex., 121, 138
Ave Maria (Florida), 116–117

**B**

Backroads Rhine River Cruise
    Bike Tour, 49
Bangkok, Thailand, 123
Banks, Internet-based, 243
Barcelona, Spain, 123
Bar Harbor, Maine, 96
Basal metabolic rate (BMR), 185
Beaufort, S. Car., 114
Belize, 115, 123, 124–125
Bend, Ore., 113
Berkshire Hathaway, 249

BestPlaces.net, 133
Best places to retire lists, 113–115
Better Business Bureau, 88
Big Brothers/Big Sisters, 39
Black Americans, 122–127
Black ExcelList (YouTube
    channel), 122–123
Blood pressure, 201–202
Blue states, 89
Blue Zones, 190–193
Bluffton, S. Car., 117, 132
BMR (basal metabolic rate), 185
Book clubs, 44
Boomer cohort, 3, 7, 10–11,
    56, 197
Boone, N. Car., 113
Bortz, Walter M., 177, 183
Boston, Mass., 130, 143
Boston College, 58, 95
Boulder, Colo., 113, 130
Bowling Green State University, 23
Bridgeville, Del., 128
Brooks, David, 301
Brown, Joel, 300
Brown, Susan, 23
Buettner, Dan, 190–192
Buffalo, N.Y., 121
Buffet, Jimmy, 117
Buffett, Warren, 249–250
Build-to-rent housing
    communities, 127–128
Burbank, Calif., 143–144
Burlington, Vt., 113

**C**

CAbi Clothing, 63
CAFE (Certified Age-Friendly
    Employer), 57

California, 10, 89, 96, 112, 114, 121, 132, 143–144, 190
Calment, Jeanne, 162
Canada, 123
Cape Coral, Fla., 111
Capital Investment Advisors, 69
Capri, Italy, 142
Car, selling your, 292–293
Carmax, 293
*Carrie* (King), 58
Carvana, 292–293
Cash investment, short-term, 243
Casinos, 60
Cayo District, Belize, 125
CCRCs (continuing care retirement communities), 134–136, 147, 151–156
CDC (Centers for Disease Control and Prevention), 189, 207
Center for Retirement Research, 58, 95
Centers for Disease Control and Prevention (CDC), 166
Certified Age-Friendly Employer (CAFE), 57
Certified Financial Planner Board of Standards, 227
Certified Financial Planners (CFPs), 224
Certified public accountants (CPAs), 224–225
CFAs (Chartered Financial Analysts), 225
CFPs (Certified Financial Planners), 224
Champlain Towers South (Surfside, Fla.), 94–95

Chapman, Gary, 13
Charitable donations, 306
Charity Navigator, 38, 306
CharityWatch, 38, 306
Charleston, S. Car., 132
Charlotte, N. Car., 114, 123
Charlottesville, Va., 114
Chartered Financial Analysts (CFAs), 225
Chattanooga, Tenn., 114, 123
Chicago, Ill., 113
Chicago Health and Aging Project, 186
Citibank, 243
Clearwater, Fla., 114
Clemens, Samuel, 301
CLEP (College Level Examination Program), 36
Cleveland, Ohio, 121
Cocoa, Fla., 114
Cognitive biases, 281–287
Co-housing, 119–120
*College Gazette*, 140
College Level Examination Program (CLEP), 36
College towns, 140–141
Colombia, 123
Colonoscopy, 201
Colorado, 76, 111–113, 128, 130, 132, 265
Communes, 149
Condo owners' associations (COAs), 94–95
Confirmation bias, 286
Congressional Research Service (CRS), 234
Connecticut, 114

Consumer Expenditure Survey (U.S. Bureau of Labor Statistics), 210
Continuing care retirement communities (CCRCs), 134–136
Continuity theory, 6
Cool Works, 65–66
Costa Rica, 123, 190
Costco, 68
COVID-19 pandemic, 21–22, 60, 81, 189, 210, 308
CPAs (certified public accountants), 224–225
Create the Good (AARP), 39, 50
Creativity, 45
Credit cards, 287–288
CRS (Congressional Research Service), 234
Cruises, 48, 51
Cruise ship, living on a, 128–129
*Crystal Serenity* (ship), 129
Cuenca, Ecuador, 115
Customer service jobs, work from home, 68

**D**
Dahlonega, Ga., 113
Dalbar, Inc., 250
Dallas, Tex., 130
DASH diet, 188
Daytona Beach, Fla., 117–118, 143
Death:
  costs of, 294–295
  leading causes of, 166
Deciding whether to move, 74–76
DeCluttr, 61–62
Defined contribution retirement accounts, 233–241

Defining the "ideal" location for retirement, 77–81
Delaware, 114, 128, 219, 265
Del Webb, 75–76, 117, 133
Dementia, 186
Democratic-leaning states, 89
Denison, Ohio, 141
Diakite, Parker, 123
Diet, 188–202
Dieting, exercise vs., 200–201
Discovery Toys, 63
Disney cruise ships, 51
Distributions, retirement account, 272–275
District of Columbia, 267
Doherty, William, 116
Dress for Success, 40
Drugs, cost of, 290–291
Duany, Andres, 143

**E**
Eagle, Colo., 113
EAs (Enrolled Agents), 225
Eating less, 193–196
EBay, 61
EBRI (Employee Benefit Research Institute), 5, 55, 207
*The Economist,* 43
Ecuador, 115
Educational travel, 50
Edward Jones (financial services firm), 19, 21, 308
Elderhostel, 50
El Paso, Tex., 132
Employee Benefit Research Institute (EBRI), 5

End of life, 299–316
  planning and important
    documents, 310–315
  regrets at, 300–301
  values and purpose, 302–307
  and virtues, 301–302
  and wills, 307–311
Enrolled Agents (EAs), 225
Epigenetics, 163–164
Equestrians, communities for, 146
Escorted tours, 48
Estate and inheritance taxes, 275–276
Ethical wills, 93–94
Etsy (Internet site), 61
Eugene, Ore., 121
Everyday Leisure Priorities list, 45
Exchange-traded funds,
  248–249, 307
Exercise, 177–185
Exercise, dieting vs., 200–201
Exercising, 43–44
Expectations about retirement, 4–7
Expenses in retirement,
  determining, 210–222
Extroverts, 96, 129–130

F
Facebook, 309
Family and friends, living
  near, 74–75
Farms, communities including, 144
FDA (U.S. Food and Drug
  Administration), 196, 201
FDIC (Federal Deposit Insurance
  Corporation), 243
FEBS acronym, 179
Federal Deposit Insurance
  Corporation (FDIC), 243

Federal Emergency Management
  Agency (FEMA), 93
Federal Trade Commission,
  253, 294
FedEx, 67
FEMA (Federal Emergency
  Management Agency), 93
Fidelity Investments, 7, 213, 242
Fidelity Retiree Health Care Cost
  Estimate, 213
15 minute cities, 143
Financial advisors, 223–227
Financial decisions,
  rational, 287–298
Financing your retirement,
  207–257
  basic cheat sheet for being
    prepared, 208–209
  Compare Your Housing Costs
    (worksheet), 254
  expenses in retirement,
    determining, 210–222
  financial advisors, using, 223–227
  How Much $$$ Do You
    Need in Retirement?
    (worksheet), 254–256
  with investments, 241–252
  with pensions and defined
    contribution retirement
    accounts, 233–241
  with reverse mortgages, 252–253
  with Social Security, 227–233
FIRE (financial independence,
  retire early), 4
The Five Love Languages
  (Chapman), 13
Fiverr, 61
Flagstaff, Ariz., 114

Flat Rock, N. Car., 138
Fleet Landing (Florida), 134–136
Florida:
  cost of living in, 111
  in-migration to, 10, 76, 77
  natural disasters in, 93–94
  and niche lifestyle communities,
    116–117, 121–123, 128, 130,
    132–136, 141–145, 147
  as one of the best places to
    retire, 111, 114
  taxes, 264, 266–269
Food delivery jobs, 60
For a Day Foundation, 41
*Forbes,* 114, 190, 242
Forever letters, 307–308
Fort Collins, Colo., 89
Fort Myers, Fla., 121, 135–136
Foundation for Intentional
  Communities, 149
Fountaingrove Lodge, 121
Framing (cognitive bias), 285
France, 115
Freelancers, 61
Frey, William, 76
"Friendships That Money Can Buy"
  (NCBI), 15
Friends of Bill W., 49
Friends of Dorothy, 49
Fuller, Ida May, 3
Funeral pre-planning, 308, 310, 312
Future discounting, 284

**G**
Gaesser, Glenn, 200–201
Gainesville, Fla., 141
Gallup poll, 308
Games, 44

Gandhi, Mahatma, 35, 38
Gaskin, Stephen, 149
Generation X, 56
Generation Z, 56
Genworth, 218
Georgetown, Tex., 146
Georgia, 11, 76, 113, 121, 123, 132
Ghana, 123
Gilbert, Ariz., 145
Giles, Lynn, 15
Glen Allen, Va., 144–145
Golden ID Program, 35–36
Goldman Sachs, 243
Golf courses, 92–93
Goodwill, 61
Gozo, Malta, 115
Gray divorce, 23
Greece, 190
Green House Project, 137
Greensboro, N. Car., 123
Greenwald & Associates, 207
Grisham, Ore., 121–122
Guardian ad Litem, 39
Gut biome, 199–200
Gym membership, 291

**H**
Habitat for Humanity, 41, 61
Hanover, N.H., 141
Happiness, 18–19
Harlow, Harry, 175
Harrisburg, Penn., 123
Harris Poll, 21, 212–213, 308
*Harry Potter* (Rowling), 58
Harvard Medical School,
  14, 161, 173
Harvard University, 304
Hawaii, 89, 96, 266

Health, before and after
   relocation, 89–90
Healthcare costs, 212–218,
   293–294
Health exams, 201–202
*Health* magazine, 190
Health Savings Accounts
   (HSAs), 295–296
Healthspan, 17
Healthy aging, 161–205
   and diet, 188–202
   and exercise, 177–185
   and learning, 185–188
   and nature vs. nurture,
      162–166
   and sleep, 167–171
   and social support, 174–176
   and stress, 171–173
Hedonic adaptation, 202
Herbalife, 63
Hero for a Day, 41
HIIT (high-intensity interval
   training), 183
Hilton Head, S. Car., 117
HOAs (homeowners' associations),
   94–95
Holmes, Thomas, 2
Holmes-Rahe Stress
   Inventory, 2, 172
Home inspection, 92
Homeowners' associations
   (HOAs), 94–95
Homesharing, 139
Hong Kong, 162
Horse lovers, communities for, 146
Hoschton, Ga., 132
Hospice Foundation of America, 40

Hospital baby cuddlers, 41
Housing costs, 254
Hovnanian communities, 133
*How to Retire Overseas* (Peddicord),
   150–151
H&R Block, 67
HSAs (Health Savings Accounts),
   295–296
Huntley, Ill., 132

**I**

Idaho, 10, 76, 77
*Ideal-LIVING* magazine, 85–87
Illinois, 10, 113, 132, 265
Income tax, 296
Index funds, 247–248
Indiana, 114, 265
Individual Retirement Accounts
   (IRAs), 234, 236–240, 242
Indo-Americans, 122
Inflation, 212
Inheritance taxes, 260,
   264, 275–278
Intentional communities, 149
Internal locus of control, 12–14
International relocation, 82–85
Interviews, 69
Introverts, 96, 130
Investing, socially responsible,
   306–307
Investments, 241–252
Investopedia, 132
IRAs (Individual Retirement
   Accounts), 234, 236–240, 242
IRS, 67
Irvine, Calif., 132
Italy, 112, 142, 190

**J**

Jackson Hewitt, 67
Jacksonville, Fla., 114, 123
Japan, 190
Jobs, Steve, 302, 304
Johns Hopkins University, 38
*Journal of Applied Gerontology,*
    181–182
*Journal of Clinical Oncology,* 178
*Journal of Epidemiology and*
    *Community Health,* 11

**K**

Kabat-Zinn, Jon, 173
Kaeser & Blair, 63
Kalish, Nancy, 175
Kansas, 112, 114
K (MLK) Day of Service, 40
Kellogg School of Management, 58
Kelly, Mark, 164–165
Kelly, Scott, 164–165
Kelly Services, 66–67
Kendal (university-based retirement
    communities), 141
Kentucky, 93, 112, 114, 265
King, Stephen, 58
Kissimmee, Fla., 132
Knoxville, Tenn., 114

**L**

Laguna Woods, Calif., 132
Lake Buena Vista, Fla, 116
Lake Wales, Fla., 116
Lakewood, Ohio, 121
La Mie, Beth, 307
Landry, Roger, 161
Las Cruces, N. Mex., 114
Las Vegas, Nev., 132

Latronico, Italy, 112
Laughing, 187–188
Learned helplessness, 17
Learn to Be, 42
Legacy letters, 307–308
Leider, Richard, 303
"Leisure Activities and the Risk
    of Dementia in the Elderly"
    (study), 182
Leisure World (Silver
    Spring, Md.), 45
Lennar communities, 133
Lewis, C. S., 13
LGBTQ+ communities,
    96, 120–122
LGBTQ+ travelers, 49
Libraries, 36–37, 40, 41, 44,
    80, 181, 295
Life insurance, 235–236
Lifelong learning, 35–38, 185–188
Life plan communities, 134–136
Lifespan, 161–165
Limon, Costa Rica, 123
Lincoln, Kans., 112
LinkedIn, 69
Lisbon, Portugal, 115, 123, 126
Livability.com, 129–130
Livability indexes, 89
"Live and Invest Overseas"
    (Peddicord), 123
*Live Long, Die Short,* 161
*Live Your Road Trip Dream*
    (White), 48
Living wills, 308–311
Locations, 109–160
    for active retirees, 112–113
    best places to retire lists, 113–115
    for low cost of living, 110–112

niche lifestyles, 115–151
  10 Questions to Bring on
    Your Senior Housing Tour
    (checklist), 151–156
Loma Linda, Calif., 190
Longevity, 161–165
Long-term care insurance, 218–222
Los Alamos, N. Mex., 130
Loss aversion, 284–285
Louisiana, 121, 218, 265
Loveland, Colo., 111
Low cost of living, locations
  for, 110–112
Lowe's, 68
Lutz, Fla., 144

**M**
Maine, 93, 96
Malta, 115
Managed funds, 248–249
Mandela, Nelson, 22
Manheimer, Ronald J., 8
Mankato, Kans., 112
Marcus (bank), 243
Margaritaville, 117–119, 131
Marketing Charts, 37
Married couples, 8
Mary Kay, 63–65
Maryland, 10, 89, 114,
  131, 142–143
Massachusetts, 114, 130,
  141, 143, 265
Massive Open Online Courses
  (MOOCs), 37
Masterclass, 38
Master-planned communities,
  130–133
Mather Institute, 134

Mayo Clinic, 169, 176
Mazatlán, Mexico, 115, 127
McKnight's Senior Living, 56
McLean, Lawrence, 49
Meals on Wheels, 39
Medellín, Colombia, 123
Medicaid, 219
Medical exams, 201–202
Medicare, 8, 56, 89, 93, 127,
  137, 181, 211, 213–219, 252,
  282, 291, 296
Medigap, 213–218
Mediterranean diet, 188, 190
Mentoring.org, 40
Merck, 176
Merrill Lynch, 45, 186, 204
Mexico, 115, 123, 126–127
Miami, Fla., 130, 143
Michigan, 265
Midwest United States, 76
Military relocation professionals
  (MRPs), 147
Military retirees, communities
  for, 147–149
Millennial cohort, 7, 56
Miller, Beatrice, 129
Milne, Melissa, 196
MIND Diet, 188, 190
Minneapolis, Minn., 113
Minnesota, 112, 113, 192–193
Mississippi, 112, 114
Missouri, 219
Mitochondria, 165
Monaghan, Tom, 117
Montana, 114, 265
Montreal, Que., 123
MOOCS (Massive Open Online
  Courses), 37

Morgantown, W. Va., 113
Morningstar, Inc., 19
Morningstar mutual fund
    ratings, 247–249
Moss, Wes, 69
MoveBuddha.com, 143
MRPs (military relocation
    professionals), 147
Multigenerational living, 133–134
Multigenerational travel, 50–51
Mutual funds, 246–250

**N**
Nalanda Estates (Tampa, Fla.), 122
NALCREST, 116
Nashville, Tenn., 132
National Association of Letter
    Carriers, 116
National Association of Personal
    Financial Advisors, 226–227
National Association of Realtors,
    81, 111, 147
National Association of
    Unclaimed Property
    Administrators, 291–292
National Center for Biotechnology
    Information (NCBI), 15
National Center for Education
    Statistics, 140
National Center for Health Statistics
    (NCHS), 189
National Federation of Professional
    Trainers, 59
National Funeral Directors
    Association, 294
National Geographic
    Expeditions, 50

National Indo-American Association
    for Senior Citizens, 122
National Institute on
    Aging, 171, 190
National Institute on Retirement
    Security, 233
National Institutes of Health
    (NIH), 142
National Low Income Housing
    Coalition, 41
National Parks, 69, 292
National Registry of Unclaimed
    Retirement Benefits, 240–241
National Vital Statistics System
    (NVSS), 166
Natural disasters, 93
Naturally Occurring
    Retirement Communities
    (NORCs), 141–142
Naturists, communities for, 144
*The Naughty Diet* (Milne), 196
NCBI (National Center for
    Biotechnology Information), 15
NCHS (National Center for Health
    Statistics), 189, 193
Netflix, 138
Networking, 69
Neuroplasticity, 35
Nevada, 76, 77, 132, 264, 269
Newcomb, Sarah, 19
*The New England Journal of
    Medicine*, 182
New Hampshire, 141, 264–266
New Jersey, 10, 92, 265
New Kent, Va., 146
New Mexico, 111, 114, 130
New Orleans, La., 121

New residence, buying a, 91
Newton, Mass., 141
New urbanism, 142–143
New York City, 130
New York State, 10, 267, 268
NexMetro, 128
Nextdoor app, 61, 90
Niche lifestyles, locations
  for, 115–151
NIH (National Institutes of
  Health), 142
Nolo Quicken Willmaker and
  Trust, 309
*Nomadland* (book and
  film), 65, 139
Nonprofits, charitable, 60
NORCs (Naturally
  Occurring Retirement
  Communities), 141–142
North American Moving
  Services, 10
North Carolina, 10, 11, 76, 77,
  111, 113, 114, 123, 130, 138,
  144–145, 265
North Carolina Center for Creative
  Retirement, 8
North Dakota, 114
Northeast United States, 76,
  88–89
North Myrtle Beach, S. Car., 114
Northwestern Mutual (financial
  services company), 223
Northwestern University, 58, 134
Nudists, communities for, 144
Nutrients, 198–199
NVSS (National Vital Statistics
  System), 166

**O**
Oahu, Hawaii, 96
OAT (Overseas Adventure
  Travel), 48
Obesity and overweight, 15,
  167–169, 177–179, 184,
  188–190, 193–196, 199–202
*Obesity Review,* 189
Ocala, Fla., 132
*Occupational Outlook Handbook,* 56
OECD (Organization for
  Economic Co-operation and
  Development), 259
Oenophiles, communities for, 146
Ohio, 121, 138, 141
Oh Solo Mio (travel company), 49
Oklahoma, 89, 112, 114
OLLI (Osher Lifelong Learning
  Institute), 36, 140
Online accounts, 308–309
Ontario, Calif., 132
Optimism, 16
Oregon, 77, 113, 114, 121–122,
  143, 265
Organization for Economic
  Co-operation and Development
  (OECD), 259
Orlando, Fla., 121
Osher Lifelong Learning Institute
  (OLLI), 36, 140
Overconfidence bias, 286
Overnight Caskets, 295
Overseas retirement, 150–151
Overweight and obesity, 15,
  167–169, 177–179, 184,
  188–190, 193–196,
  199–202

**P**

Palm Coast, Fla., 111
Palm Springs, Calif., 121
Pampered Chef, 63
Panama, 115, 123
Paris, Ohio, 138
Parks, Denise, 44–45
Parton, Dolly, 299
Part-time jobs, 56–57, 68
PBGC (Pension Benefit Guaranty
  Corporation), 234
PBS News Hour, 141
Peace Corps, 67
Pedasi, Panama, 115
Peddicord, Kathleen, 115,
  123–127, 150–151
Pennsylvania, 93, 123, 141,
  143, 265, 266
"The Penny Hoarder," 111
Pensacola, Fla., 114
Pension Benefit Guaranty
  Corporation (PBGC), 234
Pensions, 234–236, 241
PERFECT acronym, 111, 114
Personal Financial Specialists, 225
Personality, and goal setting, 32
Pets, 42, 52, 105, 116, 121–122,
  138, 139, 153, 173, 174, 314
Pew Research Center, 9, 176
Philadelphia, Penn., 123
Phoenix, Ariz., 121
Pilots, communities for, 144
Pittsburgh, Penn., 143
A Place for Us, 121
Planet Fitness, 180
Planning and important documents
  for end of life, 310–315

POA (power of attorney), 308–311
POAs (property owners'
  associations), 94–95
Podcasts, 37
Politics, 133
Portal, Ariz., 144
Port Orange, Fla., 144
Portugal, 84–85, 115, 123, 125–126
Poshmark, 61
Positive thinking, 16
Power of attorney (POA), 308–311
Prescott, Ariz., 114
Price-to-rent ratio, 90
Priya Living communities
  (California), 122
ProLiteracy, 39
Property owners' associations
  (POAs), 94–95
Property tax, on your
  home, 288–289
Proximity to family, 97–99
*Psychological Science,* 44
Punta Gorda, Fla., 145
Purpose, 19–22, 134, 191,
  299, 302–306

**Q**

Quebec, 123
*Queen Elizabeth 2* (ship), 129
Queen for a Day Foundation, 41
Quiz: Are You Ready to Launch
  Your Retirement?, 23–29
Quora (online site), 300

**R**

Rahe, Richard, 2
Rainbow Vista, 121–122

Raleigh-Durham-Chapel Hill, N. Car., 123
Real estate, as second career, 62
Realtor.com, 10
Recreational vehicles (RVs), 138–139
Redfin, 89
Red states, 89
Refinancing your home, 289
Regrets:
  at end of life, 300–301
  of retirees, 20–21
REI, 68
Relocating, 73–107
  and 2020 U.S. Census, 76–77
  "Aging in Place" (checklist), 99–105
  deciding whether to move, 74–76
  defining the "ideal" location, 77–81
  factors to look for, 85–97
  international relocation, 82–85
  "Retire Close to Family. . .or Not Too Close!" (checklist), 97–99
  and second homes, 81
Reno, Nev., 113
Rentals, 91
Republican-leaning states, 89
Required minimum distribution (RMD), 238–239, 272–274
Resales, 91
Resilience, cultivating, 12–14
The Resort on Carefree Boulevard, 121
Resumes, 69
Retired military, communities for, 147–149

Retirees, regrets of, 20–21
Retirement
  acronyms related to, 22–23
  and COVID 19 pandemic, 21–22
  expectations about, 4–7
  history of, 2–4
  and lifespan, 11–20
  as term, 4
  timing of, 7–11
Retirement, financing, 207–257
Retirement accounts:
  defined contribution, 233–241
  distributions from, 272–275
  individual, 234, 236–240, 242
  lost, 240–241
  rollovers, taxes on, 242
Retirement Confidence Survey, 5
2021 Retirement Confidence Survey, 207
Retirement Risk Readiness Study (Allianz Life), 18
Reverse mortgages, 252–253
Richmond, Tex., 132
RMD (required minimum distribution), 238–239, 272–274
Roads Scholar, 50
The Road to Character (Brooks), 301
Robson Communities, 133
Rochester, N.Y., 123
Roles, renegotiating, 12–14
Role theory, 6
Roosevelt, Franklin Delano, 3
Roth accounts, 238–240, 272
Rowling, J. K., 58, 304
Royal Caribbean Cruises, 129
Ruskin, Fla., 114

RV Industry Association, 138
RVing, 46–48
RVs (recreational vehicles), 138–139

**S**
St. Augustine, Fla., 142
St. Chinian, France, 115
St. George, Utah, 111, 113
Salt intake, 201
Salt Lake City, Utah, 129–130
Salvation Army, 39
Same-sex marriage, and Social
    Security, 233
San Antonio, Tex., 114, 147
San Francisco, Calif., 143
Santa Cruz, Calif., 96
Santa Fe, N. Mex., 111, 114
Santa Rosa, Calif., 121
Sarasota, Fla., 114, 132
Sardinia, Italy, 190
SAT (Scholastic Aptitude Test), 36
Saving money, 281–298
    and cognitive biases, 281–287
    and making rational financial
        decisions, 287–298
Scholastic Aptitude Test (SAT), 36
School systems, 90
Scottsdale, Ariz., 130
Seaside, Fla., 142
Seasonal/temporary work, 65–67
Seattle, Wash., 113
Second homes, 81, 267–269
Section 401(k) plans, 236–241
Section 403(b) plans, 236–241
Section 529 college education
    plans, 305–306
Self (financial technology
    company), 92

Self-efficacy, 12–14
Self-storage units, 291
Seligman, Martin, 16–17
Selling your home, 91–92, 260–263
Senegal, 123
Senioradvice.com, 121
SeniorLiving.org, 114, 121
Seventh Day Adventists, 191
ShantiKiketan, 122
Shareholder benefits, 297
SHIELD acronym, 166–167
Short-term rentals, 94
"Should I Stay or Should I Go?"
    (song), 10
*Shrek* (movie), 14
Sierra Club outings, 51
Silent Generation, 56
SilverSneakers, 181
Silver Spring, Md., 131
Sinclair, David, 161
Single people, 9
Singles' travel, 49
Singles Travel International, 49
Six Secrets for a Successful
    Retirement, 12–20
Size of community, 90
Sleep, 167–171, 186–187
SMART acronym, 34
Smart Asset (financial technology
    company), 76–77
Smart Tours, 49
Smithsonian Journeys, 50
Snopes (fact-checking site), 44
Social connections, 192
*Social Psychology and Personality
    Science*, 18
Social Security, 3, 227–233,
    241, 270–271

Social support, 14–16, 174–176
Sodium intake, 201
Solo agers, 9
*Somnio* (residential ship), 128–129
South Carolina, 10, 11, 77, 114, 132, 143, 145
South Dakota, 112, 264
Southeastern United States, 85–87
*Southern Living Magazine,* 146
Southern United States, 76
Southwestern United States, 89
Spain, 123
Special Olympics, 41–42
Staging your home, 91
Stanford Center on Longevity, 161
Stanford University, 177, 302
Staples, 68
Starbucks, 68
Starting your own business in retirement, 58–59
State College, Penn., 141
State tax rates table (2021), 277–278
State tax rules, 264–278
State University of New York at Stony Brook, 9
Status quo bias, 283–284
Steiner, Clyde, 74
Steiner, Shari, 74
Steuteville, Robert, 143
Stewart, Potter, 303
Stewart, Rod, 161
Stocks and bonds, 243–246, 250, 296–297
Stonewall Gardens, 121
Stress, 171–173
Summertown, Tenn., 149
Sun City, Ariz., 88

Sun City, Fla., 114
Surfside, Fla., 94–95
Surprise, Ariz., 147
Sussex County Community College (New Jersey), 36
Swimming, 181

**T**
Tampa, Fla., 121, 122
Target-date funds, 245
Taskrabbit, 62
Tauck Bridges tours, 51
Tavares, Fla., 122
Tavira, Portugal, 115
Tax Counseling for the Elderly (TCE), 40
Tax Cuts and Jobs Act, 238–240
Taxes, 259–279
  average lifetime payment, 92
  estate and inheritance, 275–276
  and financial advisors, 224–225
  on retirement account distributions, 272–275
  on retirement account rollovers, 242
  and reverse mortgages, 252
  on Roth accounts, 238–239
  and selling your home, 260–263
  on Social Security income, 270–271
  state tax rules, 264–269
Tax Foundation, 265, 267
Tax Freedom Day, 267
Tax preparation, 40, 67
TCE (Tax Counseling for the Elderly), 40
Teaching in retirement, 63
TED talks, 149

Television, 289–290
Telomeres, 164–165
Tempe, Ariz., 141
"The 10 Best College Towns for
    Retirement," 140
"Ten Great Outdoor Towns
    for Retirement (Top
    Retirements), 113
Tennessee, 10, 77, 93, 114, 132,
    149, 264–266
Tennis, 43
Teresa, Mother, 304
Texas, 10, 76, 77, 93, 121,
    128, 130, 132, 138, 146,
    147, 264, 269
Thailand, 83–84, 123
Thermostats, smart, 293
"The Ten Best Places for African
    Americans to Move Abroad"
    (Parker), 123
Time, unscheduled, 32
Time management, 31–53
  learn new skills, 43–45
  and lifelong learning, 35–38
  and travel, 45–51
  and volunteering, 38–43
Time on your Hands (quiz), 52–53
Tiny homes, 137–138
"Tiny House Nation" (Netflix
    series), 138
TNDs (traditional neighborhood
    developments), 142–143
Tomas, William H., 137
*The Top Five Regrets of the Dying*
    (Ware), 300
Top Retirements, 113–114
"Top 10 Regrets in Life by Those
    About to Die" (Brown), 300

Touchstone Crystal, 63
Traditional neighborhood
    developments (TNDs), 142–143
Transamerica Center for
    Retirement, 22
Travel, 45–51
Travel Channel, 113
Traveling Vineyard, 63
*Travel Noire,* 123
Traverse City, Mich., 113
*The Truman Show,* 142
Tucson, Ariz., 121
Tulum, Mexico, 123
Tupper, Earl, 63
Tuscaloosa, Ala., 141
Tutoring, 42
Twitter, 69

U
UBRCs (university-based retirement
    communities), 140–141
UCLA Williams Institute, 96
U-Haul, 68
Unclaimed property, 291–292
United Health Foundation,
    112, 192–193
United Nations, 162
United Parcel Service, 67
United Van Lines, 77
United Way, 41
Universal design, 97
University-based retirement
    communities
    (UBRCs), 140–141
University of California, Los
    Angeles, 96
University of Maryland, 35–36
University of North Carolina, 8

University of Pennsylvania, 16
University of Virginia, 304
UPS (United Parcel Service), 67, 68
U.S. Bureau of Labor Statistics,
    3, 56, 210
U.S. Census (2020), 76–77
U.S. Census Bureau, 2
U.S. Department of Housing and
    Urban Development, 252
U.S. Food and Drug Administration
    (FDA), 196
U.S. Geological Survey (USGS), 93
U.S. Moving Migrations Patterns
    Report, 10
*U.S. News & World Report,* 115, 190
U.S. Preventive Services Task Force
    (USPSTF), 201–202
U.S. Small Business
    Administration, 59
U.S. Social Security
    Administration, 3
U.S. Supreme Court, 233
U.S. Treasury Bonds, 292
USGS (U.S. Geological Survey), 93
Ushering, 42
USPSTF (U.S. Preventive Services
    Task Force), 201–202
Utah, 10, 76, 89, 111–113,
    129–130, 265

**V**
Values, and purpose of life, 302–307
Vanguard, 210, 225–226, 242, 245
"Vanguard's Principles for Investing
    Success," 245
Venice, Fla., 132
Vermont, 89
Veterans, communities for, 147–149

Viera, Fla., 147
Village Hearth Co-housing, 122
The Villages (Florida), 88, 132
Village-to-village
    networks, 141–142
Virginia, 114, 142, 144–145,
    268–269
Virginia Beach, Va., 114
Virtues, importance of
    living, 301–302
VITA (Volunteer Income Tax
    Assistance), 40
Vitamins, 197–198
Volunteer Income Tax Assistance
    (VITA), 40
Volunteering, 38–43
Voluntourism, 50
Voter registration, 42
VRBO, 62

**W**
Wachtstetter, Lee, 129
Walking, 182–183
WalletHub, 287
Walt Disney World Resort, 116
Ware, Bronnie, 300
Washington, DC, 123, 143
*Washington Post,* 231
Washington State, 76, 112–114,
    218, 264
Watersound, Fla., 117–118
Western United States, 76
West Palm Beach, Fla., 121
West Virginia, 89, 112–114
*Wheel of Fortune,* 118
*Where to Retire* magazine, 85
White, Carol, 46–48
White, Phil, 46–48

Wills, 307–311
Wilson, Timothy, 304
Windsor, Colo., 132
Wine, 192
Winston-Salem, N. Car., 123
Women, and retirement, 8
Working in retirement, 55–71, 241
  companies welcoming mature
    workers, 57
  core pursuits, 69–70
  customer service jobs, working
    from home, 68
  direct sales, 63–65
  health benefits, working
    part-time with, 68
  networking, resumes, and
    interviews, 69
  online sites to list skills or items
    for sale, 60–62
  part-time jobs, 56–57

Peace Corps volunteer, 67
real estate, 62
seasonal/temporary work, 65–67
and sense of self, 6
starting your own business, 58–59
teaching, 63
*The World* (residential
    ship), 128–129
Wozniak, Steve, 304
Wyoming, 89, 264

**X**
Xenophon Therapeutic Riding
    Center, 42

**Y**
You Tube, 122–123

**Z**
Zoos, volunteering in, 42